SHAMBHALA
CLASSICS

BOOKS ON TAOISM BY THOMAS CLEARY

Alchemists, Mediums, and Magicians: Stories of Taoist Mystics (2009)*

Taoist Classics: The Collected Translations of Thomas Cleary, 4 vols. (2003)*

The Book of Balance and Harmony: A Taoist Handbook (2003)*

Taoist Meditation: Methods for Cultivating a Healthy Mind and Body (2000)*

Ways of Warriors Codes of Kings: Lessons in Leadership from the Chinese Classics (2000)*

Sex, Health, and Long Life: Manuals of Taoist Practice (1999)*

Practical Taoism (1996)*

The Tao of Organization: The I Ching *for Group Dynamics*, by Cheng Yi (1995)*

The Spirit of Tao (1993)

Thunder in the Sky: Secrets on the Acquisition and Exercise of Power (1993)*

The Book of Leadership and Strategy: Lessons of the Chinese Masters (1992)*

Wen-tzu: Understanding the Mysteries, by Lao-tzu (1992)*

The Essential Tao (1992)

The Secret of the Golden Flower (1991)

Back to Beginnings: Reflections on the Tao (1990)*

Mastering the Art of War, by Zhuge Liang & Liu Ji (1989)*

The Art of War, by Sun Tzu (1988)*

Awakening to the Tao, by Liu I-ming (1988)*

The Buddhist I Ching, by Chihhsu Ou-i (1987)*

The Inner Teachings of Taoism, by Chang Po-tuan (1986)*

The Taoist I Ching, by Liu I-ming (1986)*

*Published by Shambhala Publications

Vitality, Energy, Spirit

A Taoist Sourcebook

Translated and Edited by
Thomas Cleary

SHAMBHALA
Boston & London
2009

Shambhala Publications, Inc.
Horticultural Hall
300 Massachusetts Avenue
Boston, Massachusetts 02115
www.shambhala.com

9 8 7 6 5 4 3 2 1

Printed in Canada

⊗This edition is printed on acid-free paper that meets the
American National Standards Institute z39.48 Standard.
♻This book was printed on 100% postconsumer recycled paper.
For more information please visit us at www.shambhala.com.
Distributed in the United States by Random House, Inc.,
and in Canada by Random House of Canada Ltd

The Library of Congress catalogues the previous edition
of this book as follows:
Vitality, energy, spirit: a Taoist sourcebook/translated and edited
by Thomas Cleary.—1st. ed.
p.   cm.—(Shambhala dragon editions)
ISBN 978-0-87773-519-9 (alk. paper)
ISBN 978-1-59030-688-8 (pbk.: alk. paper)
1. Taoism—Sacred books. 2. Taoism. 3. Taoism—History—Sources.
4. Taoist literature I. Cleary, Thomas. F. 1949–
BL1900.A1V58   1991   90-53387
299'.514—dc20   CIP

Contents

Introduction

Taoism is a source of some of the world's oldest mind-body health and healing lore. Taoists often call their study the "science of essence and life" to represent their cultivation of those arts. The science of essence deals with mind; the science of life deals with the body. Their object is to groom and enhance what Taoists call the three bases or three treasures of human existence: vitality, energy, and spirit.

Vitality, energy, and spirit are envisioned as three centers of the individual and collective organism. Each center is twofold: there is a primal or abstract noumenon, and a temporal or concrete phenomenon. There are many differences in Taoist practices according to which aspect of what center they are primarily designed to affect.

Vitality is primally associated with creativity, temporally associated with sexuality. Energy is primally associated with movement, heat, and power, temporally associated with breath, magnetism, and strength. Spirit is primally associated with the essence of mind and consciousness, temporally associated with thought and reflection. As the three centers interact, the quality and proportion of their mutual influence relate directly to the total state of mental and physical well-being.

In terms of the individual body, vitality is associated with the loins, energy with the thorax, and spirit with the brain. These associations are invoked in some forms of Taoist yoga, where the respective areas of the body are called the lower, middle, and upper fields of elixir. These fields are used to focus attention in healing, energizing, and meditative exercises.

Vitality, energy, and spirit can also be defined in terms of three bodies: vitality is the flesh-and-blood body, energy is the electrical body within the flesh-and-blood body, and spirit is the ethereal body of consciousness within the electrical body. In yet another sense, vitality is the natural world, energy is the social world, and spirit is the psychological world.

There are many Taoist arts concerned with enhancing vitality, energy, and spirit. Included among them are sexual techniques for vitality, movements and exercises for energy, and meditations for the spirit. For historical and theoretical perspective on Taoism, therefore, it is useful to review each of the "fields of elixir" in terms of the modes of practice devised for their cultivation.

VITALITY

Taoist sexology is generally called the "bedroom art" in exoteric literature and "bedroom alchemy" in more specialized writings. Like other Taoist sciences, it is believed to have originally been articulated in antiquity. In both popular and esoteric Chinese lore, sexology is commonly associated with Huang Ti (Huang Di), the legendary Yellow Emperor, who is believed to have assembled the ancient sciences of Taoism in the middle of the third millennium B.C.E. The Yellow Emperor Huang Ti is said to have learned this particular art from someone named Su Nü, whose name means Basic Woman.

Bedroom alchemy has always been among the most controversial Taoist practices, for several reasons. From a sociopolitical point of view, there was an aspect of the art that had powerful implications apart from simple enhancement of sexual intercourse for men and women. Biologically speaking, one of the effects of the bedroom art was to maintain fertility in dominant males, who were habitually polygamous and commonly suffered from low sperm counts unless they deliberately conserved their semen. Rulers and other wealthy and powerful men with exceptionally great concerns for propagating their lineages, and exceptionally great opportunities for doing so, often became personal devotees of this aspect of Taoism, even as they discouraged it among the people at large.

An unusual and dramatic form of sexual yoga was instituted by the revolutionary neo-Taoist school of the Celestial Guides in the second century C.E. The practice, known as "joining energies," consisted of a ritual form of communal sexual intercourse. It was carried out within a religious community under the direction of Taoist healers and teachers, in the context of a comprehensive path of development.

Like some of the other activities of the controversial Celestial Guides, sacred sexual rituals were designed to offset certain imbalances that had developed in the mind and body of China. These imbalances can be defined in biological, social, and psychological terms, reflecting deterioration in the circulation of vitality, energy, and spirit of Chinese civilization.

At the time of the movement of the Taoist leaders who came to be known as the Celestial Masters, China had been subject to one political regime, the Han dynasty, for nearly four hundred years. Although Chinese society was not entirely static, as it has often been portrayed, nevertheless it was obviously stagnant and sclerotic. A small number of clans had acquired a vast majority of the wealth and power in the empire, while the social structure they supported revolved around perpetuating their privilege and authority.

This state of affairs had genetic as well as political consequences. Rich and powerful men commonly bought or stole as many teenage girls as they could, in addition to their socially appointed wives. Poor peasant men, on the other hand, were more likely to die prematurely from hunger, overwork, or violence. The sexual ritual of "joining energies" cut across long-established class lines and remixed segments of the gene pool that had been largely segregated for centuries except through the liaisons of rich men with slave girls. Socially and psychologically, it also cut through long-fixated feelings about paternity and possessiveness.

It has been said that traditional opposition of Confucian authorities to Taoist sexual arts is based on prudish or puritanical Confucian attitudes toward sex. It would appear most likely, however, that the real fears of Confucian authorities were socially and politically founded. Social and political questions were indeed the very foundation of Confucian moral thinking, and their position on Taoist bedroom arts was evidently rooted in these concerns.

Apart from the controversial collective "joining energy" rites, the bedroom arts also included a variety of techniques for individual couples, and for rites involving a man and two or more women. Taoists expressed their own reservations about sexual alchemy, but these reservations were founded on a different basis from those of Confucian orthodoxy. The concerns of the Taoists were the dangers arising from ignorant misuse, excess, and lack of appropriate preparation, context, and self-mastery before taking up the practice of sexual alchemy.

Evidence of this cautionary attitude appears fairly early in Taoist literature. Near the end of the second century C.E. the alchemical text *Ts'an-t'ung-ch'i*, or *Triplex Unity*, included a certain form of mechanically ritualized sexual intercourse in a list of mechanically ritualized practices that it rejected. Later the Complete Reality school of Taoism would regard this text as a classic of spiritual alchemy, and its caveats on practice would be widely repeated in the literature of that school. Warnings about misuse of sexual yoga were common to other forms of yoga, being based on the attitude, approach, and application; all formal practices were considered limited in any case, and mechanical performance was known to exhaust the spirit and energy of yogic practices.

The bedroom art is mentioned several times in the great fourth-century Taoist work *Pao-p'u-tzu* (*Baopuzi*), a collection of essays by Ko Hung (Go Hong, 284–363), a famous researcher and writer on secular and occult subjects. In the chapter "Subtle Doctrines," the author recommends the method of P'eng Tsu (Peng zu), the Chinese Methusalah, who is supposed to have lived for seven hundred years, due in part to his practice of bedroom arts. Ko Hung writes, "The method of P'eng Tsu is quintessential. The other texts are often complicated, tedious, and hard to practice, while the actual benefits are not necessarily as written in the books. Few people can do them. The verbally transmitted secrets, furthermore, consist of only a few thousand words."

In the chapter "Unclogging," Ko Hung elaborates further on the bedroom arts and their customary practice: "There are more than ten schools of bedroom arts. Some use them to repair damage; some use them to cure sicknesses; some use them to draw on yin to enhance yang; some use them to add years and extend life. What is most important and essential, however, is one thing alone: returning vitality to boost the brain. This practice is transmitted by real people by word of mouth, and is not written in books." Ko also mentions a few popular texts, including P'eng Tsu's manual, of which he approves, and says, "They note the crude things, but never put the most essential points down on paper."

Like the Taoist Celestial Guides of the late Han dynasty, Ko Hung also attributed the practice of bedroom arts to Lao-tzu, the legendary Taoist ancient, based on esoteric interpretations of certain passages in the classic *Tao-te Ching*. Sexual yoga was also known to have been practiced among male and female shamans, with whom certain of the Celestial Guides were undoubtedly associated. In his *Pao-p'u-tzu*, Ko Hung speaks highly of the great advantages of bedroom arts for health and longevity but is careful to avoid the inflated claims of sex gurus who even then commercialized the arts for personal profit.

In the "Subtle Doctrines" chapter, Ko writes of the arts' importance in terms of the general economy of vitality-sustaining life: "Those who do not know bedroom arts may take a hundred potions but still cannot prolong life." In the "Ultimate Principle" chapter, he writes of their function in bolstering the energy that underlies work and exercise: "For working with energy, it is also beneficial to know bedroom arts. The reason this is so is that if you don't know the yin-yang arts, you will repeatedly become fatigued and depleted, with the result that you will have a hard time gaining strength in working with energy."

Ko responds to exaggerations of bedroom arts in the "Subtle Doctrines" chapter of *Pao-p'u-tzu*:

> Some say that those who completely master the bedroom art can by its sole practice reach spiritual immortality, avert disasters and resolve misdeeds, turn calamity into fortune, and find promotion in official life or increased profit in the business world. Is this true? These are all deceptive exaggerations of shamanistic writings, which are so colored by fetishism as to lose reality. Some even deliberately make up lies to fool people of the world, concealing clues to get others to wait on them, attracting and gathering disciples, thus to encompass worldly profit. The fact is that the yin-yang arts at their highest can cure minor illnesses; at the next level, they can be used to avoid depletion. But that is all. There is a natural limit to the science; how can it produce spiritual immortality, repel calamity, and bring good fortune?

In another work, Ko Hung relates a story underscoring several points: that bedroom arts are only one part of Taoist developmental science; that only the cruder aspects of the bedroom arts are written in books; and that the essence of the bedroom arts, like other practices of the Taoist science of life, can be taught only by expert personal instruction. Typically, the point of the story is technical rather than moral in the ordinary sense of the word in such a context.

The story concerns a certain woman who made and sold wine. One day a wizard came into her shop, drank some wine, and left a book in lieu of payment. When the woman looked at the book, she found that it contained instructions for "nurturing nature" by means of sexual intercourse. She copied the essential points and began to practice the art with young men who came to her shop. Regaining and preserving her youth thereby, thirty years later she still looked like a woman in her twenties. Eventually the wizard returned and saw what had transpired. Laughing, he said to the woman, "On a purloined path with no teacher, even if you have wings you cannot fly." Then the woman closed up her shop and followed the wizard into the mountains.

From the third and fourth centuries onward, Taoism was increasingly influenced by Buddhism, which began to filter into China near the end of the Han dynasty. Following Buddhist models, Taoists composed scriptures, organized churches, and ordained clergy. Unlike the celibate Buddhist clergy, however, the Taoist clergy could marry and carry on the traditional art of bedroom alchemy as part of its religious observances.

Although Buddhism had married clergy practicing sexual yoga in other cultures, in China Buddhism was regarded by the Confucian authorities as foreign and politically suspect, so their policy was that Buddhist institutions could not be allowed to reproduce themselves biologically. During the T'ang dynasty (618–905), when greater regimentation was introduced into church Taoism, there was a trend toward celibacy among the clergy, more in conformity with the Buddhist custom. Later Taoist revival movements of the Sung dynasty (960–1276), independent of the old Taoist churches and strongly influenced by Ch'an Buddhism, took an even more ascetic turn to secure their political and economic independence.

The most influential of the Sung dynasty neo-Taoist movements, the Ch'üan-chen (Quanzhen) or Complete Reality school, took a reserved approach to bedroom alchemy for the cultivation of vitality. Generally speaking, the Northern branch of the school, known as the sect of clear serenity, recommends moderation in sexual activity and does not speak of deliberately practicing sexual yoga for energizing the body or healing sickness. In contrast to this, the Southern branch of the school, known as the sect of dual cultivation or grafting, is said to use sexual yoga for revitalization of the physical body. In most texts of this school the subject is not openly discussed in detail, but Chang Po-tuan (Zhang Boduan), the founder of the Southern branch, warns against overestimation of both celibacy and ritual sex exercises in his classic *Wu-chen p'ien* (*Wuzhen-pian*), *Understanding Reality*. The underlying principles invoked here, naturalness and freedom from obsession, are characteristic of ancient Taoism and its revival in the Complete Reality school.

One of the distinguishing marks of Complete Reality Taoism was its emphasis on integration of Buddhism and Confucianism with Taoism. This probably influenced the attitude of the school toward bedroom arts. Buddhist thought is particularly prominent in a story told of the famous Ancestor Lü in this connection. Ancestor Lü was one of the primary founders of Complete Reality Taoism, and the story illustrates something of the ethical tone of the school.

It seems there was a rich man skilled in sexual arts who always kept a seraglio of ten young women. Whenever one would get pregnant, he would throw her out and get someone else to replace her. He had sexual intercourse with these young women one after another day and night, with the result that he could go for days without eating and at the age of ninety-seven still looked like he was thirty years old. He was also a braggart.

Now Ancestor Lü, the master spiritual alchemist, went to see this man, posing as a beggar asking for alms. At first the rich man did not recognize him and sent him away, but Ancestor Lü displayed his occult power and won the man's confidence. When the man now asked Lü for some words of wisdom, the Taoist master told the story of someone who had once liked to hunt and fish, but gave up hunting in middle age. When asked why he gave up hunting and not fishing, seeing as how both involve taking life, he replied, "Hunting depends on me; fishing depends on the creatures. I couldn't give them both up at once, so I first stopped the worse of the two." And after that he gave up fishing as well.

When Ancestor Lü had recited this story to the rich man with ten concubines, he said, "I like the way he cared for beings and protected life. What are you doing with your antics?" After that Lü disappeared. The rich man felt ill at ease from that point on. Before long he vomited up gallons of silver liquid and died. This represents the accumulation of untransformed vitality, which supposedly did prolong the man's life, but did not improve him spiritually. The moral of the story reflects the Buddhist attitude of cherishing living beings, combined with traditional Taoist teachings on the need for a balanced integration of the sciences of essence and life.

Further illustrations of Complete Reality Taoist treatment of bedroom arts are found in the classic anthology known as *Chung-ho chi (Zhongho ji)*, or *The Book of Balance and Harmony*, which incorporates teachings of both the Northern "clear serene" branch and the Southern "dual cultivation" branch. In this text sexual yoga is treated along with many other practices in a wide-ranging scheme of classification. The conservative austerity of the Northern branch is combined with the qualified acceptance of auxiliary techniques more characteristic of the Southern branch. Schools of sex play exploited by charlatans and sybarites are relegated to the status of false paths, whereas controlled intercourse using the vitality of sexuality to tone and heal the body is accorded a high status among practices for warding off illness.

During the Yuan dynasty (1278–1367) a link was formed between the old syncretic school of the Celestial Guides and the Southern branch of the newer Complete Reality school. This encouraged a more liberal attitude toward practices formerly eschewed in Complete Reality Taoism, and accentuated the difference between Northern and Southern Complete Reality schools. Contact with the school of the Celestial Guides probably strengthened the practice of bedroom arts in the Southern school of Complete Reality, but followers of the latter school, apparently most interested in revitalization of the body, do not seem to have attempted eugenic programs quite like those of the ancient Celestial Guides.

Modern-day writings on Complete Reality Taoism mention the bedroom art in a general way, with particular emphasis on combining it with the practice of "clear serenity." Yü-yang-tzu, a contemporary Taoist, says, "If one wants to practice the yin-yang twin cultivation of the Southern school, unless one has sufficient grounding in the practice of clear serenity one will be unable to be unminding in face of objects; many have failed at the last moment because of this." He also says, "In the practice of the Southern school, even if one can obtain elixir from one's partner, one must then resume the practice of clear serenity, embrace the fundamental, preserve unity, return to emptiness, and go back to nothingness; only thus can one achieve final settlement. Otherwise, hopes of attaining reality will vanish in the end."

ENERGY

Energy work is probably the most popular aspect of Taoism in both East and West, particularly through the widespread use of exercise systems such as *t'ai-chi-ch'üan* (*taijiquan*) and therapeutic techniques such as acupressure and massage. The practice of special exercises for health and longevity is extremely ancient in China, and many different forms and styles developed over the course of centuries.

As early as *Chuang-tzu*, the famous Taoist classic of the fourth century B.C.E., mention is made of life-prolonging exercises generically known as *tao-yin, (daoyin)*, or "(energy) induction." The point emphasized by Chuang-tzu in this connection, however, is that these exercises have a limited scope: " 'Swaying like a bear, stretching like a bird' is only for longevity." Western scholars have claimed, on the basis of such remarks, that Chuang-tzu was opposed to yogic exercises, but this conclusion may be overdrawn; from the point of view of practical Taoist tradition it is more likely that Chuang-tzu was simply putting energy work into perspective as something incomplete in itself without corresponding spiritual development. Later, Complete Reality Taoists commonly chided cultists in the same spirit.

One of the greatest names in the history of Taoist energy work was a leading physician of the late Han dynasty named Hua T'o (Hua To), who lived from 141 to 203 C.E. near the very end of the dynasty, when interest in Taoism was beginning to resurge from beneath the veneer of orthodox Confucianism ruling China. Hua T'o opposed superstitious explanations of disease and promoted physical training to strengthen the body and cure illness. He is credited with the invention of a popular system of exercise known as the "play of the five animals," in which the practitioner performs stylized movements said to be patterned after those of the tiger, deer, monkey, bear, and crane.

Another type of exercise, based on a kind of shadowboxing and later associated with martial arts, is attributed to an Indian Buddhist monk named Bodhidharma, who is believed to have come to China as a missionary in the late fifth or early sixth century C.E.

Bodhidharma is traditionally considered the founder of Chinese Ch'an Buddhism, which is known for its absorption of classical Taoism and influence on later neo-Taoism. Bodhidharma supposedly introduced his exercise system to monks specializing in meditation, in order to keep the body from deteriorating from long vigils in absolute stillness. He is also associated with two other forms of exercise commonly used by Taoists, the *hsi-sui-ching* (*xisuijing*) or "course in washing the marrow," and the *i-chin-ching* (*yijinjing*) or "course in easing the sinews." The former is a set of mind-body exercises for profound relaxation and purification; the latter, of which various versions are current, is a course in elemental physical training.

Another popular type of exercise, called *pa-tuan-chin* (*baduanjin*) or "eight step brocade," is said to have been originated by one of the great neo-Taoist wizards, Chung-li Ch'üan (Zhongli Quan) of the T'ang dynasty (618–905). Chung-li is sometimes said to have been a warrior and general of the Han dynasty who gave up his career and went into the mountains to study Taoism; he is also said to have been a man of the T'ang dynasty because he is known as the teacher of the great Ancestor Lü, who is commonly said to have lived in the T'ang dynasty. Ancestor Lü is regarded at the forerunner of both Northern and Southern branches of Complete Reality Taoism; both he and his teacher Chung-li Ch'üan are familiar figures in popular Taoist iconography, and Chung-li's "eight-step brocade" exercises are widely practiced in the public domain.

Like the "play of the five animals" and other ancient systems, the "eight-step brocade" has been modified over the ages, with the result that it now exists in numerous different forms. Generally speaking, however, it can be said that this type of exercise is distinguished by simplicity and flexibility; it can be readily adjusted to suit the physical condition of and it requires little space or time. There are standing and sitting versions, hard and soft versions. Overall, the "eight-step brocade" system of energy maintenance is typically characteristic of the devices of the Complete Reality school descended from Chung-li in being easy to learn and easy to practice, simple yet remarkably effective.

Perhaps the most famous of all Taoist exercise systems, *t'ai-chi-ch'üan* or "absolute boxing," is also traditionally associated with the powerful and influential school of Complete Reality. *T'ai-chi-ch'üan* is said to have been invented by Chang San-feng (Zhang Sanfeng), one of the most popular figures of Taoist legend. Although standard writings on this type of exercise are relatively late productions and there seems to be no hard historical evidence supporting Chang's alleged authorship of the system, the traditional attribution does affirm popular recognition of a link between Taoism and *t'ai-chi-ch'üan*.

The historical Chang San-feng is something of a mystery; he is said to have lived in the thirteenth and fourteenth centuries, but through his wanderings and use of different names his identity has been somewhat diffused. Besides his fame as the legendary originator of *t'ai-chi-ch'üan*, Chang is associated with both external material alchemy and internal spiritual alchemy, and also is credited with the development or elaboration of other programs, including mental, physical, and psychosomatic exercises.

Health and longevity exercises seem to have penetrated and permeated the fabric of Chinese custom more than any other aspect of Taoism. Modern works from Communist China on *ch'i-kung* (*qigong*, "energy work" or "energetics") preserve many elements of traditional Taoist (and Buddhist) mind-body hygienics, albeit from a typically mechanical and materialistic point of view, stripped of metaphysical and religious concepts and vocabulary. Although the political and intellectual biases of communism prejudice understanding of the mind-body relationship and do not admit of certain Taoist-Buddhist perceptions and experiences of that relationship, nevertheless the practice of Taoist therapeutics would seem to be an indelible mark of Chinese culture regardless of the temporal intellectual orthodoxy or otherwise of Taoist thought.

SPIRIT

Taoist mental exercises for grooming the spirit generally involve some sort of meditation or contemplation. The practices fall into two basic categories: those that employ defined objects or images, and those without defined objects or images. In early Taoist literature predating the entry of Buddism into China, explicit references to meditation suggest great simplicity of technique. As the Buddhist presence in China grew to massive proportions in the centuries following the fall of the Han dynasty in 220 C.E., the elaborate mental science of Buddhism stimulated the articulation and development of parallel methods in Taoism.

Although the use of imagery and visualization in Taoist meditation seems to have ancient precedents, it would appear that the popularity of this particular type of exercise in Taoism is largely due to the influence of Buddhism, which is very rich in practices involving visualization and deliberate cultivation of the imagination. On the whole, the use of such practices by Taoists seems to focus on several categories of phenomena. There are many visualizations involving stars, clouds, and vast distances; occult dramas whose imaginary enactment within the body is structured to induce specific states of mind; and images of exemplary people of myth and history associated with special knowledge or attainments. There are also special contemplation stories that illustrate, and help prepare the mind for, unfamiliar uses of consciousness.

The literature of church Taoism, strongly influenced by Buddhism in the development of elaborate rituals and grandiose worldviews, is very rich in material designed for visualization exercises. The reform movement of Complete Reality, on the other hand, was more interested in formless enlightenment and placed less emphasis on this type of meditation. This new orientation was adopted by the Complete Reality school in much the same spirit as it liberated itself from rigid attachment to all the formalized routines of church Taoism.

The Complete Reality subordination of visualization as a temporary expedient is articulated in a famous document claiming to record the teachings given by Chung-li Ch'üan to Ancestor Lü. As mentioned earlier, Chung-li is considered the inventor of the "eight-step brocade" exercise system, and his disciple Ancestor Lü is revered as the grandfather of Complete Reality Taoism. In the text purporting to report what Lü learned from Chung-li, there is a most revealing discourse on the purpose and place of visualization practice. In one chapter of this collection, Ancestor Lü asks Chung-li about the principle of "inward gazing," by which is meant visualization of special images in the mind and body. The master wizard replies,

> The method of sitting forgetting [the outside world] while gazing inward and sustaining images was used by some sages and not by others. Considering how the mind and thoughts run and jump around ceaselessly, the ancient sages feared that the will would be lost because of objects, so they set up images in the midst of nothingness, to cause the ears not to hear, the eyes not to see, the mind not to go wild, and the thought not to ramble.
>
> In such cases, visualization of phenomena in inward gazing while sitting forgetting is indispensable. Unfortunately, ignorant people of little learning who don't understand the process expect visualization to accomplish the work, and they form the alchemical elixir in their minds and cull the medicine in their imaginations. This is why outstanding adepts tear down sitting forgetting with inward gazing at a certain point, saying that materials gotten in a dream cannot be used in actuality, as a picture of a cake cannot satisfy hunger.
>
> Nevertheless, there are those who should use this method, namely those who are easily stirred and have trouble controlling their minds.

The text also includes general descriptions of imagery used in visualization practice, then leads into the process of transcending this phase of meditation:

> The rising of yang is often visualized as a man, a dragon, sky, clouds, a crane, the sun, a horse, smoke, mist, a car, a chariot, a flower, or energy. Images such as these are held in inward gazing to correspond to the image of yang rising.
>
> The descending of yin is often visualized as a woman, a tiger, water, earth, rain, a tortoise, the moon, a cow, a spring, mud, a boat, a leaf. Images such as these are held in inward gazing to correspond to the image of yin descending.
>
> There are also such images as a blue dragon, white tiger, red sparrow, dark warrior, five mountains, nine states, four seas, three

islands, the gold man and jade woman, the waterwheel, the multi-storied tower. There are innumerable such terms, all images set up in nothingness as means of stabilizing consciousness.

Before the purpose is achieved, the means is necessary; the cart that goes afterward must go in the tracks of the cart that goes before, and when a great instrument is completed it will be a model for later instruments. So the practice of inward gazing cannot be neglected. Also, one should not hold to it for a long time and stop it suddenly.

If you cease thought and have no conceptions, this is true thought. True thought is true emptiness. The realm of true emptiness is the gradual way of transcendence, leaving the city of darkness and going to the court of reality.

Later spiritual descendants of Chung-li Ch'üan and Ancestor Lü in the school of Complete Reality seem to have placed relatively little weight on visualization practices such as these, although their currency is well documented in *The Book of Balance and Harmony*, which was compiled centuries after the time of the founders. In the more abstract and transcendental emphasis of the Complete Reality school may be seen the influence of Ch'an, its Buddhist counterpart, which was concerned more with essence than with form and color. This characteristic of Ch'an, in turn, although rooted in certain Buddhist teachings, was reinforced by the influence of ancient Taoism, in which meditation without defined images is central to the praxis.

In classical Taoism as well as its revival in the form of Complete Reality Taoism, meditation without defined images is also generally twofold. There is the practice of emptying and quieting the mind in order to observe the flux of events without subjective distortion by personal emotions and ideas, as described in the ancient *Tao-te Ching*. The same text speaks of states of abstraction without defined objects or images that do not simply clear the mind for objective perceptions of the ordinary world, but usher the mind into another form of consciousness in which elementals (such as elemental vitality, energy, and spirit) are perceived by an inner sense.

Mental posture, or the disposition of the spirit, is also an important element in exercises primarily associated with the development of vitality and energy. The most advanced form of sexual yoga, for example, is said to be completely mental. The various kinds of energetics also include specific points of mental focus or patterns of mental exercise to go along with the physical movements. Visualization is used not only in training the mind but in healing the body, and even the most abstract formless meditation states are also esteemed for their value in restoration and maintenance of physical health. Thus there are ultimately no rigid boundaries among the domains of vitality, energy, and spirit; they are in fact regarded as originally one, and it is an aim of Taoist praxis to reunify them into a harmonious whole.

Complete Reality Taoism draws a distinction between the primal and temporal manifestations of the three treasures. In this case, greater emphasis is placed on grooming the primal vitality, energy, and spirit. According to the theoretical basis of the praxis, the primal unity of these three centers can be restored by a process described as refining vitality into energy and refining energy into spirit. This stage of unification is called "the three flowers gathered on the peak." From there, spirit is refined into emptiness, and emptiness is broken through to unite with the Tao, whereupon the practitioner is "mentally and physically sublimated."

THE TRANSLATIONS

The present anthology contains a variety of traditional Taoist educational materials dealing with the theory and practice of the "inner alchemy" by which vitality, energy, and spirit are unified, groomed, refined, and purified, a process believed by Taoists to restore the original wholeness and health of the natural human being. The anthology is divided into eight sections, covering a range of teachings from ancient classics to modern talks.

The first section, on classical sources, draws on the major Taoist texts of the pre-Christian era. The second section, on tales of inner meaning, presents a collection of symbolic stories. The third section gives an overview of the principles of spiritual alchemy. The fourth section introduces the teachings of the historical founders of the

Complete Reality school of neo-Taoism. The fifth section consists of extracts from contemplative Taoist literature. The sixth section presents writings of the greatest of the late medieval masters. The seventh section contains commentaries on classical and neoclassical texts by an outstanding premodern adept. The eighth section presents excerpts from recorded sayings of modern Taoists.

Notes on Sources

Selections from Classic Sources

My complete annotated translations of the *Tao-te Ching* and the "Inner Chapters" of *Chuang-tzu* are to be found in *The Essential Tao* from HarperCollins Publishers, 1992. My abridged translation of *Huainan-tzu* is to be found in *The Tao of Politics: Lessons of the Masters of Huainan,* from Shambhala Publications, 1990.

Tales of Inner Meaning

The tales have been taken from the following sources, with added material from oral tradition: *Zhongxi shide shenjing, Xianzhuanshiyi,* and *Gaodaozhuan.*

Ancestor Lü

Materials attributed to Ancestor Lü have been taken from the following sources: *Luzu huiji* and *Yulu daguan.*

The Founding of the Southern and Northern Schools

My complete translation of Chang Po-tuan's *Understanding Reality,* explained by Liu I-ming, is to be found in *Understanding Reality: A*

Taoist Alchemical Classic, from University of Hawaii Press, 1987. My complete translation of Chang Po-tuan's *Four-Hundred Character Treatise on the Golden Elixir,* explained by Liu I-ming, is to be found in *The Inner Teachings of Taoism,* from Shambhala Publications, 1986. Other material attributed to Chang Po-tuan is taken from *Wuzhen baofa jinju jing.* More information on the Northern school can be found in *Seven Taoist Masters: A Folk Novel of China,* translated by Eva Wong, published by Shambhala Publications, 1990.

Extracts from Contemplative Literature

These extracts are taken from works in *Daozang jiyao* and *Daotong dacheng.*

Chang San-feng

Materials attributed to Chang San-feng are taken from *Sanfeng quanshu* and *Zhang Sanfeng taiji tiandan bijue.*

Liu I-ming

These works by Liu I-ming are taken from *Daoshu shierzhong.* Other writings by Liu I-ming are translated in the following books: *The Taoist I Ching* (1986), *I Ching Mandalas: A Program of Study for* The Book of Changes (1988), and *Awakening to the Tao* (1988), all published by Shambhala Publications.

Selections from Classic Sources

Introduction

TAO-TE CHING

The *Tao-te Ching* is the most widely read of Taoist texts and the most universally accepted by followers of all Taoist orders. It has been dated variously, with estimates generally ranging from around 500 to 300 B.C.E. Although it is conventionally attributed to Lao-tzu, a semilegendary ancestor of Taoism, the *Tao-te Ching* is evidently not an original composition by an individual author, but contains redactions of even more ancient lore. In any case, it is one of the earliest sources for the theory and praxis of grooming vitality, energy, and spirit. The present anthology includes several key selections from the classic illustrating this aspect of its teachings.

The tenth chapter of the *Tao-te Ching*, "Carrying Vitality and Consciousness," introduces a number of important practical concepts, beginning with the union of vitality and consciousness. The text speaks of concentration, flexibility, purification of insight, naturalness, being impassive and innocent, acting without presumption: all of these came to be regarded as critical elements of Taoist spiritual alchemy in both the science of essence and the science of life.

The twelfth chapter, "Colors," is a concise statement of a traditional principle of Taoist teachings on energy, according to which stimulation of the senses tends to drain and dull the body

3

and mind. Later Ch'an Buddhists would say that "when you save power, you gain power," based on the same principle. The sixteenth chapter, "Attain the Climax of Emptiness," illustrates the corresponding practice of emptying and quieting the mind. Used by both Taoists and Ch'an Buddhists, this type of exercise has the twin function of clearing perceptions and conserving energy, thus preserving both mental and physical well-being.

The twenty-eighth chapter of the *Tao-te Ching*, "Knowing the Male," illustrates a prototype of the two-mind construct popular in later Taoism. To distinguish between the discursive, ratiocinative mind and the direct, intuitive mind, Taoists came to use the terms "human mind" and "mind of Tao" when discussing mental cultivation. In the *Tao-te Ching*, this duality is represented by the polarities of male/female, white/black, glorious/ignominious. The text says to "know" the male but "keep" the female, to master the rational mind yet remain poised in the intuitive mind.

The thirty-seventh chapter, "The Way Is Always Uncontrived," also treats the theme of naturalness, noninterference, unobtrusive simplicity, and desireless calm. While such attitudes, postures, and practices are typically defined negatively, their effects and consequences are all positive. Similarly, the fortieth chapter, "Return Is the Movement of the Way," speaks of "nonbeing" yet defines it as the source of being, which is in turn the source of "all things in the world." Thus instead of a negation, "nonbeing" is understood as an indefinable point of poise in a state of pure potential. In this way the means of conserving energy becomes the means of gaining access to energy.

The forty-sixth chapter, "When the World Has the Way," also deals with the issue of how energy is used. Like many Taoist teachings, it is phrased in terms of political economy but can be understood in terms of personal economy. It illustrates one of the most important techniques of energy enhancement using a simple process of reallocation of available resources. The fifty-second chapter, "The World Has a Beginning," pursues a similar theme in a different way, contrasting expenditure of energy on externals with conservation of energy within. This does not correspond to the

Western concepts of extroversion and introversion, however, insofar as the Taoist teaching employs both outward and inward attention in mutual balance, using both the rational and intuitive consciousness: as the text says, "Using the shining radiance, you return again to the light," illustrating how ordinary faculties of the human mind are subordinated to the higher faculty of the mind of Tao without being debased or obliterated.

Chapter fifty-five, "The Richness of Subliminal Virtue," metaphorically describes ideal combinations of flexibility and firmness, innocence and empowerment. This chapter also presents the key concepts of mastering energy by mind and sustaining power by restraint. Chapter seventy-six, "When People Are Born," illustrates the paradox of mastery in Taoism, which is accomplished not by assertion but by flexibility: "The stiff and strong are below, the supple and yielding are on top."

CHUANG-TZU

The next great Taoist classic after the *Tao-te Ching* is the equally famous *Chuang-tzu*, or *Book of Master Chuang*, attributed to the philosopher Chuang-tzu, or Chuang Chou (ca. 369–286 B.C.E.). Although it elaborates on many of the ideas of the *Tao-te Ching*, the *Chuang-tzu* is very different in its transmission and manner of presentation. Whereas the former text consists of proverbs and aphorisms, the latter is largely made up of allegorical stories interspersed with philosophical discussions. The *Tao-te Ching*, closely linked to ancient tradition, is attributed to a semilegendary sage and is very difficult to place historically with precision; the *Chuang-tzu*, on the other hand, is attributed to a clearly historical personage, and the marks of its time, during which the chaos and violence of the Warring States era rose inexorably toward a climax, are quite evident in the psychological mood and philosophical attitude of the text.

The four selections appearing here relate to the central concerns of vitality, energy, and spirit. The first, from "On Equalizing Things," the second chapter of the *Chuang-tzu*, begins with a discourse on the power of fear to influence judgment and create binding compulsions. It then introduces the idea of an underlying source, the "director" within, formless and invisible yet undeniably present. Chuang-tzu says that our day-to-day preoccupation with the effects blinds us to the cause, making it impossible to master life at its source. He then illustrates a kind of contemplative exercise, very much like certain Buddhist meditations, designed to affect the focus of mind in such a way as to make the distinction between the temporal and primal self-evident.

The second selection is one of the most famous stories from the classic, found in the third chapter, "Mastery of Nurturing Life." According to the story, an ancient king took a lesson in the Way from his butcher, whose skill was so remarkable as to draw the interest of the king. As is often the case in *Chuang-tzu*, what is perhaps the most critical point of all is raised and dropped so abruptly that it almost escapes particular notice: congratulated on his consummate technique, the butcher says, "What I like is the Way, *which is more advanced than technique*," yet because the transcendental Way is ineffable, he then backs up and says, "but I will present something of technique." Having made this critical distinction—for as the *Tao-te Ching* says in its opening line, "A way that can be articulated is not the eternal Way"—the butcher goes on to talk about his work in a metaphorical representation of the Taoist way of spontaneity and naturalness. By "going according to the natural pattern," the butcher says, he has been able to "cut up thousands of oxen" without breaking or dulling his blade; just as the Taoist wizard who lives in harmony with the design of nature can thereby handle the affairs of the world yet preserve vitality, energy, and spirit intact.

The third selection included here is taken from chapter four, "The Human World." Presented as a dialogue between the great political philosopher and educator Confucius and his foremost disciple, this section contains a number of key terms and concepts that were later to figure prominently in the practical literature of Taoist spiritual alchemy. The main topic of the piece is "mental fasting," which Confucius presents as a way of getting safely through complex and difficult situations. Mental fasting is identified with "emptiness," which is defined in terms of transcendence of the ego and detachment from conceptual knowledge. The corresponding meditation method described here is also very similar to its Buddhist counterpart: "For those who gaze into space, the empty room produces white light." This passage is often quoted in alchemical lore as a touchstone for the practice of "mental fasting."

The fourth and last selection is drawn from the end of "Freedom," the opening chapter of the *Chuang-tzu*. It illustrates the distinction between the temporal "human mentality" and the primal "mind of Tao," focusing on the freedom of the latter in contrast to the limitation of the former. Because it does not fit into categories constructed by the human mentality, in the *Chuang-tzu* the mind of Tao is often represented by images of oddity or uselessness to emphasize its transcendental nature. Ordinarily, people cannot avail themselves of the reserves of the mind of Tao, the philosopher suggests, because everything, even the idea of the mind of Tao, is habitually filtered through the perceptions of the human mentality. Thus the mind of Tao must be experienced in its own domain to be meaningful in a real sense. Speaking metaphorically of this greater potential hidden in humanity, Chuang-tzu therefore says, "Now you have a huge tree and worry that it is useless: why not plant it in the vast plain of the homeland of Nothing Whatsoever, roaming in effortlessness by its side and sleeping in freedom beneath it?"

HUAI-NAN-TZU

The next great Taoist classic after *Chuang-tzu* is the *Huai-nan-tzu* (*Huainanzi*), or "Masters of Huai-nan," composed approximately 150 years later in a very different social and political climate. Centuries of civil war had ended around 200 B.C.E. with the founding of the monumental Han dynasty, which was to rule China for the next four hundred years, with but a brief interruption in the early part of the first century C.E. Although the later impact of Buddhism was so great as to be immeasurable, nevertheless the culture of the Han dynasty left an indelible imprint, exerting a lasting influence on the development of Chinese civilization.

The early emperors of Han adopted a Taoist policy of minimalist government in order to allow the nation and its people to recover from the violence and destruction of the long era of Warring States. China had been united into an empire under the militaristic Ch'in dynasty in the middle of the third century B.C.E.; taking over from the Ch'in, the Han dynasty attempted to restore classical culture, which had been suppressed by the Ch'in government in favor of a mechanical form of legalism. One of the great patrons of this revival was Liu An, a grandson of the founding Han emperor and king of a small feudal domain. Known as the king of Huai-nan after the region where his fief was at one time located, Liu An opened his court to scholars and savants from all over the empire, developing it into a major center of learning and culture.

According to legend, the classic *Huai-nan-tzu* is the product of an inner circle of eight Taoist sages at Liu An's court. This group of wizards is said to have appeared at court when it was already in full bloom as a seat of arts and sciences. Challenged by the king to demonstrate knowledge not already represented at his illustrious court, the eight ancients proceeded to astound him with uncanny displays of occult powers. Duly humbled, the king of Huai-nan welcomed the sages and apprenticed himself to them. The *Huai-nan-tzu* purports to be records of their talks.

Because of the historical circumstances of its origin, the *Huai-nan-tzu* contains a great deal of material relating to political science and affairs of state; but it also synthesizes other aspects of Taoism, including natural and spiritual sciences. In this respect it is the richest of the early Taoist classics. The dissemination of these teachings was inhibited, however, by two events: the downfall and disappearance of Liu An, victim of an intrigue; and the official adoption of a form of Confucianism as the orthodox system of thought and education throughout the empire. The brand of Confucianism that won the imperial stamp of approval was really a hybrid of Confucianism, legalism, and a peculiar cosmology that revived the ancient doctrine of the divine right of kings and bestowed on it the dignity and authority of natural law.

Thus the liberal, egalitarian idealism of the Taoist Huai-nan masters was eclipsed by the imperial ideology of political despotism and intellectual conformism. Nevertheless, the essential vitality, energy, and spirit of Taoism remained stored within its own secret reservoirs in spite of external barriers to its effective application on a large scale: as the Huai-nan masters themselves said, "To blame the Way for not working in a polluted world is like tying a unicorn down from two sides and yet expecting it to run a thousand miles." The teachings of the *Huai-nan-tzu* may not have made the social and political impact that could have been possible under more favorable conditions, but they retained incalculable value as a basic resource for Taoist principles and practices.

Although the *Huai-nan-tzu* follows the *Tao-te Ching* and the *Chuang-tzu* in its fundamental understanding of human nature and life, because of the historical circumstances of its composition it is more positive and constructive than either of its great predecessors, especially the *Chuang-tzu*. It goes further not only in political science but also in the alchemy of vitality, energy, and spirit. Particularly noteworthy is the way in which it links these three aspects of the human being, emphasizing the interconnection of physical and psychological health.

WEN-TZU

After the downfall of Liu An, the disappearance of the Huai-nan Masters, and the establishment of Confucian orthodoxy in the second century B.C.E., the classical Taoist tradition of the *Tao-te Ching*, the *Chuang-tzu*, and the *Huai-nan-tzu* went underground. There remained considerable private interest in Taosim among the Confucian intelligentsia, but over the course of the Han dynasty their "Taoism" became mixed with superstitions and mechanical thought systems characteristic of hybrid Han Confucianism. Among Taoist purists, it is said that so-called Real People, or true

Taoist adepts, went into hiding during the Han dynasty and did not reemerge for hundreds of years.

The *Wen-tzu* (*Wen zi*) occupies a unique position in this complex historical context. Its compilation is attributed to a disciple of Lao-tzu, with virtually all of its contents presented as sayings of Lao-tzu himself. Although later Taoist literature includes many texts ascribed to Lao-tzu, they refer to the ancient master by honorific epithets attached to him as the apotheosized founder of Taoism, a transhistorical immortal reappearing in the world from age to age. *Wen-tzu*, on the other hand, uses the names Lao-tzu and Lao Tan, suggesting greater antiquity. This is reinforced by the contents of the work, which follow more closely on the classic tradition than do later texts attributed to the transcendental personalities of the founder. Non-Taoist historical evidence would seem to indicate that the text may have been compiled around 100 B.C.E., not long after the *Huai-nan-tzu*, and later augmented to form an expanded version. Linguistic evidence also suggests an early Han dynasty origin.

The *Wen-tzu* contains many extracts from its predecessors, *Tao-te Ching*, *Chuang-tzu*, and particularly the *Huai-nan-tzu*. In a sense, the *Wen-tzu* may be considered something like an early commentary on these texts, or an attempt to continue the classic tradition after its fall from political grace. In terms of format the *Wen-tzu* follows the *Tao-te Ching*; generally abstract and timeless like its model, the *Wen-tzu* does not include the kind of stories and allusions that make *Chuang-tzu* and *Huai-nan-tzu* extravagantly colorful and difficult to read. It does, nevertheless, contain many images and metaphors that are not found in the earlier texts but are effective in illustrating and vivifying the ancient teachings. Like the *Huai-nan-tzu*, its immediate predecessor, the *Wen-tzu* embraces a wide range of related topics, from physiology and health lore to social and political science.

The existence of an early version of the *Wen-tzu* is noted in the records of the Han dynasty (206 B.C.E.–219 C.E.), and the expanded version is catalogued in the documents of the Sui dynasty (588–618 C.E.). During the T'ang dynasty, when Taoism was made into a state religion by the ruling house, which claimed blood descent from the clan of Lao-tzu himself, the *Wen-tzu* was presented to the emperor by one of the ancient Taoist families and given an honorific title as a "scripture," the *T'ung-hsuan Ching* (*Tongxuan Zhenjing*), or *Scripture on Penetrating the Mysterious*. It is of great historical value as a source of information on the continuation of the classic Taoist tradition in the Han dynasty, and of great philosophical and practical value in elucidating the ancient Taoist teachings.

Tao-te Ching

Carrying Vitality and Consciousness

Carrying vitality and consciousness,
embracing them as one,
can you keep them from parting?
Concentrating energy,
making it supple,
can you be like an infant?
Purifying hidden perception,
can you make it flawless?
Loving the people, governing the nation,
can you be uncontrived?
As the gate of heaven opens and closes,
can you be impassive?
As understanding reaches everywhere,
can you be innocent?
Producing and developing,
producing without possessing,
doing without presuming,
growing without domineering:
this is called mysterious power.

Colors

Colors blind people's eyes,
sounds deafen their ears;
flavors spoil people's palates,

the chase and the hunt
craze people's minds;
goods hard to get
make people's actions harmful.
Therefore sages work for the core
and not the eyes,
leaving the latter and taking the former.

Attain the Climax of Emptiness

Attain the climax of emptiness,
preserve the utmost quiet:
as myriad things act in concert,
I thereby observe the return.
Things flourish,
then each returns to its root.
Returning to the root is called stillness:
stillness is called return to Life,
return to Life is called the constant;
knowing the constant is called enlightenment.
Acts at random, in ignorance of the constant, bode ill.
Knowing the constant gives perspective;
this perspective is impartial.
Impartiality is the highest nobility;
the highest nobility is divine,
and the divine is the Way.
This Way is everlasting,
not endangered by physical death.

Knowing the Male

Knowing the male, keep the female;
be humble to the world.
Be humble to the world,
and eternal power never leaves,
returning again to innocence.
Knowing the white, keep the black;
be an exemplar for the world.

Be an exemplar for the world,
and eternal power never goes awry,
returning again to infinity.
Knowing the glorious, keep the ignominious;
be open to the world.
Be open to the world,
and eternal power suffices,
returning again to simplicity.
Simplicity is lost to make instruments,
which sages employ as functionaries.
Therefore the great fashioner does no splitting.

The Way Is Always Uncontrived

The Way is always uncontrived,
yet there's nothing it doesn't do.
If lords and monarchs could keep it,
all beings would evolve spontaneously.
When they have evolved and want to act,
I would stabilize them with nameless simplicity.
Even nameless simplicity would not be wanted.
By not wanting, there is calm,
and the world will straighten itself.

Return Is the Movement of the Way

Return is the movement of the Way;
yielding is the function of the Way.
All things in the world are born of being;
being is born of nonbeing.

When the World Has the Way

When the world has the Way,
running horses are retired to manure the fields.
When the world lacks the Way,
warhorses are bred in the countryside.
No crime is greater than approving of greed,

no calamity is greater than discontent,
no fault is greater than possessiveness.
So the satisfaction of contentment is always enough.

The World Has a Beginning

The world has a beginning
that is the mother of the world.
Once you've found the mother,
thereby you know the child.
Once you know the child,
you return to keep the mother,
not perishing though the body die.
Close your eyes, shut your doors,
and you do not toil all your life.
Open your eyes, carry out your affairs,
and you are not saved all your life.
Seeing the small is called clarity,
keeping flexible is called strength.
Using the shining radiance,
you return again to the light,
not leaving anything to harm yourself.
This is called entering the eternal.

The Richness of Subliminal Virtue

The richness of subliminal virtue
is comparable to an infant:
poisonous creatures do not sting it,
wild beasts do not claw it,
predatory birds do not grab it.
Its tendons are flexible,
yet its grip is firm.
Even while it knows not
of the mating of male and female,
its genitals get aroused;
this is the epitome of vitality.
It can cry all day without choking or getting hoarse;

this is the epitome of harmony.
Knowing harmony is called constancy,
knowing constancy is called clarity;
enhancing life is called propitious,
the mind mastering energy is called strong.
When beings climax in power, they wane;
this is called being unguided.
The unguided die early.

When People Are Born

When people are born they are supple,
and when they die they are stiff.
When trees are born they are tender,
and when they die they are brittle.
Stiffness is thus a cohort of death,
flexibility a cohort of life.
So when an army is strong,
it does not prevail.
When a tree is strong,
it is cut for use.
So the stiff and strong are below,
the supple and yielding on top.

Chuang-tzu

Small fear is fearful, great fear is slow. In action they are like a bolt, an arrow, in terms of their control over judgment. In stillness they are like a prayer, a pledge, in terms of their attachment to victory. They kill like fall and winter, in the sense of daily dissolution. Their addiction to what they do is such as to be irreversible. Their satiation is like a seal, meaning that they deepen with age. The mind drawing near to death cannot bring about a restoration of positivity.

Joy, anger, sadness, happiness, worry, lament, vacillation, fearfulness, volatility, indulgence, licentiousness, pretentiousness—these are like sounds issuing from hollows, or moisture producing mildew. Day and night they interchange before us, yet no one knows where they sprout. Stop, stop! From morning to evening we find them; do they arise from the same source?

If not for other, there is no self. If not for self, nothing is apprehended. This is not remote, but we don't know what constitutes the cause. There seems to be a real director, but we cannot find any trace of it. Its effectiveness is already proven, but we don't see its form. It has sense, but no form.

The whole body is there with all of its members, openings, and organs: with which is the self associated? Do you like any of them? That means you have selfishness therein. Then do all sometimes act as servants? As servants, are they incapable of taking care of one another? Do they alternate as ruler and subject? Evidently there is a real ruler existing therein: the matter of whether or not we gain a sense of it does not increase or decrease its reality.

Once we have taken on a definite form, we do not lose it until death. We oppose things, yet also follow them; we violate things, yet also submit to them: that activity is all like a galloping horse that no one can stop. Isn't it pitiful? We work all our lives without seeing it accomplish anything. We wearily work to exhaustion, without even knowing what it all goes back to. How can we not be sad about this? People may say at least it isn't death, but what help is that? As the physical constitution changes, so does the mind; how can this not be considered a great sorrow?

Once a butcher was cutting up an ox for a king. As he felt with his hand, leaned in with his shoulder, stepped in and bent a knee to it, the carcass fell apart with a peculiar sound as he played his cleaver.

The king, expressing admiration, said to the butcher, "Good! It seems that this is the consummation of technique."

The butcher put down his cleaver and replied, "What I like is the Way, which is more advanced than technique. But I will present something of technique.

"When I first began to cut up oxen, all I saw was an ox. Even after three years I still had not seen a whole ox. Now I meet it with spirit rather than look at it with my eyes.

"When sensory knowledge stops, then the spirit is ready to act. Going by the natural pattern, I separate the joints, following the main apertures, according to the nature of its formation. I have never even cut into a mass of gristle, much less a large bone.

"A good butcher changes cleavers every year because of damage, a mediocre butcher changes cleavers every month because of breakage. I've had this cleaver for nineteen years now, and it has cut up thousands of oxen; yet its blade is as though it had newly come from the whetstone."

Yen Hui asked Confucius, "May I hear about mental fasting?"

Confucius replied, "You unify your will: hear with the mind instead of the ears; hear with the energy instead of the mind. Hearing stops at the ears, the mind stops at contact, but energy is that which is empty and responsive to others. The Way gathers in emptiness; emptiness is mental fasting."

Yen Hui said, "The reason I haven't been able to master this is because I consider myself really me. If I could master this, 'I' would not exist. Could that be called emptiness?"

Confucius said, "That's all there is to it. I tell you, you can go into the political arena without being moved by repute. If you are heard, then speak; if not, then stop. Let there be no dogma, no drastic measures: remain consistent and abide by necessity. Then you'll be close.

"It is easy to obliterate tracks, hard not to walk on the ground. It is easy to use falsehood in working for people; it is hard to use falsehood in working for nature.

"I have heard of flying with wings; I have never heard of flying without wings. I have heard of knowing with knowledge; I have never heard of knowing without knowledge.

"For those who gaze into space, the empty room produces white light; auspicious signs hover in stillness. But if one does not stay here, that is called galloping even while sitting.

"If you have your ears and eyes penetrate inwardly, and are detached from conceptual knowledge, then even if ghosts and spirits come after you they will stop; how much the more will people!"

Hui-tzu said to Chuang-tzu, "I have a gigantic tree, but its trunk is too gnarled for the plumb line and its branches too twisted for the ruler: even if it were set in the middle of the road, carpenters would pay no attention to it. What you say is similarly grandiose but useless, rejected by everyone alike."

Chuang-tzu replied, "Have you not seen a wildcat? It lowers itself close to the ground to watch for careless prey; it leaps this way and that, light and low, but then gets caught in a trap and dies. A yak, on the other hand, is enormous; it can do big things, but cannot catch a rat. Now you have a huge tree and worry that it is useless: why not plant it in the vast plain of the homeland of Nothing Whatsoever, roaming in effortlessness by its side and sleeping in freedom beneath it? The reason it does not fall to the axe, and no one injures it, is that it cannot be exploited. So what's the trouble?"

Huai-nan-tzu

Heaven is calm and clear, earth is stable and peaceful. Beings who lose these qualities die, while those who emulate them live.

Calm spaciousness is the house of spiritual light; open selflessness is the abode of the Way.

Therefore there are those who seek it outwardly and lose it inwardly, and there are those who safeguard it inwardly and gain it outwardly.

The Way of heaven and earth is enormously vast, yet it still moderates its manifestation of glory and is sparing of its spiritual light. How then could human eyes and ears work perpetually, without rest? How could the vital spirit be forever rushing around without becoming exhausted?

Don't be surprised, don't be startled; all things will arrange themselves. Don't cause a disturbance, don't exert pressure; all things will clarify themselves.

Human nature is developed by profound serenity and lightness, virtue is developed by harmonious joy and open selflessness. When externals do not confuse you inwardly, your nature finds the condition that suits it; when your nature does not disturb harmony, virtue rests in its place.

If you can get through life in the world by developing your nature and embrace virtue to the end of your years, it can be said that you are able to embody the Tao.

If so, there will be no thrombosis or stagnation in your blood vessels, no depressing stifling energy in your organs. Calamity and fortune will not be able to disturb you, censure and praise will not be able to affect you. Therefore you can reach the ultimate.

When the mind neither sorrows nor delights, that is supreme attainment of virtue. To succeed without changing is supreme attainment of calm. To be unburdened by habitual desires is supreme attainment of emptiness. To have no likes and dislikes is supreme attainment of equanimity. Not getting mixed up with things is supreme attainment of purity.

Those who can accomplish these five things reach spiritual illumination. Those who reach spiritual illumination are those who attain the inward.

Therefore when you master the outward by means of the inward, all affairs are unspoiled.

If you can attain this within, then you can develop it outwardly.

When you attain it within, your internal organs are peaceful and your thoughts are calm; your muscles are strong, your eyes and ears are alert and clear. You have accurate perceptions and understanding, you are firm and strong without snapping.

In a small domain you are not cramped, in a large domain you are not careless. Your soul is not excited, your spirit is not disturbed. Serene and aloof, you are the toughest in the world. Sensitive and responsive, when pressed you can move, infinitely calm and inscrutable.

Human nature is generally such that it likes tranquillity and dislikes anxiety; it likes leisure and dislikes toil. When the mind is always desireless, this can be called tranquillity; when the body is always unoccupied, this can be called leisure.

If you set your mind free in tranquillity and relinquish your body in leisure, thereby to await the direction of nature, spontaneously happy within and free from hurry without, even the magnitude of the universe cannot change you at all; even should the sun and moon be eclipsed, that does not dampen your will. Then you are as if noble even if lowly, and you are as if rich even if poor.

When the spirit controls the body, the body obeys; when the body overrules the spirit, the spirit is exhausted. Although intelligence is useful, it needs to be returned to the spirit. This is called the great harmony.

The mind is the ruler of the body, while the spirit is the treasure of the mind. When the body is worked without rest, it collapses. When the spirit is used without cease, it becomes exhausted. Sages value and respect them, and do not dare to be excessive.

Sages respond to being by nonbeing, unfailingly finding out the inner pattern; they receive fullness by emptiness, unfailingly finding out the measure. They live out their lives with calm joy and empty tranquillity. Therefore they are not too distant from anything and not too close to anything.

What sages learn is to return their nature to the beginning and let the mind travel freely in openness. What developed people learn is to link their nature to vast emptiness and become aware of the silent infinite.

The learning of ordinary worldlings is otherwise. They grasp at virtues and constrict their nature, inwardly worrying about their physical organs while outwardly belaboring their eyes and ears.

Sages send the spirit to the storehouse of awareness and return to the beginning of myriad things. They look at the formless, listen to the soundless. In the midst of profound darkness, they alone see light; in the midst of silent vastness, they alone have illumination.

When the perceptions are clear, with profound discernment free from seductive longings, and energy and will are open and calm, serenely joyful and free from habitual desires, then the internal organs are settled, full of energy that does not leak out. The vital spirit preserves the physical body inwardly and does not go outside. Then it is not difficult to see the precedents of the past and the aftermath of the future.

Outwardly go along with the flow, while inwardly keeping your true nature. Then your eyes and ears will not be dazzled, your thoughts will not be confused, while the spirit within you will expand greatly to roam in the realm of absolute purity.

When the spiritual light is stored in formlessness, vitality and energy return to perfect reality. Then the eyes are clear, but not used for looking; the ears are sharp, but not used for listening. The mind is expanded, but not used for thinking.

When vitality passes into the eyes, the vision is clear; when it is in the ears, the hearing is sharp. When it is in the mouth, speech is accurate; and when it gathers in the mind, thought is penetrating.

The energy of heaven is the higher soul, the energy of earth is the lower soul. Return them to the mystic chamber, so each is in its place. Keep watch over them and do not lose them; you will be connected to absolute unity above, and the vitality of absolute unity is connected to heaven.

There are countless sights, sounds, and flavors, rarities from distant lands, oddities and curiosities, that can change the aim of the mind, destabilize the vital spirit, and disturb the circulation and energy.

The vital spirit belongs to heaven, the physical body belongs to earth: when the vital spirit goes home and the physical body returns to its origin, where then is the self?

Wen-tzu

Lao-tzu said:

Consider the world light, and the spirit is not burdened; consider myriad things slight, and the mind is not confused. Consider life and death equal, and the intellect is not afraid; consider change as sameness, and clarity is not obscured.

Perfected people lean on a pillar that is never shaken, travel a road that is never blocked, are endowed from a resource that is never exhausted, and learn from a teacher that never dies. They are successful in whatever they undertake, and arrive wherever they go. Whatever they do, they embrace destiny and go along without confusion. Calamity, fortune, profit, and harm cannot trouble their minds.

Those who act justly can be pressed by humanitarianism but cannot be threatened by arms; they can be corrected by righteousness but cannot be hooked by profit. Ideal people will die for justice and cannot be stayed by riches and rank.

Those who act justly cannot be intimidated by death; even less can those who do not act at all. Those who do not act deliberately have no burdens. Unburdened people use the world as the marker of a sundial: above they observe the ways of perfected people to delve deeply into the meanings of the Way and virtue; below they consider the behaviors customary in the world, which are enough to induce a feeling of shame.

Not doing anything with the world is the drum announcing learning.

Lao-tzu said:

Those who are known as Real People are united in essence with the Way, so they have endowments yet appear to have none; they are full yet appear to be empty. They govern the inside, not the outside. Clear and pure, utterly plain, they do not contrive artificialities but return to simplicity.

Comprehending the fundamental, embracing the spirit, thereby they roam the root of heaven and earth, wander beyond the dust and dirt, and travel to work at noninvolvement. Mechanical intelligence does not burden their minds; they watch what is not temporal and are not moved by things.

Seeing the evolution of events, they keep to the source. Their attention is focused internally, and they understand calamity and fortune in the context of unity. They sit unconscious of doing anything, they walk unconscious of going anywhere.

They know without learning, see without looking, succeed without striving, discern without comparing. They respond to feeling, act when pressed, and go when there is no choice, like the shining of light, like the casting of shadows. They take the Way as their guide; when there is any opposition they remain empty and open, clear and calm, and then the opposition disappears.

They consider a thousand lives as one evolution, they regard ten thousand differences as of one source. They have vitality but do not exploit it; they have spirit but do not make it labor. They keep to the simplicity of wholeness and stand in the center of the quintessential.

Lao-tzu said:

Those whom we call sages rest peacefully in their places according to the time and enjoy their work as appropriate to the age.

Sadness and happiness are deviations of virtue; likes and dislikes are a burden to the mind; joy and anger are excesses on the way.

Therefore their birth is the action of nature, their death is the transformation of things.

When still, you merge with the quality of darkness; when active, you are on the same wave as light.

So mind is the master of form, spirit is the jewel of mind. When the body is worked without rest, it collapses; when vitality is used without rest, it is exhausted. Therefore sages, heedful of this, do not dare to be excessive.

They use nonbeing to respond to being, and are sure to find out the reason; they use emptiness to receive fullness, and are sure to find out the measure. They pass their lives in peaceful serenity and open calm, neither alienating anyone nor cleaving to anyone.

Embracing virtue, they are warm and harmonious, thereby following Nature, meeting with the Way, and being near Virtue. They do not start anything for profit or initiate anything that would cause harm. Death and life cause no changes in the self, so it is called most spiritual. With the spirit, anything that is sought can be found, and anything that is done can be accomplished.

Lao-tzu said:

Rank, power, and wealth are things people crave, but when compared to the body they are insignificant. Therefore sages eat enough to fill emptiness and maintain energy, and dress sufficiently to cover their bodies and keep out the cold. They adjust to their real conditions and refuse the rest, not craving gain and not accumulating much.

Clarifying their eyes, they do not look; quieting their ears, they do not listen. Closing their mouths, they do not speak; letting their minds be, they do not think. Abandoning intellectualism, they return to utter simplicity; resting their vital spirit, they detach from knowledge. Therefore they have no likes or dislikes. This is called great attainment.

To get rid of pollution and eliminate burdens, nothing compares to never leaving the source. Then what action will not succeed?

Those who know how to nurture the harmony of life cannot be hooked by profit. Those who know how to join inside and outside cannot be seduced by power.

Beyond where there is no beyond is most great; within where there is no within is most precious. If you know the great and precious, where can you go and not succeed?

Lao-tzu said:

Those who practiced the Way in ancient times ordered their feelings and nature and governed their mental functions, nurturing them with harmony and keeping them in proportion. Enjoying the Way, they forgot about lowliness; secure in virtue, they forgot about poverty.

There was that which by nature they did not want, and since they had no desire for it they did not get it. There was that which their hearts did not enjoy, and since they did not enjoy it they did not do it.

Whatever had no benefit to essential nature they did not allow to drag their virtue down; whatever had no advantage for life they did not allow to disturb harmony. They did not let themselves act or think arbitrarily, so their measures could be regarded as models for the whole world.

They ate according to the size of their bellies, dressed to fit their bodies, lived in enough room to accommodate them, acted in accord with their true condition.

They considered the world extra and did not try to possess it; they left everyone and everything to themselves and did not seek profit. How could they lose their essential life because of poverty or riches, high or low social status?

Those who are like this can be called able to understand and embody the Way.

Lao-tzu said:

The energy that people receive from nature is one in terms of the feelings of the senses toward sound, form, scent, and temperature. But the way in which it is managed differs: some die thereby, and some live thereby; some become exemplary people, some become petty people.

The spirit is where knowledge gathers; when the spirit is clear, knowledge is illumined. Knowledge is the seat of the heart; when knowledge is objective, the heart is even.

The reason people use limpid water for a mirror, not a moving stream, is that it is clear and still. Thus when the spirit is clear and the attention is even, it is then possible to discern people's true conditions.

Therefore use of this inevitably depends on not exploiting. When a mirror is clear, dust does not dirty it; when the spirit is clear, habitual cravings do not delude it.

So if the mind goes anywhere, the spirit is there in a state of arousal; if you return it to emptiness, that will extinguish compulsive activity, so it can be at rest. This is the freedom of sages. This is why those who govern the world must realize the true condition of essence and life before they can do so.

Lao-tzu said:

Sages close up together with darkness and open up together with light. Able to reach the point where there is no enjoyment, they find there is nothing they do not enjoy. Since there is nothing they do not enjoy, they reach the pinnacle of enjoyment.

They use the inner to make the external enjoyable, and do not use externals to make the inner enjoyable; therefore they have spontaneous enjoyment in themselves, and so have their own will, which is esteemed by the world. The reason it is so is that this is essential to the world in the world's own terms.

It is not up to another, but up to oneself; it is not up to anyone but the individual. When the individual attains it, everything is included.

So those who understand the logic of mental functions regard desires, cravings, likes, and dislikes as externals. Therefore nothing delights them, nothing angers them, nothing pleases them, nothing pains them. Everything is mysteriously the same; nothing is wrong, nothing is right.

So there is consistent logic for men and consistent behavior for women: they do not need authority to be noble, they do not need riches to be wealthy, they do not need strength to be powerful; they do not exploit material goods, do not crave social reputation, do not consider high social status to be safe and do not consider low social status to be dangerous; their body, spirit, energy, and will each abides in its proper place.

The body is the house of life; energy is the basis of life; spirit is the controller of life: if one loses its position, all three are injured. Therefore when the spirit is in the lead, the body follows it, with beneficial results; when the body is in the lead, the spirit follows it, with harmful results. Those people whose lives are gluttony and lust are tripped and blinded by power and profit, seduced and charmed by fame and status, nearly beyond human conception.

When your rank is high in the world, then your vitality and spirit are depleted daily, eventually to become dissipated and not return to the body. If you close up inside and keep them out, they have no way to enter. For this reason there are sometimes problems with absentmindedness and work being forgotten.

When the vitality, spirit, will, and energy are calm, they fill you day by day and make you strong. When they are hyperactive, they are depleted day by day, making you old.

Therefore sages keep nurturing their spirit, make their energy gentle, make their bodies normal, and bob with the Way. In this way they keep company with the evolution of all things and respond to the changes in all events.

Their sleep is dreamless, their knowledge is traceless, their action is formless, their stillness is bodiless. When they are present, it is as if they were absent; they are alive, but are as if dead. They can appear and disappear instantaneously, and can employ ghosts and spirits.

The capabilities of vitality and spirit elevate them to the Way, causing vitality and spirit to expand to their fullest effectiveness without losing the source. Day and night, without a gap, they are like spring to living beings. This is harmonizing and producing the seasons in the heart.

So the physical body may pass away, but the spirit does not change. Use the unchanging to respond to changes, and there is never any limit. What changes returns to formlessness, while what does not change lives together with the universe.

So what gives birth to life is not itself born; what it gives birth to is what is born. What produces change does not itself change; what it changes is what changes. This is where real people roam, the path of quintessence.

Tales of Inner Meaning

Introduction

Fables, stories, and jokes have been used by practical philosophers for thousands of years as a means of conveying ideas and impressions to the receptive mind. They are particularly useful for subtleties that do not translate well into formal logic, and for making a direct impression, bypassing intellectual prejudices in the mind of the reader. Several examples of such tales of inner meaning are presented in this section of the present anthology.

The first group of stories is drawn from the *Lieh-tzu* (*Lie zi*), a well-known classic and source of numerous popular tales whose currency has long since expanded beyond the realm of Taoism per se. There is a wide range of opinion about the date of this text, a question to which there would appear to be no satisfactory solution in conventional historical terms. For the purposes of the present translations, the extent of the significance of this matter is that there appear to be additions and comments that flatten some of the tales and tend to diffuse rather than clarify their inner Taoist meaning. Therefore the stories from *Lieh-tzu* are rendered here in forms reflecting a synthesis of the written text and oral tradition.

A number of the tales of *Lieh-tzu* are pithy and amusing. The first one presented here, the story of Confucius and the two boys ("The Learned Man"), illustrates the limitations of discursive reason, thus hinting indirectly at a more comprehensive mode of consciousness. Presented as a joke at the expense of Confucius, it illustrates how logic can be coherent within the bounds of its postulates yet be ineffective or inaccurate in a larger context. While this is well understood today in the context of physics, it is not generally applied to the whole realm of cognitive knowledge as it is in practical Taoism.

The next story presented here, "The Story of Old Mister Shang," capped by the remarks of Confucius, illustrates the metaphysical basis of the extraordinary powers attributed to concentration, the idea that subjective and objective worlds are relative and respond to each other as they change and evolve through their mutual interaction.

"The Poor Man and the Gold" deals with the negative aspect of concentration. The joke about the man who stole the gold reinforces the observation that too much concentration on one thing can cause a person to overlook something else of equal or greater importance; and that focus on only one aspect of a situation can blind a person to other significant features of the total reality. This story can also be taken to show how concentration on transcendental matters at the expense of common sense leads to loss in both worlds.

"Who for Whom" also revolves around the theme of one-sided concentration and biased awareness. In this case, the prejudice in question, what is now termed anthropocentrism, has to do with the relativity of importance and point of view. Like Christianity and communism, Confucianism is essentially an anthropocentric way of thought. The Taoist *Lieh-tzu* ridicules the Confucian attitude in this story, where a youth at a banquet of self-satisfied feasters makes a bold attack on human conceit, showing how assumptions about the order of nature reflect subjective biases and lose their presumed validity when examined in the larger perspective of the universe. This perception is central to ancient Taoist teachings on ecology, which antedate Western concern on the subject by thousands of years.

The tale of the missing axe ("Suspicion") presents another view of the workings of subjectivity, one that also readily beckons insight into matters near at hand today. "Ups and Downs," on the aged laborer and his employer, illustrates mechanisms of compensation and balance, whose beginnings spring from a vantage point beyond one-sided views. The last two tales from the *Lieh-tzu* presented here illustrate the technique of "mental fasting" and the distinction between timeless and temporal aspects of consciousness.

Following these tales, all of which are distinguished by their brevity, are three much longer stories from later literature of the type commonly known as hagiography. Ordinary academic and sectarian conceptions of hagiography are based on the premise that the subject of the sketch is being described (fictionally or truthfully) in such a manner as to justify or prove his or her authority or sanctity within a religious or cultural tradition. When one looks beyond this superficial understanding to observe the structure of the tales, however, it becomes clear that certain hagiographies contain inner meanings relating to principles and practices of spiritual sciences.

The first "biographical" story presented here, "The Story of Wan Baochang," is of a master musician who lived in the Sui dynasty, near the end of the sixth century C.E. Music has been a matter of serious concern in Chinese thinking since ancient times, and Taoists in particular attributed profound power to its energy, as illustrated in an essay on the subject translated on page 153. This story of the master musician Wan Baochang graphically portrays the intimate connection between the state of a society and its music, as observed by ancient Confucians and Taoists alike. It also contains a traditional warning for Taoists, in the master's separation from his wife and tragic end, that there is no possibility of ultimate success when the "science of life," which deals with energy, becomes a passion in itself, divorced from the "science of essence," the ultimate refinement of spirit.

The next story, "Golden Butterflies," is about a Japanese immigrant living in T'ang dynasty China (619–905), probably one of the many Japanese students and pilgrims who went to China during the early T'ang to learn Chinese arts and sciences for their own newly developing nation of Yamato (Japan). The name of this particular individual, Han Shih-ho (Han Shiho, or in Japanese, Kan

Shiwa), would seem to indicate that he was in fact of fairly recent Chinese or Korean ancestry, as were many families among the upper classes of ancient Japan and in the craft guilds they patronized. Kan Shiwa was a master craftsman, one of the professional pursuits traditionally associated with Taoism. Although stories about him mention no details on this point, he was evidently also a martial artist, another profession with traditional Taoist connections, for he served in the imperial guard of the ruling house of the T'ang. His story illustrates a number of Taoist ideas. His ability to make lifelike moving replicas of insects, animals, and birds represents what is sometimes called taking over creation, the power to infuse inert matter (the physical body) with vitality, energy, and spirit. The relationship between the color of his mechanical insects and the "food" he gives them illustrates the way personality is formed by education and environmental influences. The story of the golden butterflies represents the Taoist theory of "equalizing things" in worldly terms, through redistribution of wealth by nonviolent means.

The last story in this section portrays the life of Nieh Shih-tao (Nie Shidao), a distinguished priest in one of the Taoist religious orders. The story contains several important themes. One is the idea that the highest adepts can be found only by people with certain inner qualities, and that the visible face of Taoism is only one link in a sort of spiritual hierarchy connecting the human world to the celestial. Another is the distinction between immortality of spirit and immortality of energy. This story also uses the familiar Taoist "time warp" theme to illustrate the coexistence of different modes of experience possible to humankind.

Tales of Inner Meaning

The Learned Man

One day Confucius was walking along with some disciples when they came upon two boys arguing. Confucius asked the boys what the dispute was about. They told him they were arguing about whether the sun was nearer at dawn and farther away at noon, or farther away at dawn and nearer at noon.

One of the boys argued that the sun appeared larger at dawn and smaller at noon, so it must be closer at dawn and farther away at noon.

The other boy argued that it was cool at dawn and hot at noon, so the sun must be farther away at dawn and closer at noon.

Confucius was at a loss to determine which one was correct. The boys jeered at him, "Who said you were so smart?"

The Story of Old Mister Shang

Old Mister Shang was a poor peasant whose strange fate began to unfold on the day his ramshackle little house was commandeered by a couple of arrogant young men belonging to the establishment of a local gangster.

At that time wealthy families, with many followers and hangers-on, could be as if a law unto themselves. Some families might have thousands of armed men on their estates. The gangster in question was the head of one such clan, and his followers were all young bullies from local well-to-do families. They spent their time dressing up in costly attire and gallivanting around, doing as they pleased.

The boss of the clan was well known for being able to make a poor man rich or a rich man poor with a single word or a nod of the head. Even the government had him on the payroll, though he had no regard whatsoever for law and order and contributed nothing at all to the general well-being. Countless were the deluded young men who had been maimed or killed in senseless duels staged to fire the ambitions of yet other deluded young men, and to amuse the gangster and his gang.

Old Mister Shang thought he had discovered his chance to become a success when he overheard the two young men that had taken over his house talking about their leader. The very next day old Shang set out for the residence of the gangster, who was such a big man that even the government paid him not to secede from the empire.

When old Shang arrived, he was greeted with hoots and hollers of laughter and derision. Who was this bumpkin, come to join their gang? Clearly he was going to be no fun for a duel, so the boys decided to see how it looked when an old man hit the ground after a fall from a building seven stories high.

A number of young men took poor old Shang up this high tower and told him the boss was offering a hundred pieces of gold to anyone who would jump off. Several of them made for the railing, as if to be the ones to get the prize, so old Shang hurriedly jumped over.

The hooligans held their breaths for a moment as they prepared to see the old man plummet to a gruesome death. What met their eyes instead was the sight of old Shang drifting lightly to the earth like a feather in the air.

Unable to believe what they had seen, the young men dismissed it as a fluke, due perhaps to the sudden gust of wind that everyone had noticed.

Next they decided to take him to the river bend, where there was an infamous rapids full of holes with unmeasured depths. They told him of an enormous pearl lying at the bottom of a deep hole under the swift current, and said the boss had offered it to anyone who could fish it out.

Old Shang plunged into the current without a moment's hesitation, only to surface moments later holding a huge pearl in his hand.

This could no longer be passed off as a fluke, and old Shang was now given a place among the guests of the master of the house.

Not long after that, a fire broke out in the storehouse. The boss told his followers that he would reward anyone who could retrieve his silk. Old Shang rushed right into the burning building and emerged unscorched with the silk.

At this point, the hooligans were convinced that old Shang must be one of those who had attained the Tao, and they all begged forgiveness for having tricked him. They said, "We played tricks on you, not realizing you were one of those imbued with the Tao. We derided you, unaware you were a man of the spirit. You must think us ignorant, deaf, and blind indeed, but we wish to ask about your Way."

Old Shang said, "You mean you were joking?"

When this was reported to Confucius, he said, "Someone who is perfectly sincere can affect things thereby. Old Shang believed in falsehoods, and things did not betray his trust. How much the more effective would truth and sincerity on both sides be. Make a note of this."

The Poor Man and the Gold

A poor man decided one day to get rich, so he put on his hat and coat and went to town.

As he walked through the center of town, pondering the question of how to obtain riches, his glance happened to fall on someone carrying a quantity of gold.

The poor man rushed up and grabbed some of the gold. He was caught as he tried to flee.

The magistrate asked the poor man, "How did you expect to get away with the gold, with all those people around?"

"I only saw the gold," explained the poor man, "I didn't see the people."

Who for Whom

Once a man held a huge banquet with a thousand guests. When someone presented a gift of fish and fowl, the host said appreciatively, "Heaven is generous to the people indeed, planting cereals and creating fish and fowl for our use." The huge crowd of guests echoed this sentiment.

A youth about twelve years old, however, who had been sitting in the most remote corner of the banquet hall, now came forward and said to the host, "It is not as you say, sir. All beings in the universe are living creatures on a par with us. No species is higher or lower in rank than another, it's just that they control each other by differences in their intelligence and power; they eat each other, but that does not mean they were produced for each other. People take what they can eat and eat it, but does that mean that heaven produced that for people? If so, then since mosquitoes bite skin and tigers and wolves eat flesh, does that not mean that heaven made humans for the mosquitoes and created flesh for tigers and wolves?"

Suspicion

Once a man found that his axe was missing, and suspected his neighbor's son of having taken it. Observing the youth walking around, the man was convinced that his was the walk of a thief. The youth looked like a thief and talked like a thief; everything he did pointed to his having stolen the axe.

Then one day the man happened to find his missing axe. After that, he noticed his neighbor's son wasn't behaving like a thief anymore.

Ups and Downs

Mr. Yin of the state of Chou was a prosperous businessman. His employees worked without rest from early morning until late at night.

Among them was an old laborer whose physical strength was virtually exhausted, yet who worked all the harder for that. By day he did his work huffing and puffing, grunting and groaning; by night he slept soundly, thoroughly exhausted.

As the old worker slept, his spirit relaxed and expanded. Every night he dreamed he was a king, a leader of the people, commanding the affairs of the nation, roaming at leisure and reveling in villas, enjoying whatever he wanted, his delight beyond compare. When he woke up, he would go back to work.

When someone expressed pity at how hard the old man toiled, he responded, "People may live a hundred years, but that is divided half and half into day and night. In the daytime I work like a slave, and I can't deny that it is miserable. At night, however, I am a king, and my pleasure is incomparable. So what have I got to complain about?"

As for the boss, Mr. Yin, his mind was occupied with his business, his thoughts concentrated on his affairs, so his body and mind were both tired. At night he also collapsed with fatigue into a deep sleep. Every night he dreamed he was a servant, rushing around all the time doing one chore after another, being scolded and beaten time and again. So he used to huff and puff and grunt and groan the whole night through.

Mr. Yin was unhappy about this state of affairs and consulted a friend about it. His friend said, "You have status and wealth far beyond that of most people, but at night you say you dream you are a servant. Well, the alternation of suffering and ease is normal; if you want to have it good both in working life and dream life, I'm afraid that is asking too much."

After that Mr. Yin lightened his workers' load and reduced his own concerns, so both got a bit of relief.

Forgetfulness

A man named Hua-tzu suffered from forgetfulness when he reached middle age. He would forget by nighttime what he had gotten during the day, and he would forget by morning what he had given at night. On the road he would forget to walk, at home he would forget to sit down. At any given time he was unconscious of what had gone before, and later he would not know what was going on at the present.

His whole family was distressed by his condition. They called on a fortune-teller to figure it out, but there was no prognosis. They called on a shaman to pray for him, but that did not stop it. They called on a doctor to treat him, but that did not cure it.

Now there was a Confucian who reckoned he could heal the man, and his wife and children offered him half of their estate for the remedy. The Confucian said, "This cannot be figured out by omens, cannot be alleviated by prayer, cannot be treated by medicine. I will try to transform his mind and change his thought, in hopes that he will get better."

Now when the Confucian tested him by exposing him to the elements, the man asked for clothing. When he starved him, the man asked for food. When he shut him up in the dark, the man asked for light. The Confucian joyfully announced to the children, "This sickness can be cured. My remedy, however, is secret and not to be revealed to others. Please clear everyone out and leave me alone with him for seven days." The family did as he said, so no one knew what measures the Confucian took, but one day the ailment from which the man had suffered for years was all gone.

When the man woke up, he flew into a rage. He threw his wife out of the house, punished his children, and went after the Confucian with a hatchet. The local people grabbed him and asked him what it was all about. He said, "In my past forgetfulness I was clear and free, unaware even of the existence or nonexistence of

44

heaven and earth. Now that I am suddenly conscious, all these decades of gains and losses, sorrows and joys, likes and dislikes, suddenly occur to me in a welter of confusion. I am afraid that future gains and losses, sorrows and joys, likes and dislikes, will disturb my mind like this. Will I ever have a moment's forgetfulness again?"

The Ailment

Lung Shu said to the physician Wen Chi, "Your art is subtle. I have an ailment; can you cure it?"

The physician said, "I will do as you say, but first tell me about your symptoms."

Lung Shu said, "I am not honored when the whole village praises me, nor am I ashamed when the whole county criticizes me. Gain does not make me happy, loss does not grieve me. I look upon life as like death, and see wealth as like poverty. I view people as like pigs, and see myself as like others. At home I am as though at an inn, and I look upon my native village as like a foreign country. With these afflictions, rewards cannot encourage me, punishments cannot threaten me. I cannot be changed by flourishing or decline, gain or loss; I cannot be moved by sorrow or happiness. Thus I cannot serve the government, associate with friends, run my household, or control my servants. What sickness is this? Is there any way to cure it?

The physician had Lung Shu stand with his back to the light while he looked into his chest. After a while he said, "Aha! I see your heart; it is empty! You are nearly a sage. Six of the apertures in your heart are open, one of them is closed. This may be why you think the wisdom of a sage is an ailment. It cannot be stopped by my shallow art."

The Story of Wan Baochang

Wan Baochang (Pao-ch'ang) was a man of unknown origin. A born genius, he had a subtle understanding of music and crafted all sorts of musical instruments.

Once when he was in the wilds, he saw a group of ten people dressed in beautiful clothes riding on magnificent bannered chariots. They were standing in rows, as if waiting on someone.

Wan moved to get out of their way, but they sent someone to summon him to them. When he approached, they said to him, "You have been given a musical nature, and you are going to hand on eight kinds of musical instruments in a degenerate age, to save its music from imminent corruption. But you do not yet completely know all the sounds of correct beginnings, so the supreme God has sent officers of the highest heaven to show you the mysterious and subtle essentials."

Then they had Wan sit there while they taught him the music of the ages, the sounds of order and disturbance. They set forth everything in detail, and Wan recorded it all. After a while, the group of immortals took off into the sky, and Wan went back home. When he returned, he found that he had been gone for five days. After this he studied all the music of the human world.

During the Northern Zhou and Sui dynasties in the latter sixth century, Wan gained recognition for his unusual talent and learning. He did not serve in government, however, and lived a bohemian lifestyle.

In the early 590s, when a certain nobleman completed a musical composition and submitted it to the throne for official adoption as court music for the newly established Sui dynasty, Emperor Wen summoned Wan to consult him. After listening to it, Wan said, "This is the sound of the destruction of a nation: sad, bitter, fleeting, scattered. It is not the sound of true elegance. It will not do for classical music."

The emperor had Wan make musical instruments. All of the instruments he made were low-keyed, different from those in use hitherto. Wan also said there was a mode in the ritual music of the ancient Chou dynasty nearly two thousand years earlier that none of the experts had been able to understand for centuries. When he composed a piece in this mode, people all laughed in derision, but when he had it performed, everyone marveled.

Subsequently Wan readjusted countless musical instruments, but their resulting tone was elegant and serene, not in accord with popular tastes; so they never became fashionable.

When Wan heard a musical composition called "Forever and Ever," he wept and told people, "It is licentious, harsh, and sad; it won't be long before people are killing each other everywhere."

Now at this time there was peace throughout the land and the economy was flourishing, so everyone who heard this statement of Wan's thought he was all wrong. But by the end of the era of Great Works [618, when the Sui dynasty collapsed], Wan's words proved to be true.

Wan Baochang had no children and was abandoned by his wife. He passed away in loneliness and sorrow, intimating that he had been punished by heaven for becoming too passionately involved with the world.

Golden Butterflies

In the time of the emperor Mu-tsung (Muzong) of the T'ang dynasty, in the ninth century, among the members of the elite corps of the imperial guard was a Japanese man named Kan Shiwa.

Kan Shiwa was a most extraordinary sculptor. He could fashion any sort of bird and make it so that it could drink water, hop around, stretch out its neck and call, and so on, all in the most beautiful and charming manner. He put machinery in the bellies of the birds he made, so that besides having beautiful plumage they could also fly one or two hundred feet in the air.

Also, Shiwa sculpted cats that could do even more; they could run around and even catch small birds.

Now the captain of the guard thought this was truly marvelous, and wrote to the emperor about it. Emperor Mu-tsung summoned Kan Shiwa into his presence, and he too was captivated by Shiwa's skill.

The emperor asked Shiwa if he could carve something yet more marvelous. Shiwa told the emperor he would make a "dais for seeing dragons."

Several days later, the dais was done. It was two feet high and looked like an ordinary footstool. When he saw it, the emperor wondered what was so special about it. Shiwa told him he would soon see if he stepped up onto the dais.

Not without misgivings, the emperor stepped up. The moment he did so, a gigantic dragon appeared in the sky. It was about twice the size of a man and had scales, a mane, claws, and horns; it flew into the clouds and rode on a mist, dancing in the sky. Its energy and appearance were such that one would never think it to have been made by human hands.

The emperor was flabbergasted. Frantically he jumped off the little platform and said, "Fine, fine, very good—now take it away with you!"

Strange to say, the moment he got off the dais the big dragon disappeared. All that remained was to put it back in its place.

Now Shiwa apologized to the emperor for startling him so, and offered to make good by doing something amusing.

The emperor, after protesting that he had not been frightened but merely surprised, asked Shiwa what he intended to fashion.

"Something small," replied Shiwa, producing a box from his pocket. When he opened it up, inside were little scarlet bugs.

"What are they?" the emperor asked.

"They're like spiders," said Shiwa. "They're flycatchers."

"Are they real?" the emperor asked, amazed by their lifelike quality.

"No, they're manmade," Shiwa answered.

"Then why are they scarlet?" asked the emperor.

"Because I feed them cinnabar powder," Shiwa explained. "Similarly," he continued, "if I fed them sulfur they'd be golden, and if I fed them powdered pearl they'd be pearly."

Then the emperor asked what the insects could do. Shiwa said, "They will dance for Your Majesty. And so that we may have Your Majesty view the dance, I have invited the musicians to play 'The Song of Liang-chou,' which is the insects' favorite tune." Now as the musicians prepared to play, the little red spiders scrambled out of the box and arranged themselves in five rows. They now stood in formation, waiting for the music to start.

When the orchestra began to play, the spiders began a very orderly dance in harmony with the music. They went forward, then backward; the rows came together, then rearrayed at angles, now suddenly shifted to form a circle.

The choreography was beautiful indeed, resembling an intricate and picturesque brocade, truly dazzling to the eye. And as the music played, the spiders also made a humming sound, as loud as the buzzing of a fly, keeping time with the music.

Finally, when the music ended, the spiders went back to their beginning position, arrayed in five rows; in unison they bowed to the emperor, and then went in orderly files back into the box.

The emperor exclaimed his delight. Shiwa went on to explain that the spiders were, as their name suggested, indeed flycatching bugs. To demonstrate, he took one of them and placed it on the palm of his hand; pointing to a fly near a tree, he said, "Grab it." The spider caught the fly just as a hawk might catch a sparrow. Then spiders leaped from Shiwa's hand to catch flies alighting on people's shoulders, or even flies buzzing through the air. Catching the flies, one by one they returned to Shiwa's palm.

The emperor marveled at this. He gave Shiwa a big reward of silver, which Shiwa ungrudgingly gave away to poor people in the city. Now the rumor passed around among the people of the city was that Kan Shiwa was a spiritual immortal from the Isles of the Blest in the Eastern Sea. Just when this gossip reached its peak, Kan Shiwa disappeared from the imperial guard, and no one ever saw him again.

Meanwhile, Emperor Mu-tsung had planted his garden with the finest and most luxuriant peonies, which filled the palace with their fragrance in season. Every evening, myriads of butterflies danced and chased each other amidst these blossoms.

Strange to say, the butterflies were all golden or pearly, and their dazzling brilliance made the palace seem as beautiful as the celestial realms. Countless thousands of them appeared in the evenings, but not one was to be found in the morning.

Every evening the palace ladies would vie with one another to catch these beautiful butterflies, and they found them very easy to do so. They used silk thread to tie the butterflies to their bosoms, or to their hairpins.

These shining butterflies, used as ornaments, were very pretty indeed, but when morning came, they were found to have lost their sheen, so the girls took them off. Then the following evening the butterflies would come to life again, flashing their brilliant lights as they danced among the flowers.

At these times Emperor Mu-tsung would roam around the garden happily, but what he liked most was to catch several hundred of the butterflies, let them loose in the palace, and enjoy watching the palace girls chase them.

The emperor enjoyed this sport every evening, never tiring of it, until one day the butterflies did not return to the flower garden. Emperor Mu-tsung and his ladies thought they had caught them all, but that wasn't so. Wherever flowers grew throughout the city, there now began to appear these strange and beautiful butterflies. They proved to be especially easy to catch among the flowers and trees planted by poor people; and so the poor would often catch them and sell them to rich people for a high price, using the proceeds to purchase things they needed.

One day the emperor went to his treasure house to get a certain dish made of gold. When he got there, he found that this precious article had already been smashed to pieces, and so had other items of gold and pearl.

From the midst of the fragments he could vaguely discern the pattern of a butterfly, and at that moment realized that the missing butterflies were the work of Kan Shiwa. He immediately searched the whole treasure house, but could find no trace of the wizard. After that he had the palace and the whole capital city, from its avenues to its alleyways, searched thoroughly, but the man was never found again.

And the butterflies never returned.

The Story of Nieh Shih-tao

Nieh Shih-tao was styled One Who Had Penetrated the Subtle. He was a brilliant man, yet simple and straightforward. Modest

50

and prudent in his speech and behavior, he was known for taking
care of his parents well in their old age, and was highly respected
in his community. When he was young, he became the student of
one of those beyond convention. At the age of thirteen, he was
ordained as a Taoist priest, and at the age of fifteen received an
esoteric symbol of a method for cultivating reality.

According to his own account, once when he was reading Taoist
books he came across a prescription for eating pine sap and decided
to climb Hundred Fathoms Mountain with a Taoist colleague to
gather some sap.

This mountain was very steep and high, and from its peak one
had a view of all four directions. At night the two Taoists rested
under the pines on the summit of the mountain; the sky was clear,
the moon was bright. Suddenly they heard immortal music coming
from Purple Cloud Mountain to the southeast, far far away, slowly
passing Stone and Metal Mountain, which was the same height as
Hundred Fathoms Mountain and, though ten miles away on the
surface of the earth, seemed very close from peak to peak.

When they heard the immortal music reach them, it stopped a
while; then there were three beats of a small drum, and a whole
orchestra was clearly heard to play again. Though percussion
instruments kept a beat, it was impossible to determine the
melody. The sounds were high and clear, not like the music of the
human world. It continued from midnight until dawn, finally
stopping at cock crow.

Later they heard from the villagers who lived at the foot of the
mountain that they had all heard it. Nieh's colleague said, "When
we were gathering mystic medicine, we suddenly heard immortal
music. This must mean that our intentions have been felt in the
other world. I also regard it as a sign that you will attain the Tao."

After that, Nieh traveled around, then went to Nanyue, the
southern Holy Mountain, where he prostrated himself before the
altars of Jade Purity and Blue Jade of the Heaven of Light.
Subsequently he stayed at the Immortal Summoning Observatory
and entered the Wellspring of the Spirit of Open Clarity.

Now it was springtime, and he heard that the old hermitage of

Real Human Ts'ai (Cai), a famous adept of centuries past, was not far away. He also heard there were strange flowers and trees around there, and that woodcutters sometimes saw Real Human Ts'ai.

Nieh Shih-tao, delighted at the prospect of possibly getting to see Real Human Ts'ai, fasted for seven days to purify himself, then rose early one morning and went alone into the mountains.

As he went along, he smelled an unusual floral fragrance. Before he realized it, it was already evening, and he found himself by a large valley stream. He saw a woodcutter sitting on the sand, facing the water. Nieh quickened his steps, heading over toward the woodcutter, who now picked up his bundle and began to go down the valley.

The woodcutter turned around and looked at Nieh, then put his bundle back down and asked, "Where are you going, all alone?"

Nieh replied, "I'm doing my best to learn the Tao and find the immortals. I've heard Real Human Ts'ai is hidden in these mountains, and I just want to meet him once."

The woodcutter said, "Master Ts'ai's abode is extremely deep—people can't go there."

Nieh said, "I've already come this far, climbing vines up cliffs—if there are mountains to cross, what does distance matter?"

The woodcutter said, "Anyway, it's getting late, almost nightfall; for now, go past this mountain, and to the east you'll find a home where you can stay."

Nieh wanted to go along with the woodcutter, but the woodcutter quickly stepped into the stream. It seemed quite shallow when the woodcutter walked in, but the moment Nieh stepped in the stream turned out to be extremely deep, with a swift current. So Nieh did not dare try to wade across.

The woodcutter said, "You'll be able to cross this stream fifty years from now."

Nieh watched as the woodcutter walked across the water and disappeared out of sight on the farther shore.

Nieh then went several miles around the mountain and saw in the distance a rustic cottage with a fenced yard, chickens, and dogs. Approaching nearer, he saw a pale man who looked like a farmer, about thirty years old, living alone.

When this man saw Nieh, he thought it very odd that anyone would be traveling alone deep in the mountains. Suddenly he said, "The troubles of the family come out together; who is in charge?" And he asked Nieh, "Where are you going?"

Nieh said, "I'm looking for the hermitage of Real Human Ts'ai."

The man said, "Did you see a woodcutter on the way here?"

Nieh said that he had.

The man said, "That was the Taoist adept Ts'ai, who just passed by."

When Nieh heard this, he prostrated himself in prayer and said, "When an ordinary ignoramus meets an immortal sage and does not recognize him, that too is in the order of things."

It was already nightfall, and the mountain forest was pitch black. Nieh had no place to stay.

The man asked him, "Where do you come from?"

In reply, Nieh told him of his beginnings and his journey in search of reality. Then the man allowed him into the house and even had him sit on the platform near the fireplace.

The man said, "I happen to be out of provisions here in the mountains."

Nieh said, "I've been fasting a long time, and I'm not hungry." He saw beside the fire a kettle of hot water and several covered yellow porcelain bowls.

The host said, "You can drink what's in the bowls—feel free to take what you want."

Nieh then took the cover off one of the bowls and found that there was tea in it. The host told him to pour hot water on it and drink.

Drinking the tea, Nieh found that its energy and savor were far different from ordinary tea. After a time he again wanted some tea and went to take the cover off another bowl, but found that he could not do so. He tried all the bowls, but found that he could not uncover any of them. Realizing with some diffidence that this was not an ordinary villager's house, he did not dare say anything.

The host, who slept in another room, did not get up the next morning even though the sun was high in the sky. And there was no fire in the hearth. In his sleep, the host said, "In this solitary and desolate place, suddenly I am concerned that I have nothing to offer you. There are a lot of homes in the village up ahead—you should go there."

Nieh went a couple of miles, but didn't see any houses, nothing but cliffs and defiles. When he turned around and looked back, he found that he had lost the way to where he had stayed the night. He went about ten miles, when he suddenly saw an old man.

Nieh and the old man sat on a flat rock to talk, and the old man asked him about why he had ventured into the mountains. Nieh told him all that had happened. The old man said, "Master Ts'ai and his son both hide in these mountains. Last night you stayed with his son."

The old man also told Nieh, "You have a rich air of the Tao about you, but your immortal bones are not yet complete. You will starve and thirst in the mountains—how can you stay here long?"

Then the old man suddenly broke off a stalk of a plant and handed it to Nieh. It was shaped like a ginger sprout and was over a foot long. Nieh chewed it and found it sweet and delicious. The old man also had him drink some spring water.

When Nieh raised his head after drinking from the spring, he found the old man had already disappeared.

Now Nieh was very disappointed, but after having taken the tea and eaten the herb, he felt stronger and lighter than when he had come.

He wanted to follow the mountain trail to look for a place to stay, but the trail was already covered and blocked by brambles and vines, impossible to get through.

So Nieh returned to the Immortal Summoning Observatory, where the Taoist priests there exclaimed with surprise, "This observatory is near the spiritual crags, but there are many poisonous creatures and wild beasts, so people are rarely able to go alone. We were wondering why you suddenly left over a month ago, and we've been worrying about you for a long time."

54

Nieh said, "I just left yesterday, and only stayed overnight."

He then told all about seeing the woodcutter, the cottage where he spent the night, and also about meeting the old man. The priests were impressed. They said, "While we have been living in this observatory, we have just been studying Taoism; we knew of the existence of Real Human Ts'ai, but haven't had any opportunities to see him. You must have the Tao in you already, because you've now seen both Master Ts'ai and his son. And as for the old man, in the past it has been said that Real Human P'eng also is hidden in these mountains; maybe the old man was this Master P'eng. As soon as you go into the mountains, you meet three immortals, and spend a day and a night there that is over a month long in the human world. In reality, this is what accumulated practice has led you to."

Nieh himself was amazed. He stayed at Immortal Summoning Observatory for years. Later he decided to return to his native place because his parents were getting old; he went back to the mountain hermitage near his home, where he had stayed as a youth.

When he went into the mountains to gather firewood and herbs, if he ran into tigers or leopards, when they saw Nieh they would let their ears droop and wag their tails, crouching down to the ground. Nieh would pet and talk to them, and they would get up and follow him. Sometimes he would fasten kindling or herbs on their backs; they would carry it home for him and then leave.

There are many similar examples of how people of the Way could influence wild animals. There was a mountain nearby where Nieh lived that was notorious for being inhabited by many fierce animals that didn't harm people; this was attributed to Nieh's influence.

His parents asked him how he had benefited from his traveling studies, and he told them the whole story. His parents were very happy because not only did they receive his care on the ordinary plane, they were also enriched by the all-embracing Tao through him. They considered themselves very fortunate to be the parents of Nieh.

Later he went traveling again, having heard that Real Human Mei and Administrator Siao were hiding on Jade Tube Mountain, and that many people of the time had seen them. Mei was Mei Fu, and had been an official; Siao was a prince of the Liang dynasty (sixth century C.E.), Siao Tzu-yun. When the governor of their district fled the rebellion of the infamous Hou Ching, whole families went into the mountains, and these two had both attained the Tao here.

Nieh, staying for a while at the Observatory of Pure Space on Jade Tube Mountain, wanted to look for Mei and Siao, so he made a special trip in hopes of seeing them. He set off with determination and went very deep into the mountains. Suddenly he saw a man dressed in muslin, with a black silk cap. By his face, he appeared to be about fifty years old.

Nieh paid his respects to this man and asked him who he was. At first the man said he was a worker and asked Nieh where he was going. Nieh told him he was looking for Mei and Siao. The worker said, "We have heard you are very diligent in your quest for the Tao, traveling to all the famous mountains. This is not easy at all. If you want to see those two masters, I can take you there. Your past deeds are very pure, already worthy of a name on the Jade Register; though you will not go on the ultimate flight right away, you will still cross over the world."

The workman also said, "I am Hsieh T'ung-hsiu (Xie Tongxiu). You may not know me, so I introduce myself. I have been living in seclusion in the mountains with the immortals P'eng and Ts'ai for three hundred years now. I know you have traveled to the Spring of Clear Awareness; I happen to have been ordered by the Master of the Eastern Flower to take charge of the mountain, forest, and earth immortals on Jade Tube Mountain, and am also in charge of the sanctuary shrines of the Observatory of Pure Space, so you and I have a spiritual connection already. That is why we have been able to meet. As for Master Mei and Master Siao, during the day they were called by the king of the Heaven of Little Existence, and I doubt that they will be back soon, so there is no use in waiting for them."

Nieh now bowed respectfully and said, "Mortals in the ordinary world search for the Tao in the wrong way, freezing their spirits and concentrating their thoughts from morning to night without yet knowing the essential wonder. They are like people adrift in a shoreless ocean. This unexpected meeting with you today is really a rare bit of good luck for me, as I have gotten to see a master of the Tao."

T'ung-hsiu said, "Your sincere devotion is very touching. You haven't finished your tasks in the world, so I am going to show you a way out of the mountains. We'll go to where I stay."

Nieh followed T'ung-hsiu for a couple of miles, when suddenly he saw a two-room reed house, very new and clean. Inside were low platform seats and a little kettle over a fire, with water boiling in it. It looked like a scholar's studio, with no one there.

T'ung-hsiu had Nieh come in and sit on a wooden horse, while T'ung-hsiu himself sat on a white stone deer. Suddenly a child came in and gave Nieh a cup of hot water. When he drank it, Nieh felt very clear and refreshed.

T'ung-hsiu also had him take a book from the shelf. He said, "This is the Basic Book. Be diligent in learning it, and you will attain the essence of reality."

Nieh wanted to stay there and learn from T'ung-hsiu, but before he said anything, T'ung-hsiu, aware of what Nieh was thinking, said, "You have parents who are getting old, and though you have an older brother who can take care of them, I cannot tell you to stay, in case you may want to travel to study more. I have a disciple living on a certain mountain; if you go see him, give him a message for me, and also show him the Basic Book. Then you will be able to find out what it means. If you don't see him, just throw the Basic Book in the cave above a certain ravine, and scratch my message on a rock there. Then my disciple will teach you the essential Way himself."

After he had said this much, T'ung-hsiu sent Nieh back. All of a sudden Nieh found that T'ung-hsiu had disappeared, and he himself was near the place he had started from. He went back to the Observatory of Pure Space, where the Taoist priests said in astonishment that he had been gone for seven days. Where did he go?

Nieh told them the whole story, and two of the priests were so excited that they begged to go back with him. They did go, and when they reached the place where Nieh had been, the rock formations and vegetation were as he had seen them, but they could not find the reed house. They looked around all day in dismay and finally returned to the observatory.

Anyway, Nieh had the Basic Book, which was written in readable characters, telling about the true secret of the esoteric essentials used by the Queen Mother of the Celestial Court to order and educate the Community of Immortals. When those immortals put it into practice, they should attain the ability to ascend to heaven; when mortals in the world receive it, while on earth they participate in the Inner Government. There were some points, however, whose meaning eluded him, so he later went to the Observatory of Reality and stayed there for a month looking for traces of Hsieh T'ung-hsiu's disciple.

Some people said there was a hermit who lived around the ravine T'ung-hsiu had mentioned, but no one knew his name, though sometimes people saw him. Nieh went into the mountains time and time again looking for him, but did not see him. At length he did as T'ung-hsiu had told him, throwing the book into the cave and scratching the message on a rock face. After that he dreamed that a spiritual man named Purple Sacred Mushroom, the disciple of T'ung-hsiu, taught him in such a way that his mental blocks melted away. Then he awoke.

A year or more later, he again returned to his original hermitage on the mountain near his hometown, and lived there for over twenty years. He regarded the Real Humans T'sai, P'eng, and Hsieh as his occult mentors, and personally oversaw the collection of tales about these immortals from among the Taoist priests and the general populace.

Eventually Nieh Shih-tao was recognized as a Taoist adept of great powers, respected by all. His prayers were always answered, and he had over five hundred disciples, at least fifteen of whom also attained adepthood and graced the Mystic School. People came from all around to study with him, and he taught them according to their natures and perceptions. He died at the age of sixty-eight, but like many of the Real People was seen from time to time for years and years afterwards.

Ancestor Lü

Introduction

Lü Yen (Lü Yan), commonly known in folklore as Lü Tung-pin (Lü Dongbin), is also called Lü Tsu (Lü Zu), or "Ancestor Lü," in recognition of his place in Taoist history as a progenitor of the school of Complete Reality. In Taoist tradition he is believed to have lived in the T'ang dynasty (618–905 C.E.). Some sources place his birth as early as the year 646, but other materials suggest much later dates. He is one of the greatest figures of folk Taoism and esoteric Taoism alike, and an enormous body of literature is attributed to his spiritual inspiration. His own work, along with later writings ascribed to him, is particularly noteworthy for its integration of Confucianism and Buddhism with classical, religious, and alchemical Taoism.

The story of Lü Yen's initiation is also one of the most famous of Taoist tales, rich in inner meaning. His first initiation, with Chung-li Ch'üan, the wizard who was to be his main teacher, took place at an inn, as did many such encounters described in Taoist recitals. For thousands of years hospitality has been one of the traditional Taoist crafts, and inns were established along pilgrimage roads and trade routes, including those linking China with Central Asia. Although they were later imitated and commercialized, originally the inns could be working Taoist circles disguised as places of rest and refreshment for travelers. For this reason many meetings with wizards in Chinese folklore take place at inns, not simply because such meetings are a folkloric motif in themselves, but because they were one of the ulterior purposes of the inns to begin with.

People are naturally in a special state when they travel, a state in which they are detached from the reinforcement of their customary environment and are therefore particularly exposed, sensitive, and vulnerable. Such a condition offers wizards an enhanced opportunity to see into people's hearts; since the spiritual alchemists could not be found by amateurs and so had to find their apprentices themselves, they also used the inns for this purpose, to help them in the way of their duty as master workers to pass on the art to worthy successors.

In common rooms of old inns, travelers could and would share their stories and their company. This too was a part of their ulterior design, to help maintain a general flow of common knowledge and information through the interaction of people from all over the country. Legend says that alchemists would mix in with the people in common rooms as part of their own training, as well as for the express purpose of looking for special individuals who might be able to receive the esoteric teaching.

When Lü Yen first met the alchemist Chung-li, he was mesmerized by the light in the stranger's eyes and by the indefinable aura of power that seemed to emanate from the man. Aware that he had caught Lü's attention, the mysterious stranger wrote a verse on the wall:

> Sitting or reclining, I always have
>   a jug of wine with me:
> I don't let both eyes perceive
>   the imperial city.
> Heaven and earth are so vast,
>   I have no name or clan:
> I wander aloof in the human world,
>   an independent man.

Chinese people, especially scholars, habitually used poetry to exchange ideas and find out what others were thinking. Individuals could be judged professionally, intellectually, morally, and spiritually by their sensitivity to subtle nuances in the symbolism of poetry. Struck by the stranger's extraordinary verse, Lü Yen saw that it bore the stamp of alchemy and immortalism, esoteric Taoist sciences. Now the man urged Lü to reply with a verse of his own. A Confucian scholar then in his middle age, Lü expressed his weariness with politics and his interest in spiritual elevation:

> When I was born, the scholars
> lived in a time of peace.
> The regalia of office hang heavy, restrictive;
> ordinary clothing is light.
> Who can struggle for name and gain
> in this world?
> I would serve the Jade Emperor
> up in the highest pure heaven.

Reading Lü's lines, the mysterious stranger said they would talk, but first he would prepare some gruel for their evening meal. As the wizard then rose to cook some cereal, Lü Yen suddenly felt himself overcome by an unfamiliar drowsiness. Unable to keep his eyes open, he lay his head on the table and fell asleep.

In his sleep, Lü Yen dreamed that he went to the capital and became a successful scholar. Obtaining a succession of government appointments, he went from one position to another. Sometimes his new assignment was to a higher position, sometimes he was demoted. Gradually he worked his way through decades of ups and downs. In the meanwhile, he married a woman from a wealthy clan and raised a large and prosperous family.

After forty years of government service, Lü was finally promoted to the rank of prime minister, one of the highest positions of the land. He held this office for ten years, and became accustomed to its privileges and powers. Then, at the zenith of his career, Lü was charged with a crime and stripped of both rank and property. His family was broken up, and he drifted off into the mountains alone. Before long he was on the very brink of starvation. Finding himself at length deep in the mountains, freezing in the wind and snow, he heaved a sigh that seemed to come from the very depths of his being.

At that moment he awoke. Looking around, he saw the mysterious stranger sitting at the table with him. The gruel hadn't even finished cooking. The stranger smiled and said, "The cereal isn't even done, and you've already dreamed yourself to paradise."

Lü was amazed. Incredulous, he said, "You know what I dreamed?"

The stranger said, "In the dream you just had, you experienced fifty years of ups and downs, all in a short while. Whatever you got is not worth rejoicing over, and whatever you lost is not worth regretting."

Lü Yen was at a loss for words. "There is also," the stranger added, quoting a classic, "a great awakening, after which you realize this human world is one big dream."

After he had seen through the vanity of political ambitions, the Confucian scholar Lü Yen conceived a strong desire to be free from all worldly concerns. He realized that the mysterious stranger must be one of the spiritual alchemists, for only such people could read the innermost thoughts of others, even in dreams. Without any further hesitation, Lü asked the stranger to teach him "the art of transcending the world."

The alchemist saw that the scholar was still ambitious and demanding, even if his thoughts had turned from government offices to the celestial realms. Observing that Lü needed more trying to refine his aspirations, the stranger said, "You are still unformed. Your will and your actions are not stable yet. It will take you several generations to transcend the world."

Lü Yen begged to be given at least a way to get started, but the wizard refused, telling the scholar that he still had unfinished business in society. With that, the stranger abruptly left the inn and disappeared.

The scholar was devastated. According to some stories, Lü was already over sixty years old at this time. Some say he returned to professional life for a while, others say he abandoned his career and went into isolation.

It was several years before the scholar again crossed paths with the wizard. Lü had now learned one of the esoteric arts from a Taoist adept he had met in the mountains, and he seemed to be ready for the "great transmutation."

Accepting the scholar Lü Yen as an apprentice, the wizard Chung-li Ch'üan showed him how to set up the alchemical operation, a deeply encoded process believed to stabilize the individual human consciousness and fuse it with what alchemists called impersonal awareness of the primal source of creative energy.

Three times Lü Yen set about the work; all three times he failed to complete the "great cycle." Something was not quite right. Apprentices of alchemy ordinarily studied the whole process before they began to carry out the operation, for the wizards always said that "a small error results in a big slip."

Lü Yen was unable to determine where he had gone wrong, so he went back to the maestro for help. Chung-li told him, "Your human mentality is not yet dead, so you have not been strict enough in the process of refinement." Then he had the apprentice turn off his thoughts, "darken his mind," and enter into a profound state of trance. When the scholar had done this, the wizard used his hypnotic powers to put the detached consciousness of the apprentice through ten ordeals, "turning up the fire to refine the gold from the ore."

In a vision, the entranced scholar came home one day to find that everyone in his family had died of the plague. Undisturbed, knowing that death was the natural lot of every living thing, he set about making preparations for their funerals. When he had gotten coffins for them, however, everyone rose from the dead. At that point he understood death as an awakening.

On another occasion, when he was selling some goods at the market, Lü was cheated by a merchant who paid only half of what he had promised. Seeing the way of the world, Lü didn't argue. In fact, he took nothing at all; he left his goods there and went away empty-handed.

When New Year's Day arrived, a beggar came to the door of Lü Yen's house, looking for a handout. Lü gave him some money, but the beggar kept asking for more, railing at the scholar all the while as he continued his importunate demands. Lü bowed to the vagabond again and again, asking for his pardon. He knew how close destitution was. At length the beggar laughed and went away.

Once Lü was herding sheep in the mountains, when he happened to encounter a tiger, one of the fierce predators that used to roam vast areas of Asia. The tiger went after the sheep, chasing them to the edge of a precipice. To save his wards from being driven over to their death, Lü stood in the tiger's way to block its advance. Now the tiger gave up and left.

Another time, Lü found himself staying alone in a mountain cottage studying his books, when a young woman appeared at his door. She was seventeen or eighteen years old, radiantly beautiful and prettily dressed. She said she was on her way to visit her mother. Since it was evening and she was tired from traveling, the scholar agreed to her request to let her stay at the cottage to rest. After a while the young woman began to flirt with the solitary scholar, and when night fell she pressed him to sleep with her and make love. Although he was courteous to the young woman, the meditating scholar remained unmoved by her seduction.

Another day, when Lü returned from a trip out of town, he found that all of his belongings had been stolen by thieves, leaving him penniless. Evincing no signs of anger, he took to gardening and gathering herbs for a living. One day he happened to find several dozen pieces of gold buried in the ground where he was hoeing. Refusing to take them for himself, Lü hurriedly reburied the gold deeper in the earth so that it wouldn't bother anyone else either.

The scholar was to have further encounters with the lure of material gold. Once when he bought some bronze vessels at the market, he found that they had turned to gold by the time he got home. He immediately took them back to the market and returned them to the merchant.

On another occasion, the scholar saw a mad Taoist monk in town selling medicine. The lunatic claimed that whoever took the potion would die at once and attain the Tao in the next life. Not surprisingly, he had not sold any of his elixir for some time. Lü Yen bought some of the brew and swallowed it, but nothing happened. He realized it was only phantom elixir, an imaginary potion of dreams without power.

When spring came, one day the scholar poled a small boat down a swollen river. All of a sudden wind and waves arose, nearly capsizing the boat in the torrent. Lü sat there unworried, aware that nothing lasts. Presently all was calm.

Then one day as Lü was sitting alone in his room, he suddenly saw a gang of bizarre monsters, a countless number of ghosts and ghouls. Some of them were threatening to attack him, some were making as though to kill him. In spite of the horror of the scene, Lü found himself unruffled. Perhaps he had already seen worse in the thoughts and deeds of his fellow men. Several dozen ghouls now appeared with a prisoner on a rack, squeezing the blood from his flesh. The prisoner cried out to the scholar, "You killed me in a past life; now ransom me off."

Lü Yen said, "Why refuse to repay a murder with my life?" Justice was one of the higher virtues of Confucianism, and one of the elementary virtues of Buddhism and Taoism; Lü's mind was steeped in all three traditions. Obtaining a dagger and a rope, the scholar was about to kill himself, when all of a sudden he heard a voice from the sky rebuking the players in the ghastly scene. All at once the ghosts and ghouls disappeared; there was a clap, and the master alchemist Chung-li Ch'üan appeared before the scholar Lü Yen.

Now the wizard said to his apprentice, "It is hard to put mundane concerns aside, and it is hard to propagate the material of which immortals are made. I seek people more than they seek me.

"I have tested you ten times, and you have remained unmoved each time. You are certain to attain the Way, but you haven't finished your active service in the world.

"I will give you the secret art of making gold, which you can use to balance society and help people. When you have seen three thousand accomplishments through to fulfillment and have carried out eight hundred undertakings to perfection, then I will come and take you over to the other side."

Boldly, the scholar asked the alchemist whether or not the gold made by this art would ever undergo change. The maestro replied that it would revert to its original substances in three thousand years. The scholar said that he didn't want to fool people, even three thousand years in the future. The wizard laughed and said, "Herein lies your sincerity in the three thousand accomplishments and eight hundred undertakings." This had been Lü's final test. He was now a full-fledged apprentice of spiritual alchemy. He followed Chung-li back to a remote ridge on a mountain known as an ancient site of esoteric learning, both Buddhist and Taoist. There he finally mastered spiritual alchemy.

As the story of Nieh Shih-tao illustrates, Taoist traditions of immortalism distinguish adepts who attain immortality of spirit and those who attain immortality of both spirit and energy. Ancestor Lü is generally considered one of the latter category. His spirit is believed to be accessible to people of the appropriate sensitivity and attunement; and he "himself" is believed to have reappeared over the ages in response to local conditions. A vast body of literature resulted from the accumulation of these beliefs. Such mystical revelations of Lü Yen, now known as Lord Lü, were forthcoming in particular abundance during the eighteenth century, when China was in desperate straits.

Almost all of the writings and sayings attributed to Lü Yen are evidently products of mediums and other workers in the *T'ien-hsien-p'a,* or Sect of the Celestial Immortals, an offshoot of the Southern school of Complete Reality Taoism tracing its ancestry back through Lord Lü to the ancient Taoist schools of the Han and Chou dynasties. The present anthology contains works from both what would seem to be the original body of the writings of Ancestor Lü, who founded the Complete Reality school, and what are later developments in the literature of the Celestial Immortals Sect.

The most accessible of the core works that seem to be attributable to the original Ancestor Lü may be the *Hundred-Character Tablet,* for which we are also fortunate to have detailed commentaries by later adepts. In this volume *The Hundred-Character Tablet,* which as its title indicates is a very short work, is presented in two interpretations. The first commentary translated here is attributed to Chang San-feng, who is universally recognized as being among the greatest Taoist masters of all time and is closely associated with the spirit and teachings of Ancestor Lü. The second is written by Liu I-ming (Liu Yiming), an outstanding adept of the late eighteenth and early nineteenth centuries. Two readings of the original work by Lü Yen are presented here, with commentaries, in the sections devoted to Chang San-feng and Liu I-ming.

The sayings and writings translated in the present section are taken from the larger body of work deriving from the later activity of Lü's followers and the mediums of the Celestial Immortals Sect. They are particularly useful for the elegant simplicity with which they introduce the broad range of traditional teachings to which they are heir in a manner that makes the principles accessible to the lay person without sacrificing inner meaning.

The first group of writings translated here is from a text called *Ch'ing-wei san-p'in ching (Qingwei sanpin jing),* or *Scripture on the Three Pure Subtle Natures,* which is represented as a reformulation of the teaching projected in the human world at the behest of the celestial government in response to deterioration in the quality of life on earth. The second group of writings is from *Yu-lu ta-kuan (Yulu daguan),* or *Great Display of Records of Talks.*

The Hundred-Character Tablet

Nurturing energy, forget words and guard it.
Conquer the mind, do nondoing.
In activity and quietude, know the source progenitor.
There is no thing; whom else do you seek?
Real constancy should respond to people;
in responding to people, it is essential not to get confused.
When you don't get confused, your nature is naturally stable;
when your nature is stable, energy naturally returns.
When energy returns, elixir spontaneously crystallizes,
in the pot pairing water and fire.
Yin and yang arise, alternating over and over again,
everywhere producing the sound of thunder.
White clouds assemble on the summit,
sweet dew bathes the polar mountain.
Having drunk the wine of longevity,
you wander free; who can know you?
You sit and listen to the stringless tune,
you clearly understand the mechanism of creation.
The whole of these twenty verses
is a ladder straight to heaven.

Sayings

THE THREE TREASURES

The human body is only vitality, energy, and spirit. Vitality, energy, and spirit are called the three treasures. Ultimate sagehood and noncontrivance are both attained from these. Few people know these three treasures, even by way of their temporal manifestations. What is inconceivable is their primordial state—is it not lost? If you lose these three treasures, you are incapable of noncontrivance, and so are unaware of the primordial.

THE PRIMORDIAL

Not only is the primordial uncontrived, it has nothing to it that could be contrived. When you reach nonexistence of even uncontrivance, there is no nonexistence of noncontrivance, and so no nonexistence of nonexistence. This nonexistence of nonexistence is the primordial, yet the primordial contains everything. It is because there is the primordial that there is the temporal. The primordial of everything is one single primordial. The unique primordial is the primordial state of each thing, each individual, and thus it forms the temporal. Thus we get the three treasures. These three treasures are complete as a human being.

VITALITY

In heaven, vitality is the Milky Way, it is the light of the sun, moon, and stars, it is rain and dew, sleet and hail, snow and frost. On earth it is water, streams, rivers, oceans, springs, wells, ponds, and marshes. In people it is vitality, the root of essence and life, the body of blood and flesh.

ENERGY

In heaven, energy is substance and form, yin and yang, the movement of the sun, moon, and stars, the processes of waxing and waning; it is clouds, mist, fog, and moisture; it is the heart of living beings, evolution and development. On earth, it is power, fuel, the pith of myriad beings, the source of mountain streams; it is lifegiving and killing, activating and storing; it is the passage of time, flourishing and decline, rising and falling, sprouts and sprout sheaths. In humans it is energy, physical movement, activity, speech, and perception; it is use of the body, the gateway of death and life.

SPIRIT

In heaven, spirit is the pivot, the true director, the silent mover; it is the essence of the sun, moon, and stars; it is the wind blowing, thunder pealing; it is compassion and dignity; it is the force of creation, the basis of the origin of beings. On earth, it is ability, communion, opening; it is the shapes of myriad species, mountains and waters; it is peace and quietude, the source of stability; it is calm, warmth, and kindness. In humans, it is the spirit, the light in the eyes, thought in the mind; it is wisdom and intelligence, innate knowledge and capacity; it is the government of vitality and energy, awareness and understanding; it is the basis of the physical shell, the foundation of the life span.

STABILIZING VITALITY

The three treasures are not easily obtained. Since they are not easy to obtain, how can we not take care of them? They are to be taken care of, and this is accomplished by purity and tranquillity, not agitating the vitality, not letting it leak, so that it abides peacefully in its original home, true to reality as it is, circulating three hundred and sixty-one times in a day and night, returning to its original home, true to its own nature, immutable, forming the stabilizing ingredient of the elixir of immortality.

GUARDING ENERGY

Vitality is always controlled by energy. Once energy runs outside, vitality eventually leaks out. Therefore, to stabilize vitality one should guard the energy. How is energy to be guarded? This requires freedom from craving, clear openness and serenity, not acting impulsively. The energy is to be placed in the mysterious pass, where it is brought to be nurtured and calmed. Always free, the energy is then unified, whole, unfragmented, all-pervasive, without gaps. After the energy is thus developed, it is brought down to merge with the vitality, unobstructed, like water and milk blending into one. Then the medicinal ingredients of the great elixir are naturally completed. Now just add the firing, and the effect will appear in the crucible.

PRESERVING SPIRIT

The firing is the spirit. Vitality cannot be concentrated except by energy, but vitality and energy cannot be operated without the spirit to stabilize the vitality, and nurturing the energy is just a matter of preserving the spirit. In the work of preserving the spirit, it is important to stop rumination, with nothing coming out from within and nothing coming in from outside. With all signs of emotion gone, one plunges into a state of boundlessness, lightness, blissful fluidity, tranquil independence.

75

EMERGENCE OF THE SPIRIT

When the spirit is preserved in this way, it abides in its chamber. The chamber of the spirit is in the alchemical storehouse. Once the alchemical storehouse is firmly secured, the spirit is calm and collected: controlling and operating the vitality and energy, thereby it crystallizes the great elixir, which is in the form of an infant resembling oneself. This then emerges from the forehead to travel through the universe; in the interval of an exhalation and inhalation, it travels unhindered through the ten directions, inconceivably serene and content.

If you stick to this, however, and do not hear of the Great Way or meet Real People, you will be affected by three calamities. Then if you do not awaken, the accomplishment that has been achieved will all go to waste.

THE THREE CALAMITIES

What are the three calamities? One is called the hard wind. The hard wind is sharp, cutting, and piercing; it enters through the forehead and penetrates the bones and joints, right down to the bottom of the feet. The limbs and hair fall apart, becoming wispy threads floating about loose.

If the hard wind cannot invade you, then there is a poisonous fire, which rises from below and enters through the top of the head, attacking the internal organs and burning the limbs. The pores and the hairline are instantly turned into ashes.

If your achievement is not harmed by this wind and fire, then it can be said to be consummate, unless you still have not learned the Way. Then there are five thunders, each with accompaniments, which circle and attack. As long as you have not learned the Great Way, the vital spirit will scatter in a moment, never to stabilize and unify.

Therefore it is imperative to study the Great Way, for if you do not study the Great Way you cannot escape these three calamities and will lose your three treasures. So it is only people of understanding who know this and therefore go in search of elevated Real People who will teach them the Great Way so that they can be forever free from the three calamities.

THE GREAT WAY

The Great Way is very difficult to express in words. Because it is hard to speak of, just look into beginninglessness, the beginningless beginning. When you reach the point where there is not even any beginninglessness, and not even any nonexistence of beginninglessness, this is the primordial. The primordial Way cannot be assessed; there is nothing in it that can be assessed. What verbal explanation is there for it? We cannot explain it, yet we do explain it—where does the explanation come from? The Way that can be explained is only in doing. What is doing? It is attained by nondoing. This nondoing begins in doing.

DOING

How is doing applied? To study its application, one must ask the autonomous mind. The autonomous mind is imbued with great understanding; it observes the changes of movement and stillness of yin and yang, looks to absolute yang and emulates its firm action, looks to absolute yin and communes with its process. The autonomous mind also studies the four seasons and models itself on their cycle. Silently comprehending the ultimate, it plumbs the original source.

Thus extensively observing all processes of creation and evolution, sitting calmly with the mind in trance, the energy of trance exists alone, calm sitting exists alone. Now there is nothing whatsoever in the autonomous mind, and the infant resembling the self that was previously cultivated and crystallized by the alchemical elixir communes with heaven and earth.

TRANSMISSION

It is necessary, however, to seek the guidance of elevated real people. If you do not meet real people who can point out the refinements and subtleties, you will not understand the Great Way. In that case, whatever you understand will still be superficial, and you will ultimately fail to attain the mysterious profundities. If you do not attain the profundities, how can you understand the Great Way? So we know that the Great Way requires us to seek true transmission.

This true transmission is received individually from a teacher; there is an opening up in the darkness, resulting in clear understanding. Once you are capable of clear understanding, you eventually realize the hidden mystery. Upon realizing the hidden mystery, you know the Great Way. This is called having knowledge and is regarded as attainment. When you attain this ultimate mystery, then nondoing is finally possible.

UNDERTAKINGS AND WORTHY DEEDS

Even if you have attained nondoing, you should still carry out undertakings, fulfilling them and realizing their proper results. After many undertakings, you should accomplish worthy deeds, fulfilling them completely and realizing their proper results.

Those whose worthy deeds are great realize great fruits of their causes; they may become incorruptible immortals and take their places in the ranks of the celestials, or they may remain in the human world as masters of all things, or they may live in a state of pure bliss.

Those whose worthy deeds rank next also lie in highest heaven as nondoing immortals, roaming in ecstasy, or they may live on special mountains, or they may travel in the polluted world as guides to the Way.

Those whose worthy deeds are shallow abide eternally in natural settings, among the springs and rocks, unborn and undying, forever free from the three calamities.

Some know that there is a distinct order in learning the Way. There is neither difficulty nor ease, but for the proper results look to deeds and undertakings; the deeds and undertakings accumulated each produce their proper results, but if you want the proper results you must learn the Great Way.

ORDER ON THE WAY

If you want to learn the Great Way, you must value the three treasures. Without the three treasures you cannot live long, and deep attainment cannot be reached in a limited time; so you will not learn the Great Way. Without learning the Great Way there is no purpose to accumulating deeds, so deeds thus accumulated are not great achievements. If you immediately think of the elevated sages and thereupon grasp the Great Way without establishing great works or fulfilling great undertakings, it is as though you have gained nothing.

ENTERING THE WAY

Observe what people who arrived did to enter the Way. They strove mightily, as if they feared they wouldn't reach it, and looked all over for elevated Real People to teach them the mysterious wonder. Plunged into danger, they were not cowed; plunged into difficulty, they were not disturbed; faced with obstacles, they were not confused; confronted with hardships that refined them, they had no regrets. Such was their sincerity that they moved the Real People to teach them the essential, and thus they were able to attain penetrating understanding, without distortion. Then they came back and sat, silently carrying on mystic work, gazing above and examining below, realizing the mystery of mysteries.

Yet they still did not become complacent: they mixed in with the ordinary world and carried out various undertakings and performed various deeds in the cities, towns, and villages. Thinking their works were still shallow, they made yet broader commitments, to carry out unlimited undertakings and accomplish unlimited deeds. They vowed that all people through the ages, those with knowledge and those without, would hear of the Great Way and ascend to the ultimate goal.

THE ULTIMATE GOAL

So this undertaking could not be finished even in ten million eons. If this were ever fully accomplished, it would be truly supreme, reaching nondoing, reaching to where there is not even any nondoing. This nondoing is coextensive with heaven and earth, but not coterminous. This is because both heaven and earth are created, and they consist of that which is created, so they must end. Because heaven does something, it too must suffer wastage. People who have arrived on the Way have no doing, and nondoing cannot suffer wastage or aging.

These ultimate people exist before heaven and earth exist, and emerge once heaven and earth come to exist. While heaven and earth wear out, these ultimate people are safe. This is very subtle indeed; I can hardly describe such ultimate people, but in the final analysis all people are like this. How are they like this? Because of the primordial. The primordial is inherent in everyone.

THE PRIMORDIAL AND THE ACQUIRED

People have the primordial, but are mostly unaware of it. What is the reason for this? It is because while there is the primordial, there is also the acquired. Since there is that which is temporally acquired, there are six organs of sense. Once there are sense organs, they produce six consciousnesses.

What are the six organs? One is the eye; this eye organ looks at color and form and produces various states of mind that obscure the primordial. Another is the ear; this organ listens to sounds and produces various states of mind that obscure the primordial. Another is the mouth, which utters judgments that produce various states of mind that obscure the primordial. Another is the nose; this organ smells odors and produces various states of mind that obscure the primordial. Another is the tongue; this organ tastes flavors and produces various states of mind that obscure the primordial. Another is the body; this experiences situations and produces various states of mind that obscure the primordial.

Therefore these six organs are called the six robbers. If you want to learn the Great Way, first remove the six organs. As long as the six organs are not removed, they produce wrong consciousness.

REMOVING THE SIX ORGANS

How are the six organs removed? In ancient times there were adepts who knew the way to remove them. They did not dwell on any objects of sense: they saw without using their eyes, heard without using their ears, shut their mouths and withdrew their tongues, being like imbeciles all day long. They breathed from their heels, set their bodies aside unused, and performed all actions by the operation of the spirit. In this way the six organs were all there, yet it was as if they did not exist.

If one does not have the six organs, how can bad tendencies arise? There being no such tendencies of consciousness, as a result there is no obstruction. There being no obstruction, the mind is at peace. With the mind thus free from defilement and attachment, you set up the furnace and put in the three treasures; they can crystallize the great elixir, because that is what is produced by their conjunction.

MAKING THE ELIXIR

Using real knowledge, harmony, and awareness, combine them with the three treasures. When the three become one, the great elixir is made. Once you have made the great elixir, essence and sense submit, and the earthly and celestial are in their places. It is necessary, however, to seek elevated Real People to indicate to you the hidden subtleties in order that the proper results be attained.

MALPRACTICE

Lesser people do not know the basis and so act out erroneous ideas. They carry out various deviant practices, turning further and further away from the Way. Because of this aberration, they are beset by various bedevilments and obstacles. They incur the anger of heaven above and violate civil laws below.

If they take to seclusion, addicted to natural settings, as they know about the aforementioned type, they refine their energy and tranquilize the spirit, gathering the three treasures in hopes of producing the great elixir. But if they do not obtain directions in genuine method, ultimately they will be afflicted by the three calamities.

DISSIPATION

The human body is only vitality, energy, and spirit. If you do not care about your vitality and waste it arbitrarily, that is like putting water into a leaking cup; it will not fill the cup, but will gradually leak away. Finally it will be all gone, not a drop left. If you do not care about your energy but let it go whichever way it will, that is like placing incense on a red-hot brazier, letting it burn away; add more fuel and fire, and the incense will become ash. If you do not care about your spirit and dissipate it arbitrarily, that is like placing a lone lamp in the wind, letting it be blown by the wind, uncovered, so that it goes out.

THE SEED OF EMOTIONS

Because of the six organs, people produce the six consciousnesses; and because of the six consciousnesses they produce emotions. They hardly realize that emotions confuse them in regard to fundamental reality. Once fundamental reality is lost sight of, then emotions run wild. But the seed of all emotions is craving. Why is this? Because craving is at the root of emotions. If you don't crave anything, you don't want anything; if you don't want anything, how can you be attracted to anything? If you are not attracted to anything, you are not repulsed by anything; if you have neither attraction nor repulsion, what anger can there be? When there is no anger, fear does not occur; without fear, sadness disappears.

So we know that craving is the root of emotions. If you try to control emotions forcibly without extirpating the root, you control nothing but outgrowths. This is like a flood of water: if you try to dam it without stopping the source or clearing the flow, eventually you'll be drowned. It is also like a blazing fire: if you try to beat it out without removing its fuel or cutting off its path, you'll just increase the force of the flames, so that you'll be threatened at every turn. It is also like the waves of the ocean, one following another endlessly.

Feeling emotions and evoking them, they all accompany the mind, growing according to circumstances. Only developed people, knowing the seed, use the sword of wisdom with great aspiration and fierce determination to cut through the root and sprouts, extirpate undesirable syndromes, and prevent emotions from growing on them like parasites.

DISORIENTATION

The emotions are a huge bolt, and craving is the lock on the bolt. When you cut through the lock and take away the bolt, you can get beyond the barrier and go in peace, freely, without hindrance. Mastering understanding of the ultimate Way, you then ascend to exalted reality. I pity people who create all sorts of demons and obstacles because of craving. They are confused and disoriented all their lives, rarely taking stock of themselves. Even when people of high attainment try to enlighten them, it is like beating a drum for the deaf, like presenting a lamp to the blind. After all they do not wake up. What a pity! Still they feign interest in the Way, but their interest is misguided—what they seek is immortality. This is like opening Pandora's box—it's not that they don't find anything, but there is harm in it.

REMOVING EMOTIONS

How can you remove emotions? The way to remove them is to think there is no self. What is called no self? The self is originally not self; we are not these selves. So what does the self cleave to?

Once there is self and you cling to it as yourself, when clinging to the self as yourself, then nothing is not self. When nothing is not self, there is nothing to which the self does not cleave. The country is not one's own, yet one will die for love of it; the home is not one's own, yet one will die for love of it. Things are not one's own, yet one dies for them, like flies seeking ordure, like ants gathering in putrid flesh, like bees trying to get through a closed window, smashing themselves against it when they see the sunlight. Gluttony and greed make people like vultures, insatiably voracious. But try to think of the self; before the self existed, it wasn't like this: it must have been clear and cool. The self is transient, like a fleeting shadow, like the morning dew—in a moment the self is gone. Since the self has no self, what is the purpose of self-love? You will grab your heart and laugh in astonishment; when you meditate in this way, what craving will not disappear?

DETACHMENT

Once craving is eliminated, everything will disappear—desire, aversion, attraction, sorrow, fear, anger, ego, emotion. All will end with this craving. But people stick to craving as though they have fallen into an abyss. Though they try to swim out, there is no shore. What is needed first is patience, which means that you should think to yourself and reflect with increasing intensity.

In ancient times there was a rich man with many wives and children, surrounded by every luxury. One day he lost everything dear to him, and his mind was impressed with the Way. At this point he was surrounded by demons calling to him enticingly, trying to hold him back, taunting him, weeping, encircling and embracing him, not letting him go free. But this high-minded man remained patient and unconcerned. He looked upon what he had lost as like a broken pot, like worn-out shoes. Quietly disappearing into the mountains, stilling his breath and plunging into profound silence, not seeing or hearing anything, he caused his mind to be entirely free of emotion, vastly expanded, open and empty.

Yet when one has reached this stage, it is still necessary to go into the ordinary world with all its clamor and toil, experience all kinds of situations, observe all sorts of phenomena, and become familiar with people. When you can roam playfully, going in and out of the world without becoming influenced or attached, then you humbly seek the secret of the mysterious pass and refine the three treasures.

GOVERNING THE MIND

Since the refinement of the three treasures requires removal of emotions, it is necessary to govern the mind. What is governing the mind? The mind is originally pure, the mind is originally calm; openness and freedom are both basic qualities of mind. When we govern the mind, this means we should keep it as it is in its original fundamental state, clear as a mountain stream, pure, fresh, unpolluted, silent as an immense canyon, free from clamor, vast as the universe, immeasurable in extent, open as a great desert, its bounds unknown.

In this way, the mind with nothing in it is like charcoal or still water: charcoal can burn, still water can reflect. It may also be likened to a clear mirror, with no images in it once objects are gone. It is also like enlightenment, constituting the root of the Way. When the clear mirror is always polished and enlightenment is refreshed from time to time, the clear mirror is cold, and the heart of enlightenment leaves its impression. Being cold means all objects disappear; when the heart leaves its impression, all paths arise.

SITTING FORGETTING

I know without knowing, see without seeing; I have no ears, no eyes, no mind, no thought, no cognition. Thus having nothing, then reaching absence of even nothingness, after that the mind cannot be disturbed by anything. Being imperturbable is called sitting forgetting.

Once you can forget, you can be given the Way. You can thus pass through the barriers, tame essence and sense, establish the foundation of enlightenment and make it accessible to consciousness. If, however, in forgetting things you can battle with things but cannot settle them, and you seek to learn the secrets of the Way in this condition, it will not only be of no benefit, it will even be harmful.

THE CHIEF HOODLUM

To learn the Way we first kill off the chief hoodlum. What is the chief hoodlum? It is emotions. We need to wipe out that den of thieves to see once again the clear, calm, wide open original essence of mind. Don't let conditioned senses spy in.

What is this about? It is about quelling the mind. One removes emotions to quell the mind, then purifies the mind to nurture its great elixir.

ESSENCE

Some people practice aberrant techniques that not only obscure the Way but also obscure their own essence. Essence is that which is bestowed by Nature. Therefore quelling the mind is done for the sake of this essence. When the mind is surely quelled, how can essence be obscured?

So the effort to nurture essence is not to be relaxed. How is essence to be nurtured? This essence is rooted in the beginningless, espied in the absolute, and becomes fragmented in the temporal.

In the temporally conditioned essence there is inner design and energy. Inner design is divided into real and false; the false has lost the natural reality. Energy is divided into pure and polluted; the polluted is murky, and being murky and degraded cannot be called essence any more but is called temporally acquired conditioning.

THE ABSOLUTE

In the absolute, inner design and energy are whole and integrated; there is nothing false, and no pollution. This is the celestial state

86

of nature. Now when it comes to the beginningless, we cannot say it is essence and cannot say it is life; it being neither essence nor life, how can we say nature is rooted in the beginningless? We must realize that the beginningless is neither essence nor life, it is a seed in the absolute void. This seed becomes the root of the ultimate, whereupon there is life and essence. To nurture this essence is to nurture this seed.

NURTURING THE SEED

The seed of the beginningless is undefinable, imperceptible, formless; how does one set about nurturing it? The way to nurture it is to nurture the temporal first. The temporal nature has inner design and energy, pure and polluted, real and false, which cannot be equated; what can be nurtured? Nurturing and quelling means to get rid of the false and purify the polluted. Getting rid of the false is not easy, purifying the polluted is difficult. Out of pity for people, I will point out the way to start.

Where do you start? From pure desirelessness. When you have no desire, there is reality. Reality is without fabrication; when there is no fabrication, there is purity. When pure, you can be clear; when real, you can understand. What can you clearly understand? The attainment of pure reality illumines everything; the clarity of illumination understands every way.

REMOVING FALSEHOOD AND POLLUTION

How are falsehood and pollution removed? On the lower terrestrial plane, falsehood and pollution are mixed together; therefore I will give directions. It is necessary to be buoyant, to rise on high, making a profound effort to avoid entanglement in worldly objects. Sit in deep tranquillity with eyes downcast. Do not see, do not hear, and the mind will be clear and calm, without any garbage in it. After that you can get rid of falsehood and clean away acquired pollution. Once acquired pollution is cleared away, the mind is pure and no externals can adhere to it.

MASTERING MIND

In order to master the mind it is necessary to banish five kinds of consciousness, thereby get rid of five obstacles, and thus understand five natures and penetrate five mysteries.

CAUSELESS CONSCIOUSNESS

When people sit quietly in total stillness, with no images appearing to them, their ears not receiving anything, their eyes not making contact with anything, in a state of profound silence, undifferentiated, with steadily concentrated awareness, it may happen that suddenly a thought arises, drawing forth an outburst like wild animals galloping in all directions, out of control. This is very harmful to the Way, so students of the Way first get rid of this kind of consciousness. Where does this consciousness come from, and how does one get rid of it? The way to get rid of it is to eliminate falsehood and maintain truthfulness.

CONSCIOUSNESS OF THE FUTURE

Before situations have been experienced, before matters arise, you should make your mind clear and calm. Clarity and calm are roots of the Way, but it can happen that you may for no reason get caught up in all sorts of before-the-fact considerations, assailed by a hundred thoughts; then when you go through situations, dealing with people and events, they turn out differently than you thought, and so you try to make your thoughts fit them. This depletes the vitality, wearies the spirit, and exhausts the energy. It is better not to be conscious of the future, letting it be as it may. Therefore students who do not get rid of this consciousness can hardly learn the Way. The way to get rid of this consciousness is to forget objects, dismiss concerns, and clear the mind so that it is like space.

CONSCIOUSNESS OF SOUND AND FORM

What the ear hears and what the eye sees may be beautiful or ugly, fair or foul, may have any of a countless variety of features. You view them subjectively, like dreams, yet you do not understand this and become actually attached to them. First conscious of what is pleasing and displeasing, you devise strategies, uneasy and anxious, agitated and restless, so the luminous essence of mind is covered by shadows and you become feebleminded, unable to attain clarity. How can you study the great Way in this condition? You will on the contrary destroy yourself.

Therefore students of the Way silence the superficial intellect and cause the inner mind to be ever alert, realizing that if this consciousness remains it produces affliction, with no prospect of getting out of the confusion caused by affliction, anxious and insecure. When the autonomous mind emerges, it will get rid of this, clearly aware, free from entanglement or dependence, thoroughly equanimous outwardly and inwardly. Using ears for eyes and eyes for ears, no matter how extreme the situation may be, you do not see or hear.

CONSCIOUSNESS OF THE PAST

Whether there is good or bad fortune, if feelings are forgotten along with situations, what gain or loss is there, what weakness or strength? The ignorant are bound up in many concerns, upset and uneasy, confused and worried, going mad by losing their minds for no reason. To try to comprehend the Way in this condition is like trying to cross the ocean in a tub, leaving you helplessly adrift; it is like trying to descend into an abyss of a thousand fathoms by means of a well rope, which is not only impossible but dangerous. Therefore students of the Way must clear away this consciousness and not be fixated by it, so that nothing retards them and they are in a state of wholeness, everything evaporating, leaving no more false awareness mixing up true awareness.

CONSCIOUSNESS OF PERSONAL KNOWLEDGE

Considering oneself to be intelligent and enlightened is not going by the right Way. Unaware that presumption of personal knowledge greatly obstructs the Way, you go back and forth in a fog, stagnant, without expanding. This not only obstructs the Way, it actually destroys essential life. Therefore students of the Way work to eliminate this consciousness, because if they do not eliminate this consciousness they will never clarify true consciousness even if they eliminate other consciousnesses.

THE LEVEL ROAD

The Great Way is like a level road. If you do not proceed to traverse the level road by way of true consciousness, you fall into sidetracks. When people get mixed up in any of the countless cults, even if they are admonished they can rarely wake up, and even if there is true guidance they do not follow it. Even if causeless consciousness, consciousness of the future, consciousness of sound and form, and consciousness of the past are all forgotten, still if the consciousness of personal knowledge is kept you will be lost after all.

SPONTANEITY

Serenely accord with spontaneity; don't act willfully, or you'll lose the fundamental. What is the fundamental? It is the essence of mind. The awareness in this essence is called true awareness. The awareness of true awareness is called accurate awareness. The awareness of accurate awareness is great awareness. This great awareness is primal awareness; it doesn't depend on calculation or reasoning, it is not willful, insistent, fixated, or egotistic. If you follow its basic truth and let it be as it spontaneously is, then you will understand the beginningless and endless, penetrating the universe.

This is very subtle and abstruse. Taoists call it the knowledge of sages, Confucians call it spiritual communication, Buddhists call it silent illumination. These are all terms for true awareness, accurate awareness, great awareness, primal awareness. Consciousness without this awareness is called false consciousness. Unless false consciousness is eliminated, it will obscure true awareness.

But to eliminate false consciousness, it is best to get rid of five obstacles.

BEDEVILMENT

The obstacle of bedevilment may arise in the mind, may attach to objects, may operate through other people, or may pertain to the body. Bedevilments arising in the mind are ideas of self and others, ideas of glory and ignominy, ideas of gain and loss, ideas of right and wrong, ideas of profit and honor, ideas of superiority. These are dust on the pedestal of the spirit, preventing freedom.

Bedevilment in the body is when it is invaded by illness, hunger, cold, satiation, pain and pleasure; when one becomes comfortable, one becomes lazy, repeating vicious circles into which one becomes trapped and bound. There is disharmony in action, which carries over into the way one deals with situations. There are both pleasant and unpleasant situations: the pleasant are considered easy, the unpleasant are considered difficult. To enter the world is easy, to leave the world is hard; when confronted with fine things, then jealousy, willfulness, and attraction take over.

Everyone has such bedevilments; if students of the Way do not get rid of this obstacle, they will never be able to learn the Way. So get rid of these obstructing bedevilments one by one.

DOUBT

What is the obstacle of doubt? The Great Way is easy to know, simple to do; the indications of an illumined teacher are a lamp in a dark room, bright and clear, like a crystal globe. Nevertheless, the obstacle of doubt plants its roots. When one person talks about the Way, many people add their remarks and opinions, until the influence of the clamor becomes blinding, and people turn from that which is accurate to that which is deviant, confusing the true with the false. This is like falling off a tree into a deep canyon.

The words of the sages are supreme indeed: "The open spirit does not die; it is the entry to all marvels." The Way of the sages is great indeed: open and free, responding to cause, pure and serene. What is the use of different doctrines? Arbitrary indulgence in fuss and confusion makes the obstacle of doubt, by which people impede themselves. What a pity that they do not understand and wind up subject to pernicious influences.

It is necessary for practitioners to learn from genuine teachers; don't be confused by false doctrines, and don't take to sidetracks. Clear openness, calm stability, nurturing vitality, nurturing spirit, the mysterious pass, mystic receptivity, pure attention, nascent enlightenment, yin and yang, real knowing and conscious knowing, overcoming pitfalls, illumination, creative strength and receptive tranquillity—all are in the mind. What is the use of names? Forms do not remain. It is so simple and easy—what doubt is there? If you do not get rid of the obstacle of doubt, there will be a thicket of confusion.

THE OBSTACLE OF PRINCIPLE

Even when the obstacle of doubt is removed, there is still the obstacle of principle, which is even more harmful to the Way. The obstacle caused by individual clinging to partiality prevents comprehensive perception. The obstacle of Confucians is in reification, the obstacle of Taoists is in nothingness, and the obstacle of Buddhists is in emptiness.

REIFICATION

Those obstructed by reification cling to their partial principle; while they act in illusory situations, deal with illusory affairs, and see illusory persons, they take them all to actually exist. They belabor their minds, wear out their bodies, and exhaust their energy, considering all this obligatory in principle, unaware that these ideas are obstacles.

Now in human life, benevolence, duty, kindness, generosity, loyalty, respect, restraint, and vigor are all the abundant energy of heaven and earth; they are to be practiced genuinely and should not be considered vain. If the principles one observes are not fully digested, however, and one clings only to partial principles, then this will degenerate into a bad cause.

Sentimental benevolence, ostentatious dutifulness, petty loyalty, and ignorant respectfulness are criticized even in Confucianism, to say nothing of Taoism. It is lamentable how people are obstructed by reification; they fall into a pit of fire, without real understanding. The psychological certitude of sages is comprehended and penetrated by silent recognition and thorough investigation; there is nothing idle in it at all.

NOTHINGNESS

Those obstructed by nothingness, clinging one-sidedly to this principle, sit blankly to clear away sense objects and think that the Way is herein. None of them seeks the secret of nurturing the three treasures. Though they speak of reaching nothingness, this is really not the Way. The ultimate Way is not in reification, nor simple nothingness. The mystic essential is to balance openness and realism.

EMPTINESS

Those obstructed by emptiness cling to this partial principle; not knowing true essence, they vainly talk of empty emptiness, and emptiness is not voided, so it becomes nihilistic emptiness. Ultimately they are unaware of the independence of original true suchness.

SECTARIANISM

All those obstructed by the three obstacles of reification, nothingness, and emptiness are unable to reconcile the three teachings of

Confucianism, Taoism, and Buddhism. This results in sectarian differences and disputes. Confucians criticize the nothingness of Taoism, Taoists criticize the emptiness of Buddhism, Buddhists criticize the path of Confucianism—and so it goes on endlessly, back and forth. They do not realize that the basis is really one, even though the doctrines may be different. Their perception is divisive because they are obstructed by their principles.

INTEGRATION

The obstacle of reification leads to delusion, which makes it hard to wake up. The obstacle of nothingness leads to withering, in which there is no realism. The obstacle of emptiness leads to quietism, which reverts to nihilism. The ancient sages were realistic yet open, empty yet realistic. They saw that emptiness is not empty, that emptiness does not void anything. This is the supreme Way. It is attained by integration. It is only because of succumbing to the obstacle of principle that no one knows this. So students of the Way should be careful.

THE OBSTACLE OF WRITINGS

For the obstacle of principle to be removed, there is an obstacle whose roots derive from writings. But in reality, the obstacle of writings is an obstacle of mind. The mystic sayings of the *Tao-te Ching* all come from profound enlightenment: if you view them literally and lose their inner sense, if you fail to understand and succumb to this obstacle, then all sorts of false statements, aberrated doctrines, curiosities, and fantasies enter your mind, causing damage to the nature and body.

So what ancient adepts set up as truths were mostly in the form of indirect allusions. For example, the terms water and fire, furnace and cauldron, girl and boy, dragon and tiger, yin and yang, and mysterious female—all are allusions to something else. People who are obstructed by words often do exercises without knowing the Great Way is in vitality, energy, and spirit. Nurturing these three treasures is nurturing the seed; this seed is the root of the ultimate. What all those terms refer to is this one energy; the basis of the energy is this seed. When you recognize the seed, all the various explanations are dregs. Why consume the dregs?

So writings are not real explanations of the Way. When you personally realize the Way, you can dispense with all the writings.

THE OBSTACLE OF TRADITION

If you do away with writings but still stick to a teacher's tradition, this very teacher's tradition becomes a source of obstruction. You should by all means examine clearly and go to visit adepts who can transmit the profound marvel. If you don't find such a person, you will suffer from obstruction all your life. Generally speaking, beginners have dreams about the Way; once they make a mistake in choosing a teacher and are given false teachings, they are confused and cannot attain enlightenment. They follow false teachings all their lives, thinking them true guidance. Their bodies and minds become imprisoned, so that even if real people point out true awakening to them, they may repudiate it and turn away. Once they have tasted fanciful talk, they sell falsehood by falsehood, believe falsehood through falsehood. All sorts of obstructions arise from this.

Therefore students of the Way should be careful to choose high illuminates, to get rid of obstructions of body and mind. When these obstacles are eliminated, all obstructions disappear. Once obstructions dissolve, the spiritual base is clear and clean; then one can be given explanation of the subtleties of the five natures.

FIVE NATURES

The earthy nature is mostly turbid, and the turbid are mostly dull. The metallic nature is mostly decisive, and the decisive are mostly determined. The wooden nature is mostly kind, and the kind are mostly benevolent. The fiery nature is mostly adamant, and the adamant are mostly manic. The watery nature is mostly yielding, and the yielding are mostly docile.

The docile tend to wander aimlessly. The manic tend to undergo extremes. The benevolent tend to harmonize warmly. The determined tend to be strong and brave. The dull tend to be closed in.

The closed-in are ignorant; the strong and brave are unruly; those who wander aimlessly are shifty; those who harmonize warmly fall into the traps; those who are adamant and can endure extremes are cruel.

Therefore each of the five natures has a bias, so it is important to balance each with the others. By yielding one can overcome being adamant, by being adamant one can overcome yielding. Benevolence is balanced by effectiveness, effectiveness is balanced benevolence. The ignorance of earthy dullness is to be overcome by developed understanding. If developed understanding is not dominant, one loses the function of yielding.

Those who are too yielding tend to be lazy. Those who are too benevolent are foolish, and being foolish tend to be blind. Those who are too adamant tend to be rebellious. Those who are too determined tend to be stubborn. Those who are too dull do not have clear understanding and become alienated from reality.

BALANCED PERSONALITY

In terms of social virtues, the water nature corresponds to wisdom, the fire nature corresponds to courtesy, the wood nature corresponds to benevolence, the metal nature corresponds to righteousness, and the earth nature corresponds to trustworthiness. In a balanced personality, these five natures should be able to produce and control one another.

Wisdom should be able to produce benevolence. Benevolence should be able to produce courtesy. Courtesy should be able to produce trustworthiness. Trustworthiness should be able to produce righteousness. Righteousness should be able to produce wisdom.

Wisdom should control courtesy. Courtesy should control righteousness. Righteousness should control benevolence. Benevolence should control trustworthiness. Trustworthiness should control wisdom.

When these five natures produce and control each other thus in a continuous circle, then no element of personality dominates; they all interact, balancing each other, resulting in completeness of the five natures.

Those who know this truly understand the ultimate design; then when they are told of the subtleties of the five mysteries, they can understand them on their own.

THE FIVE MYSTERIES

The five mysteries are the mystery of heaven, the mystery of earth, the mystery of natural law, the mystery of the Way, and the total mystery of mysteries.

When you penetrate the mystery of heaven, then you know the course of heaven; emulating its spontaneity, you can be uncontrived. When you penetrate the mystery of earth, then you know the pattern of earth; emulating its firmness and flexibility, you can master balanced interaction. When you penetrate the mystery of natural law, you know cause and response, and assess unexpected changes before they become apparent. When you penetrate the mystery of the Way, then you comprehend the subtleties of the temporal and the primordial, of doing and nondoing; this is penetration of the mystery of mysteries.

Heaven above, earth below, the natural law of the Way, the refined and the profound—you will then know them all. You know, yet have no knowledge; and still there is nothing you do not know. Knowing all events but really having no knowledge is called attaining the Way.

THE MYSTERY OF HEAVEN

The deep blue of heaven spreads all over; it has shape but is not shape, has form but is not form. Its shape and form have a certain appearance; this is called substantiality. Yet that appearance is vague and ungraspable; substantiality has no definite form, but is open and traceless, and can only be called empty.

Only by emptiness can one be aware, only by substantiality can one cover all. Now empty, now substantial, changing most marvelously, is that whereby one penetrates the mystery of heaven. When you know how to be both empty and substantial, there is no congestion; emulating nature, you work and adapt at will, in a comprehensive cycle that never ceases. Then the great elixir of life is made.

THE MYSTERY OF EARTH

Earth is thick, broad, boundless. Insofar as it is empty above and substantial below, myriad beings are born from it; insofar as it is substantial above and empty below, myriad beings return to the root. Now empty, now substantial, it lasts forever with heaven. Its body is still, its function flows; mountains manifest its wonderful substance, rivers reveal its spirit.

By its substance it supports being, by its spirit it gathers consciousnesses. Without spirit there is no substance, without substance there is no spirit. Spirit is active, substance receptive; substance acts through spirit. Emptiness and substantiality interact and balance each other, subtly combining into one whole.

Taoists who master understanding of this principle combine the qualities of firmness and flexibility; as emptiness and substantiality produce one another, they penetrate the mystery of earth. Also, by understanding the basis of this, creativity and receptivity are established in their proper places, and the great elixir of life is made.

THE MYSTERY OF THE WAY

The mystery of the Way is not explained by words. If you consider it substantial, still all substance is empty. If you consider it empty, still all emptiness is substantial. If you want to talk about its alternating and interacting emptiness and substantiality, where does the substantiality exist, where is the emptiness clarified?

The substantiality within emptiness cannot be called substantial, the emptiness within substantiality cannot be called empty. Substantiality is not to be considered substantial, emptiness is not to be considered empty; yet though they are not to be considered empty or substantial, ultimately they are not nonexistent. Now empty, now substantial, it is difficult to express in words. Now empty, now substantial—it is subtle indeed.

Though you cannot consider it empty, it really is empty; though you cannot consider it substantial, it really is substantial. It cannot be called alternating emptiness and substantiality, yet it is really none other than alternating emptiness and substantiality. Ultimate indeed is the mystery of the Way! It has no name or form. So profound are its depths that it is difficult to fathom. Therefore if you understand this mystery, the elixir of life is thoroughly refined.

THE MYSTERY OF NATURAL LAW

The mystery of natural law is learned from a teacher, but it is based on the celestial order, which circulates throughout the earth. Once the Great Way is accomplished, then miracles, at the extreme end of natural law, are manifested at will, and supernatural powers are unfathomable. Then sky and earth are like a pouch, sun and moon are in a pot, the minuscule is gigantic, the macrocosm is minute; you can manipulate the cosmos at will, looking upon the universe as a mote of dust. Now integrating, now vanishing, now detached, now present, you enter the hidden and emerge in the evident; space itself disappears. You can even employ spirits and ghosts and make thunder and lightning.

You might call this emptiness, but there is nothing it doesn't contain; you might call this substantiality, but nothing in it really exists. When you attain it in the mind, activity corresponds; mind and activity reflect each other. The mind has no such mind; nothing is added by action. It is not attained in action, but operates in accord with the mind, changing unpredictably like a dream.

Heaven and earth are the witnesses; it is most subtle, endlessly creative. Only when you penetrate the mystery of the Way do you then arrive at this essence; thereby you penetrate the mystery of natural law, and then the Way is completed.

THE MYSTERY OF MYSTERIES

There is no way to explain the mystery of mysteries in words, for it is even beyond thought. It is very subtle, ungraspable, extremely rarefied. From heaven up to the infinite heaven there are perfected people, most mysterious, by whom heaven is directed and earth controlled. They understand people and things, the hidden and the obvious, to the furthest possible extent. They operate time without any fixed track, and are invisibly in charge of the accounting of the ages. Sages cannot recognize them as sages, spirits cannot recognize them as spirits.

The mystery of mysteries is nonexistent, yet exists; it is empty, yet substantial. It is not more in sages, not less in the ignorant. Heaven is within it, yet even heaven does not know it; earth receives its current, yet even earth does not recognize it. It penetrates the depths of all things, yet they go on unawares. Its presence is not presence, its passing is not passing. How can this mystery of mysteries be conceived of, how can it be imagined? If you penetrate the essence, it is mystery upon mystery.

LEARNED IGNORANCE

In the absence of understanding, all sorts of different arguments, opinions, and theories arise, resulting in different schools and sects that each hold to one point and repudiate others. Stubbornly holding on to their theories, they attack and goad each other; each maintaining one view, they argue and assert their own doctrines. They all want to be protectors of the Way, but though they speak out, they go to extremes.

The mind that understands the Way is entirely impartial and truthful. But because Taoist tradition has gone on so long, personalistic degenerations have cropped up. People attack one another and establish factions of supporters; they call themselves guardians of the Way, but they are really in it for their own sakes. When you look into their motivations, you find they are all outsiders. People like this are rot in Confucianism, bandits in Taoism, troublemakers in Buddhism. They are confused and obsessed.

A DAYFLY

Human life in the world is no more than that of a dayfly. This is true not only of ordinary people but also of the wizards and buddhas of all times as well. However, though a lifetime is limited, the spirit is unlimited. If we look on the universe from the point of view of our lifetime, our lifetimes are those of dayflies. But if we look on the universe from the point of view of our spirit, the universe too is like a dayfly.

HIGH MINDS

People should have lofty vision and broad minds. They should be hesitant to accept favor and patient in ignominy. With a capacity vast as the ocean, a mind open as space, if they are to receive much they should do so without considering it glorious, and if they should refuse something small they should do so without making excuses. Ancient sages ruled without taking it personally, or even abandoned rulership like a worn-out shoe. When did they ever keep wealth or poverty on their minds? Nowadays many people tie up their minds with such thoughts, unable to change. If some day they should be given high rank and a large salary, I don't know what they would be like.

MOTHERS

A woman carries a child in the womb for ten months, then gives birth in pain. Breast-feeding for three years, she watches over the infant with great care, aware of when it is sick, in pain, uncomfortable, itching. Whatever she does, even when she is not there, she always thinks of the baby. She is happy when she sees it laugh and worries when it cries. Seeing it stand and walk, she is at once anxious and exhilarated. She will go hungry to feed her child, she will freeze to clothe it. She watches, worries, and works, all for the child's future. How can one ever repay the debt one owes to one's mother?

FATHERS

Fathers should not be too indulgent, nor be too strict. Only when there are wise fathers are there good children. Only when there are kind fathers are there respectful children. How many people could ever become talented without teaching, act on their own without encouragement, gain a sense of purpose without study? Fathers should be aware of this.

GOOD DEEDS

Don't be concerned about whether merit in helpful deeds is great or small, much or little. Just be completely sincere. Then if you save even one insect, or care for one plant or tree, doing whatever you can, there is immeasurable merit in this.

STABLE PERCEPTION

People's minds need stable perception. If the mind is unstable, you cannot apply it usefully to the realm of true enlightenment. Eventually you will become biased and opinionated and will not believe good words. Craftily employing mental tricks, contesting against others, unwilling to tame the crazy mind and return it to unity, you will be out of harmony with true enlightenment. As a result, though there be some good in what you do from time to time, since the mind is the root, if the root is defective a little goodness won't help.

Those who have this affliction should endeavor to change. Do not flaunt personal knowledge, do not cling to biased views. Purify your mind through and through, so there is no obstruction or attachment; act with all your heart. People of true enlightenment perform deeds of true enlightenment. Going higher with every step, wherever they go there is profit. To seek this in yourself, just fully exert your own sincerity. All the sages are ultimately one; once you understand, you receive blessings without end.

THE TRUE ETERNAL TAO

Whenever I see those whom the vulgar call devotees of the Tao, I find that all of them seek to be taken in by spirits and immortals, or they seek lasting life and preservation of wealth by the practice of material alchemy or sexual yoga. When it comes to the great Tao of true eternity, pure and open, tranquil and dispassionate, there are few who are interested in it.

ENTERING THE TAO

The Tao is entered by way of sincerity. When you reach complete sincerity, the Tao is not far off. Therefore a classic says, "Before practicing the way of immortality, first practice the way of humanity."

What does practicing the way of humanity mean? The Tao is fundamentally empty, yet it fills the universe. People should embody the Tao in action, making the extent of their minds reach everywhere and encompass everything, so that all living creatures are embraced within the mind of the individual.

Also one should investigate the root of consciousness and the nature of intelligence, from time to time looking inward and using the mind to ask the mind whether one's actions are in accord with truth, and whether one is really contributing positively to society.

LIFE AND DEATH

People usually fear death, but when they become seriously ill they long for a quick death to relieve them of their misery, and when they are utterly exhausted in a perilous situation they want to die quickly to escape their suffering. When you look at life and death in reverse this way, you break right through the mental block.

RESTORING THE MIND

To restore the mind to its unfragmented origin, sit quietly and meditate. First count the breaths, then tune the breath until it is imperceptible. Sense the body as like the undifferentiated absolute, and you won't hear anything. Those who can regain their composure after a mountain crumbles before them are second best; not even being startled is expertise.

A TEMPORARY DEVICE

As long as there is any thought left unterminated, one's essence is not whole. As long as the breath is even slightly unsettled, one's life is not secure. It is necessary to reach the point where mind and breath rest on each other, and thoughts are forgotten in the midst of thought. In essence it requires relaxation and patience. The secret is put this way: "No need to stay by the furnace and watch the firing. Just settle spirit and breath, and trust nature. When exhalation and inhalation stop and the body is as though dead, you will realize meditation is just a temporary device."

JOYFULNESS

One should not be happy or delighted when the spiritual work takes effect, for when the mind is delighted the energy floats up and one becomes greedy. When sitting meditating, joyfulness in the mind is the blooming of the mind blossom—it is best to nurture it.

STATES

As for the states experienced through the exercise of quiescence, first there is dullness, oblivion, and random thought. Then there is lightness and freshness. Later it is like being inside curtains of gold mesh. Finally it is like returning to life from death, a clear breeze under the bright moon coming and going, the scenery unobstructed.

NOT HEARING

As for the exercise of sitting until one does not hear, at the extreme of quiet stillness, the mind is not drawn into movement by the ears. One hears only sound, not tone. This is not hearing.

THREE LEVELS OF ATTAINMENT

There are three levels of attainment of the Tao. One is the alchemy of nondoing. Another is the alchemy of spiritual power. The third is the alchemy of preserving unity.

In the alchemy of nondoing, the mind is the crucible. The intent is the fire. Walking, standing, sitting, and reclining are the laboratory. Joy, anger, sadness, and happiness are the firing process. Humanity, justice, loyalty, and truthfulness are culling and ingesting the elixir. Spring, summer, autumn, and winter are extraction and addition. Essence and sense are the medicinal ingredients.

In this alchemy, a month is condensed into a day, and the elixir takes one year to refine. When you use it all your life, you go beyond the heavens, leave being, and enter nonbeing. This is the method of unsurpassed true adepts, in which myriad practices are completely fulfilled. Tranquil, open, empty, mystery of mysteries, one joins the ancestor of heaven and earth. Working for the benefit of all people, participating in evolution, one joins the origin of heaven and earth. Even before the achievement is complete, the humane heart is universal; even before the virtue is consummate, the mystic wonder is inconceivable. Thus one is an assistant of heaven and earth. This is the highest level.

In the alchemy of spiritual power, heaven and earth are the crucible. The sun and moon are the medicinal ingredients. Spirit, energy, and vitality are culling and ingesting the elixir. Exhalation and inhalation are extraction and addition. The inner circulation of energy through the psychic channels is the firing process. This is the path of spiritual immortals. It is not easy to fulfill. One year is concentrated into one month, and it takes ten years to cultivate. When you use it all your life, you transcend the realms of desire, form, and formlessness, and become the same as heaven. If its highest attainment is consummated, three thousand practices are fulfilled and one becomes a spiritual immortal able to liberate people. In the middling grade there are eight hundred lofty achievements, and one becomes a flying wizard able to rescue people. In the lower echelon, one gathers medicine that boosts and enhances, and becomes a celestial wizard able to bring one's whole family to heaven. This is the second level.

In the alchemy of preserving unity, truthfulness is the crucible. Works are the medicinal ingredients. Humanity and duty are the firing process. Chronicles and history are culling and ingesting the elixir. Speech and action are extraction and addition. This is the path of the lower adepts. The method is easy to practice, but hard to perfect. Ten years are concentrated into one day, and it takes one hundred years to cultivate to completion. The higher echelons forget themselves for the public welfare and are deputies of heaven. The lower echelons include the benefit of others in what they do for themselves and are lesser functionaries of heaven. The very lowest ones ingest herbs for long life and become earthly wizards. These are the lowest of the three levels, the dregs of the path of immortality.

Those on the foremost level leave being and enter nonbeing and are unfathomable, not trapped by life or death. Those on the second level can transform and die at will. They plunge into the origin, embrace the pristine, free the spirit, leave the body, and disappear from the world. They have birth but not death. Those on the third level work hard and accumulate achievement, becoming immortal after death. Even if they live a long time, it is not more than five hundred years.

WALK SLOWLY

Walk slowly, at a relaxed pace, and you won't stumble. Sleep soundly and you won't fret through the night. Practitioners first of all need serenity and patience. Second, they need dispassion, not to think about the past or be concerned about the future. If you think about the past, your former self will not die. If you think about the future, the road seems long and hard to traverse. It is better to be serene and relaxed, not thinking of past or future but just paying attention to the present, acting normally. Each accomplishment is an achievement, and this will build up. If you are eager for completion and vow to do so many deeds or practices, this is still personal interest, calculating merit and striving for gain. Then the mind cannot be pure. This is the root of inconsistency.

The Founding of the
Southern and Northern Schools

Introduction

The Taoist school of Complete Reality descended from Ancestor Lü specialized in the grooming of vitality, energy, and spirit, coordinating the teachings of Buddhism and Confucianism with Taoism around these themes and the corresponding practices. Thus Taoist spiritual alchemy was revived in a purified form and harmonized with the mainstreams of Chinese religion and philosophy. This powerful new Taoist movement spread and thrived through the work of two great masters following Ancestor Lü: Chang Po-tuan (Zhang Boduan) and Wang Che (Wang Zhe), who were later to be honored as the respective founders of the Southern and Northern sects of Complete Reality Taoism.

Chang Po-tuan (983–1082 C.E.) learned the secret of Taoist alchemy from Liu Ts'ao (Liu Cao), a disciple of Ancestor Lü. Chang is famous primarily for two outstanding works: the *Four-Hundred-Character Treatise on the Golden Elixir* and *Understanding Reality*. The latter is particularly esteemed as one of the two primary "ancestors of alchemical books" read by all serious students of Complete Reality Taoism. Chang's own prefaces to his two major works are translated and presented here for their value in elucidating the orientation of his teaching. Their crypticism is more apparent than real, and their meanings can be gleaned simply by removing the symbolic cloak formed of such terminology as "water" and "fire," thus extracting the essence of Chang's ideas.

Although Chang's Southern school is known for cultivation of both mind and body, his original emphasis as illustrated in these prefaces clearly subordinates everything to spiritual enlightenment. Although he does not completely repudiate Taoist health and longevity practices, he notes their limitations and clarifies his primary interest in the spiritual from that perspective. Legend nevertheless portrays Chang Po-tuan as a master of vitality and energy as well as spirit, and so the present anthology also includes *The Secret of Opening the Passes,* a short work attributed to him on an exercise for enhancing the flow of energy through the body.

Although he was born more than twenty years after the death of Chang Po-tuan, Wang Che (1113–71 C.E.) is believed to have learned alchemy from both Ancestor Lü himself and Lü's own teacher, Chung-li Ch'üan. There is, of course, no way to resolve the historical questions raised by this legend, at least in the terms of ordinary academic thought and method. If nothing else, it illustrates the belief that some alchemical masters (like Chung-li Ch'üan, Lü Yen, and the later Chang San-feng) have not died, while others (like Chang Po-tuan and Wang Che) attained spiritual immortality but did die physically.

Wang Che was originally a scholar-warrior from northern China. As a young man he mastered the Confucian classics and dynastic histories, and also learned archery and swordsmanship. He achieved election to public service not through Confucian scholarship but by virtue of his martial prowess. At that time northern China was going through a period of progressive loss of territory to aggressive foreign powers. At the age of forty-seven Wang gave up his military commission, left home, and became a Taoist monk.

Wang later traveled to Mount Chung-nan (Zhongnan), a famous resort of Taoist immortals later associated with the development of Taoist martial arts. Also an ancient center of Buddhist *vinaya* or conduct teaching, Mount Chung-nan was steeped in the atmosphere of both traditions of spirituality. Wang is supposed to have met the old masters Chung-li and Lü on two occasions, receiving the secret of the "gold pill," or Taoist enlightenment, on their second meeting.

Later, Wang Che himself taught seven apprentices, including Sun Pu-erh (Sun Buer), one of the most famous female illuminates of all time. Through the activities of these seven adepts, Wang's School of Complete Reality became tremendously influential, especially in northern China, where it largely supplanted the aging and moribund schools of Ch'an Buddhism. An enormous quantity of Wang Che's writing has been preserved, most of it in the form of didactic poetry in alchemical style addressed to his disciples. The present anthology presents a translation of Wang's most historically important work, which is also his most straightforward and accessible writing, namely his opening statement on the founding of his school.

Chang Po-tuan

INTRODUCTION TO THE FOUR-HUNDRED-
CHARACTER TREATISE ON THE GOLDEN ELIXIR

The alchemical gold is what we call the great elixir of gold liquid reverted seven times and restored nine times.

Seven is the number associated with fire, nine is the number associated with metal. Fire is associated with spirit, metal is associated with the unconscious. When metal is refined by fire, so that it reverts to its origin and is restored to its source, it is called gold elixir.

Body and mind are divided into two poles, upper and lower; spirit and energy are distinguished into two extremes, winter and summer. The joining of body and spirit, yin and yang, is represented by the trigrams water ☵ and fire ☲ .

Joining the celestial and earthly souls with the spirit and vitality through the medium of the will is called gathering the five elements.

Containing the light of the eyes, freezing the tones of the ears, tuning the breath in the nose, sealing the energy of the tongue—this is called combining the four signs.

When the eyes do not look, the ears do not listen, the tongue doesn't speak, the nose doesn't smell, and the limbs do not move, this is called the five energies returning to the source.

When vitality is transformed into energy, energy is transformed into spirit, and spirit is transformed into space, this is called the three flowers gathered on the peak.

When the celestial soul does not leak out through the eyes, the earthly soul does not leak out through the nose, the spirit does not leak out through the mouth, the vitality does not leak out through the ears, and the will does not leak out through the pores of the limbs, it is said that the nonleaking vitality, spirit, celestial soul, earthly soul, and will merge and transform into one energy, which cannot be seen or heard and has no name or form. This is why we speak of vacuity.

Refining the vitality means refining the basic vitality. It does not refer to the vitality felt through sexuality. Refining the energy means refining the basic energy. It does not refer to the energy of breathing through the mouth and nose. Refining the spirit means refining the basic spirit. It does not refer to the spirit of mind and thought.

Therefore this spirit, energy, and vitality have the same root as heaven and earth, the same substance as myriad things. When you gain them you live, when you lose them you die. Refine them with higher consciousness, and they turn into creative energy. Nourish them by subtle accord with circumstances, and they turn into supple vitality. Therefore it is said, "When you see it, you cannot use it; when you use it, you cannot see it."

The body is the house of the mind, the mind is the master of the body. Wildness of the mind is likened to a dragon, viciousness of the body is likened to a tiger. In the body there is one point of true creative energy, in the mind there is one point of true supple vitality. This is why we speak of two substances in alchemy.

Mind is associated with heaven, body is associated with earth. This is why we speak of the crucible or cauldron of heaven and earth. The creative energy is associated with fire, the supple vitality is associated with water. This is why we speak of the medicinal substances of sun and moon.

Embracing the one, keeping to the mean, refining the original, nourishing the basic, one gathers the primordial energy of the undifferentiated origin. In the morning there is beginning, difficulty, starting of growth; in the evening there is breaking through obstacles, flowing on unceasing. The cycle of the work is called the firing process.

To start gathering the medicine, you work the bellows of *heaven* and *earth,* take up the apothecary scale of *fire* and *water.* In the beginning it is like clouds filling a thousand mountains, then it is like the moon reflected in myriad rivers. Naturally there occurs a spiritual transformation and an acceleration of pace.

Yet you still do not know the dragon struggles with the celestial soul, the tiger struggles with the earthly soul, the sun battles with the vitality, the moon battles with the spirit.

In a trance you see the true lead, the inner sense of real knowledge. In darkness there is the true mercury, the inner essence of consciousness. Mix the lead and mercury in a medium of earth, true will; keep them in the central chamber, in the region of the solar plexus.

When the lead sees fire, it flies; when the mercury sees fire, it runs. Eventually you use the oil of nondoing to harmonize them, and also use the uncut jewel of namelessness to settle them. The lead returns to the palace of earth, the mercury returns to the position of heaven—the true sense of knowledge comes back to the terrestrial plane, the inner essence of consciousness goes back to the celestial plane.

Fully mixed, the true earth glows silently. If there is too much fire, it dries out; if there is too much water, it runs off. Drying out by fire and running off by water must be controlled by equilibrium.

When the development process reaches this point, a breeze arises between the eyebrows, the moon shines in the heart, fire burns in the lower abdomen, the midspine is like a cartwheel, the limbs are like boulders, the pores are like they are after emerging from a bath, the bones and blood vessels are like they are in deep sleep, the vitality and spirit are like husband and wife in joyful embrace, the celestial and earthly souls are like mother and child hugging each other. This is a real state, not a metaphor.

If you refine this by proper measure, it will stay together and not be dispelled. If you refine it with appropriate balance, it will solidify and become firmer. The celestial soul hides, the earthly soul disappears; the vitality coagulates, the spirit congeals; the unified mind is flexible, the skin is fresh and breathes freely. As time goes by, gradually congealing, gradually gathering, you produce substance from no substance, forming the spiritual embryo.

One year has twelve months, one month has thirty days, one day has a hundred intervals; so in all, one month has three thousand intervals, and ten months have thirty thousand intervals. When you continue this work uninterruptedly, the embryonic energy congeals, the spiritual infant manifests its form, the mystic jewel takes shape, the celestial spirit is imbued with reality.

Therefore these thirty thousand intervals can take the place of thirty thousand years in nature. Why? The work of one interval has inherent in it the four seasons of one year, so thirty thousand intervals can take the place of thirty thousand years. Thus one year, twelve months, has thirty-six thousand intervals. Even ignorant ordinary people can ascend to the state of sages by practicing this. Why is it that ordinary people do not realize this in their everyday lives? The original vitality is lost, the original energy exhausted, the original spirit departed.

So attunement is necessary in each of the thirty thousand intervals. If there is any deviation for even one interval, the materials for the elixir dissipate and the firing is defective. Therefore it is said that if there is even a hairsbreadth of deviation one cannot make the elixir.

Therefore one should work from moment to moment, yet without strain. The true energy congeals, the original spirit expands. Inwardly, in one year you refine the elixir of thirty thousand intervals; outwardly, your body replaces the equivalent of thirty thousand years. On the larger scale, in one day one forms an embryo of thirteen thousand five hundred breaths; on the smaller scale, over twenty-four hours one activates the energy to go eighty-four thousand miles.

This is why it is said, take the one point of yang between heaven and earth, gather up the energy of the two spheres of sun and moon, work the true water in the lead furnace, operate the true fire in the mercury crucible. Bringing mercury into contact with lead is called the flower pond, putting mercury into lead is called spirit water.

Do not cling to nondoing; do not manifest contrivance; do not get mired in meditation; do not stick to discipline; do not sit like a dead tree and reduce the mind to ashes; do not ignorantly practice blind cultivation.

Beware of not knowing where the material for the medicine comes from, and beware of not knowing the proper measure in the firing process. You should know the one aperture in the body known as the mysterious pass. This cavity is not the heart, not the kidneys, not the mouth or nose, not the spleen or stomach, not the genitals, not the bladder, not the lower abdomen, not the spot between the eyebrows.

If you know this aperture, the winter solstice, the moment of utter silence preceding the return of positive energy, is herein; the medicinal ingredients are also herein; the firing process, the course of the spiritual work, is also herein; the bathing process, to cool the fire of concentration, is also herein; release from the body is also herein.

This opening has no edges or sides, and no inside or outside. It is the root of the spiritual energy, the valley of nothingness. So seek it in the body—it is not to be found elsewhere. This aperture cannot be arbitrarily figured out by oneself—it requires mental transmission and personal instruction. Without this, all is mere falsehood and fabrication.

The purpose of writing about alchemy, embracing the foundation of creative evolution and penetrating the marrow of the complementary energies of the universe, is to enable practitioners of alchemy to follow the stream so as to know the source, to abandon the false and thereby follow the true, and not wind up forgetting the root and pursuing the branches.

Alchemy produces something out of nothing, developing the spiritual infant. One should not allow oneself to be sidetracked by getting mired in symbols and clinging to words. Now when it is said that the alchemical elixir is produced from nothing, that should not be interpreted as a blank vacantness. You should know that this emptiness is emptiness in reality; non-nothingness in nothingness is the real nothingness.

INTRODUCTION TO UNDERSTANDING REALITY

A human body is hard to get; time easily slips by. There is no telling whether one will be short-lived or long-lived. How can one escape the consequences of actions? If you didn't manage to awaken early on by yourself, all you can do is accept your lot and await the end. If a single thought goes wrong as your time is up, you fall into miserable states from which there is no hope of escape even in countless eons. Even if you feel regret now, it is too late.

This is why Lao-tzu and Buddha articulated expedient methods using the sciences of essence and life to teach people to cultivate the seed whereby to escape birth and death.

Buddha considered emptiness and silence to be the source. If you suddenly attain complete realization, then you transcend directly to the Other Shore. If you still have habitual attachments as yet unended, you continue to go along with becoming and birth.

Lao-tzu considered refinement and cultivation to be the way to realization. If you attain the critical pivot, you immediately ascend to the ranks of sages. If you do not understand your original essence, you still cling to the illusory body.

Next, the *I Ching* has the expression "find out the truth, fulfill your nature, and arrive at destiny," and the *Analects* of Confucius say he had "no willfulness, insistence, inflexibility, or egotism." Here Confucius finally reached the depths of essence and life; but why did he always speak of them laconically and not in detail? It was because he wanted to establish order in human society and disseminate the teachings of humanity, justice, etiquette, and music. Therefore he did not speak openly of the way of noncontrivance; he just put the arts of life in his sayings on the images of the

I Ching, and mixed the principles of essence in with his laconic remarks.

That brings us to Chuang-tzu, who figured out the burden of things and the essence of freedom. Mencius skillfully nurtured abundant energy. Both reached very close.

Now then, Wei Po-yang of the Han dynasty, drawing on the transformational way of the *I Ching,* the bodies of yin and yang in intercourse, composed the *Triplex Unity* to illustrate the working of the great alchemy.

[The Ch'an Buddhist master] National Teacher Chung of the T'ang dynasty caps his recorded sayings with words of Lao-tzu and Chuang-tzu to reveal the root and branches of the Way.

Is it not a fact that the doctrines [of Taoism, Buddhism, and Confucianism] may be three, but the Way is ultimately one? But that hasn't stopped the priesthoods of later generations from sole devotion to their own sects and repudiation of others, causing the basic essentials of all three philosophies to be lost in false distinctions, so that they cannot be unified and end up at the same goal.

Furthermore, people today think Taoism values cultivation of life, but do not know that the principles of the methods of cultivating life are two-sided: there is that which is easy to come by but hard to accomplish, and that which is hard to come by but easy to accomplish.

Examples of practices that are easy to come by but hard to accomplish are "refining the energies of the five sprouts," "drinking the lights of the seven stars," concentration on imagery, massage, breathing exercises, reciting scriptures, holding spells, pronouncing charms, chattering the teeth to concentrate the spirit, celibacy, fasting, keeping attention on the spirit, stilling the breathing, placing the thought between the brows, reversing the flow of vitality to repair the brain, practicing the bedroom arts, and taking mineral and vegetable potions. All of these are easy to come by but hard to accomplish.

All of the above methods ultimately fall apart on the path of cultivating the body. Therefore you may expend a great deal of effort on them without actually experiencing the anticipated results. If you practice diligently day and night with intense determination, you may just avoid disease and escape accidents. But as soon as you skip practice, your previous accomplishment gradually fades away. Thus passing the months and years, it is inevitably hard to complete the work successfully; is it not impossible to expect a permanent, once-and-for-all attainment, rejuvenation, transformation, and elevation? What a pity!

Practitioners of recent times have arbitrary fixations and do not understand the reality of the subtle teaching; then they turn around and resent the spiritual immortals for deceptive talk. They still do not know that while accomplishment of the Way is attained by refinement of the gold pill, yet it has been named after various things in fear of divulging the celestial mechanism.

Among [the aforementioned practices], the method of stilling the breathing is similar to the sitting meditation of the two vehicles [of Buddhism devoted to nirvana], if one can forget mental machinations and stop thinking. If the method is practiced diligently, it is possible thereby to enter trance and project the spirit; but the vital spirit is still dependent on an earthly abode, which can hardly be made secure, so one does not escape perpetual use of relocation techniques. As long as one has not attained the Way of restoration and recovery of alchemical gold and mercury, how can one return positive energy, change one's bones, and ascend to heaven in broad daylight?

What is hard to come by but easy to accomplish is refining the gold liquid and restoring the elixir. It is essential to understand yin and yang clearly, and to attain profound comprehension of creative evolution before you can chase the two energies into the central path, merge the three natures in the chamber of the origin, assemble the five elements and combine the four forms, so the dragon howls, the tiger roars, the husband leads and the wife follows, the water boils in the jade cauldron, and the fire blazes in the gold furnace: only then do you get the mystic pearl to take shape and the great unity to return to reality. In all, it takes only a brief period of work to permanently guarantee infinite freedom and bliss.

When it comes to warding off dangers and considering perils, being careful about the application of practice, extracting and adding, nurturing sanity and sustaining fulfillment, it is essential to keep to the feminine, embrace unity, and be natural, thus restoring the positive, life-giving energy and stripping away negative, death-dealing materialism. Once the phases of energy are complete, you are released and spiritually transformed; your name is listed in the ranks of immortals, and you are called a real human being. This is the time when the work of great people is done and their honor is realized.

Among students now, there are those who take lead and mercury for the two energies, point to the internal organs as the five elements, define the heart and genitals as fire and water, consider the liver and lungs to be the dragon and tiger, use mind and breath as child and mother, and take fluids of the body for lead and mercury. They do not recognize floating and sinking; how could they distinguish host from guest?

How is it that different from taking others' goods for your own things, or calling strangers family? And how can they know the mysterious subtlety of the mutual overcoming of metal and wood, or the profound wonder of the interaction of yin and yang? For all of them the sun and moon are off course, the lead and mercury are in different furnaces; if they want to crystallize the restored elixir, are they not far off?

I have associated with the good way since youth and read widely in the classics of the three teachings. I made attentive and detailed studies of law, writing, mathematics, medicine, divination, military science, astronomy, geography, and prognostication. But when it came to the science of the gold pill, I read through all the classics and the songs, poems, and treatises of the various schools. All of them say the gold liquid restored elixir can be made by the solar higher soul and the lunar lower soul, the tiger at the beginning of positive energy and the dragon at the climax of positive energy, the quicksilver and cinnabar, the white metal and black tin, the water man and fire woman; but they never say what the real lead and real mercury are, and they do not explain directions for the firing process, the methodical regulation, and the incubation.

Moreover, confused followers in later generations gave free rein to subjective explanation, misinterpreting the classic teachings of the ancient sages, contradicting and distorting them in myriad ways, not only throwing the classics of immortals into chaos but also deluding and misleading later students.

Because I had not met a complete human, and the verbally transmitted secret seemed impossible to find, I eventually reached a point where I could not be at peace even when sleeping and eating, and my vitality and spirit were exhausted. Even though I looked all over asking of everyone, wise and ignorant, none of them could clarify the true source and illumine the heart.

Subsequently, in the year 1069, having gone along with Mr. Lu of Lung-t'u (Longtu) into Ch'eng-tu (Chengdu, in western China), because my early determination had not changed and my original sincerity was even more earnest, I finally moved a real human being to give me the secret of the medicines and firing process of the gold pill. The words were very simple, the essentials uncomplicated. It could be called a case of "making the source known by pointing to the flow," or "making a hundred understood by speaking of one." The mist cleared, the sun shone; the dust gone, the mirror was clear: when I compared it with the classics of immortals, it was like joining matching talismans.

Based on this, I thought of how eight or nine out of ten people in the world study immortalism, yet I hadn't heard of even one or two who had arrived at the real essence. Now that I had met with a real explanation, how could I dare hide in silence? So I put all that I had attained into nine times nine or eighty-one verses, and called the collection *Understanding Reality*.

Included are a set of sixteen verses representing two eights; a set of sixty-four verses on the model of the hexagrams of the *I Ching;* one verse symbolizing absolute unity; and twelve verses on the moon over the West River, to go through a cycle of a year.

As for the cauldron and furnace, the noble and base, the medicinal substances, the measurements, the firing process, advance and withdrawal, host and guest, following and preceding, survival and destruction, being and nonbeing, luck and misfortune, regret and shame, all of them are included in these verses.

After I had completed the collection of verses, I noticed that in them I had only talked about the arts of nurturing life and stabilizing the body, and had not thoroughly explored the essence of real awareness at the fundamental source. So I read Buddhist works, including the *Transmission of the Lamp*. Coming to where one of the Ch'an masters became enlightened on hearing the sound of bamboo struck by some pebbles, I then formulated thirty-two pieces, consisting of verses in sacred style, verses in secular style, folk songs, and mixed sayings. Now I add them to the book in hopes that the way of arriving at the basis and clarifying essence is all in here. My aim is that when people with the same aspiration read this, they will understand the root on seeing the branches, and will give up illusion to follow reality.

THE SECRET OF OPENING THE PASSES

The great Tao of the gold elixir is first found through calm stability. If you are not calm and stable, your spirit and will are confused and disorderly; even if you tune the true breath, the breath will not remain, so the true energy cannot enter. Then what can you use to supply the boost to produce the great elixir?

Human life in society is always involved and full of trivialities. This means you must control your mind when dealing with things. Whatever you do, follow the natural course. Before something comes up, don't create idle imaginings about it; when something has passed, don't mull over it. Let the mind be always as if there were no concerns. With purity and clarity in oneself, the celestial lord is at peace; then the mind is calm, and when calm it is naturally stable.

With this settled mind, sit alone in a quiet room, senses shut and eyelids lowered. Turn your attention within, and inwardly visualize a pocket of energy in the umbilical region; within it is a point of golden light, clear and bright, immaculately pure.

When you have succeeded in visualizing this light in the pocket of energy, don't let it dim. The breath through your nose will naturally become light and subtle, going out and in evenly and finely, continuously and quietly, gradually becoming slighter and subtler.

The breathing will then be focused in the umbilical region, each exhalation and inhalation so subtle as to seem to be on the borderline of existence and nonexistence. After a long time at this, the true breath naturally remains, and there seems to be no flow of air through the nose.

When the energy returns to the original ocean of energy, only then can you open the passes without stirring thoughts. Then with your true spirit convey your true energy to permeate your whole body evenly. Then the positive energy has been attained, and all the passes can be opened.

The human body has three posterior passes and three anterior passes. The three posterior passes are in the coccyx, at the base of the spine; in the midspine, where the ribs join the spine; and at the back of the brain.

The pass in the coccyx, at the bottom end of the spine, connects with the channels of the genital organs. From this pass ascends the spinal cord, which is called the Zen Valley, or the Yellow River, or the Waterwheel Course, or the Mountain Range up to the Court of Heaven, or the Ladder up to Heaven.

This is the road by which positive energy ascends; it goes right up the point opposite the center of the chest, the pass of the enclosed spine, where the ribs join in back, then it goes straight up to the back of the brain, which is called the pass of the Jade Pillow.

The three anterior passes are called the Nirvana Center, the Earth Pot, and the Ocean of Energy. The Nirvana Center is the so-called upper elixir field. It is a spherical opening 1.3 inches in diameter and is the repository of the spirit. That opening is three inches behind the center of the eyebrows, right in the middle.

The space between the eyebrows is called the Celestial Eye. The space one inch inward is called the Bright Hall. The space one inch farther in is called the Hidden Chamber. One inch farther in from that is the Nirvana Center.

Below the center of the eyebrows is what is called the Pillar of the Nose, also called the Golden Bridge. Inward to the inside of the mouth are two passages, which are called the Magpie Bridge. The outside throat is hard, and this is where air passes. Inside is a soft throat, through which food and drink pass to the stomach.

The windpipe has twelve sections and is called the Multistoried Tower; it goes to the openings in the lungs, and reaches the heart. Below the heart is an opening called the Crimson Chamber, where the dragon and tiger mate.

Another 3.6 inches directly below that is what is called the Earth Pot, which is the Yellow Court, the middle elixir field. In the center of the torso, between the left lung and the liver, is an opening 1.2 inches in diameter where energy is stored. This is called the Root of Heaven and Earth, where the refined elixir is warmed and developed.

Going straight down from here to the point opposite the navel is approximately 3.6 inches. This is the reason for the saying, "Heaven above, thirty-six; earth below, thirty-six." In the middle is an opening 1.2 inches in size. From the heaven-heart is 3.6 inches, from the earth-genitals is 3.6 inches, and the middle field of elixir is 1.2 inches; so heaven and earth are 8.4 inches apart.

The umbilical opening is called the Door of Life. It has seven channels connecting with the genitals. The leaking of sexual energy takes place through these channels.

Behind the navel and in front of the kidneys, right in the middle, is the place called the Crescent Moon Jar, or the Ocean of Energy. And 1.3 inches below that is what is called the Flower Pond, or the lower elixir field.

This is where vitality is stored, and it is the place where the medicine is gathered. On the left is the lower Bright Hall, on the right the lower Hidden Room. Right in the middle is an opening, in which there are two channels, one going to the genitals and one to the coccyx; this opening is critical for the whole body.

The secret of conveying energy to open the passes is as follows:

Sit as before, closing the eyes and shutting the mouth, turning the attention inward, visualizing the pocket of energy within the body, quieting the mind and tuning the breath.

After the breath is settled, only then is it possible to produce the one true energy.

Focus your attention on visualizing this true energy arising from the arches of the feet, rising directly to the genitals, where the two streams of energy merge into one energy in the middle, which then enters the coccyx.

Steadily visualize this true energy as being like a small snake gradually passing through the nine apertures of the coccyx. When you feel the energy has gone through this pass, visualize this true energy rising up to where the ribs meet the spine, then going through this pass and right on up to the Jade Pillow, the back of the brain.

Then imagine your true spirit in the Nirvana Chamber in the center of the brain, taking in the energy.

When this true energy goes through the Jade Pillow, press the tongue against the palate. The head should move forward and tilt slightly upwards to help it. When you feel this true energy penetrating into the Nirvana Chamber, this may feel hot or swollen. This means the pass has been cleared and the energy has reached the Nirvana Center.

After that, move the spirit to the Celestial Eye between the eyebrows, drawing the true energy on to open the Hidden Room and the Bright Hall, chambers in the brain behind the brows, then finally the Celestial Eye. Then the center of the brows will throb— this means the Celestial Eye is about to open.

Then move the spirit into the center of the brows and draw the true energy through the Celestial Eye. If you see the eighteen thousand pores and three hundred and sixty joints of the whole body explode open all at once, each joint parting three-tenths of an inch, this is evidence of the opening of the Celestial Eye.

This is what is meant when it is said that when one pass opens all the passes open, and when one opening is cleared all the openings are cleared.

Once the passes have been opened, then draw the true energy down the pillar of the nose, descending the Golden Bridge. Feeling as though there is cool water going down the Multistoried Tower of the windpipe, do not swallow; let it go down by itself, bathing the bronchial tubes.

If you feel there is some backup of energy, this is a temporary reversal of the usual course, and so if there is any such irregularity, you should quietly work on tuning and harmonizing the practice; after a long time it will naturally proceed on course. Then the vital energy will bathe the internal organs and then return to the genitals. This is what is called return to the root.

From the genitals the energy goes into the coccyx, then directly back up to the center of the brain, and from the center of the brain down to the lower field of elixir, then going up and around as before. This is what is meant by returning to life.

If you practice this way for a long time, eventually you can complete a whole cycle of ascent and descent in one continuous visualization. If you can quietly practice this inner work continuously, whether walking, standing still, sitting, or lying down, then the vital energy will circulate within, and there will naturally be no problem of leakage. Chronic physical ailments will naturally disappear.

Also, once the inner energy is circulating, the breath will naturally become fine, and the true positive energy of heaven and earth will be inhaled by way of the breath and go down to join your own generative energy. The two energies will mix together, both to be circulated by you together, descending and ascending over and over, circulating up and down to replenish the depleted true energy in your body.

This true energy harmonizes and reforms, so that the vital fluids produced by the energy of daily life again produce true vitality. When true vitality is fully developed, it naturally produces true energy, and when energy is fully developed it naturally produces our true spirit.

Thus the three treasures of vitality, energy, and spirit experience a daily flourishing of life and fill the whole body, so that the great medicine can be expected to be produced naturally, whereby one can proceed onward to the process of gathering the medicine, thereby to form the golden elixir.

Wang Che

FIFTEEN STATEMENTS
ON THE ESTABLISHMENT OF A TEACHING

1. *Living in a Hermitage*

When people leave home, first they should live in a hermitage. A hermitage is a house for one person. When the body has a place to live, the mind gradually attains peace. When energy and spirit are harmonious and light, one enters the real Tao.

Whatever you do, do not work too hard. If you work too hard, it will reduce energy. But do not be inactive either. If you are inactive, energy and blood will stagnate. When activity and stillness are balanced, then you can maintain constancy and rest secure in your lot. This is the way to live in a hermitage.

2. *Traveling*

There are two ways of traveling around. One is that of the tourist, the vacationer, the opportunist. People like this may travel ten thousand miles, but it will only serve to wear them out. Seeing all the sights in the world, their minds are in confusion and their energy is sapped. These are people who travel in vain.

The second way is that of seeking essence and life and questioning their unknown mysteries, climbing high precipitous mountains undaunted to call on enlightened teachers, crossing roaring cataracts unfazed to ask about the Tao. If there is mutual understanding at a single statement, a globe of light radiates from within, and you understand the great matter of life and death and become a completely realized human. People like this are true travelers.

3. *Study from Books*

The way to study from books requires that you avoid confusing your perceptions by literalism. You should pick out the ideas, to accord with the heart. Then set the book aside to search through the ideas to cull the principles. Then set aside the principles to get the effect. When you can get the effect, you can absorb it into the mind. After a long time, if you are completely sincere, the light of mind will naturally overflow, the spirit of knowledge will leap, all will be penetrated, all will be understood. When you get to this point, you should keep it in and nurture it. Just do not let it gallop off, lest you lose in terms of essence and life.

If you do not find out the fundamental meaning of books, and merely want to have a large repertoire of information you can show off in front of people, your talents will not help you cultivate yourself. Instead they will injure your spirit and energy. Then even if you read a lot of books it will not help you on the Way.

Once you have gotten the meaning of a book, you should store it away securely.

4. *Compounding Herbal Medicine*

Medicinal herbs are the most excellent energies of the mountains and rivers, the pure essence of plants and trees. Some are warm, some are cold, some are restorative, some are purgative, some are thick, some are thin, some are to be applied as a dressing, some as a compress.

Those who would study medicine thoroughly vivify people's natural lives. Blind physicians harm people's physical bodies. People who study the Tao should be experts. Without expertise, there is no way to assist the Way.

It will not do to be attached, for that would reduce hidden

merit. To covet goods outwardly and money inwardly wastes cultivation of reality. If you do not bring on malignant disease in this life, watch out for retribution in the coming life. Let the advanced disciples in my school reflect on this thoroughly.

5. *Building*

A simple house needs to protect the body from exposure. Things like carved beams and high ceilings are not made by the best people. Big buildings with huge halls are not the livelihood of people of the Way.

When you cut down trees you interrupt the liquid of the veins of the earth. When you solicit alms you take people's blood pulse. If you only cultivate outward achievement and do not cultivate inward practice, that is like drawing cakes to satisfy hunger or piling up snow for feed. It only wastes everyone's effort and ultimately turns out empty.

People with will should lose no time in seeking out the jeweled palace within the body. Not knowing how to repair crimson towers outside the body, watch as they fall down. Let intelligent people look into this carefully.

6. *Joining Companions on the Way*

When people on the Way associate, the basic purpose is for the ailing to help one another—if you die, I will bury you; if I die, you will bury me. But it is necessary to choose people before forming associations; do not form associations first and then choose people afterwards. Do not be attached to each other, for attachment binds the mind. But do not be aloof either, for then there is estrangement. Take a middle course between attachment and aloofness.

There are three things that make for harmony, and three things that do not. Understanding mind, having wisdom, and having will are three things that make for harmony. Without understanding, you cling to external objects. Without wisdom, you are foolish and muddled. Without will, you struggle in vain. These are three things that do not make for harmony.

The basis of individual life is in the community. It all depends on mind and will. Do not follow people's feelings, do not grasp appearances. Just choose high illuminates. This is the superior method.

7. *Sitting*

Sitting does not mean physically sitting still with the eyes closed. This latter is artificial sitting. True sitting requires that the mind be unstirring as a mountain all the time, whatever you are doing, in all action and repose.

Shut off the four gates—eyes, ears, mouth, and nose—and do not let external scenery get inside. As long as there is the slightest thought of motion or stillness, this is not what I call quiet sitting.

Those who can sit quietly in the real sense may be physically present in the material world, but their names are already in the ranks of the immortals. It is not necessary for them to call on others, for the century of work of the saints and sages in the body is fulfilled, and they shed the shell to climb to reality; a pill of elixir is made, and the spirit roams throughout the universe.

8. *Overcoming the Mind*

If the mind is always calm and still, dark and silent, not seeing anything, indefinable, not inside or outside, without a trace of thought, this is the settled mind, and is not to be overcome. If the mind gets excited at objects, falling all over itself looking for heads and tails, this is the disturbed mind, and should quickly be cut away. Do not indulge it and let it go on, for it will harm spiritual qualities and cause a loss of essential life. Whatever you are doing, always strive to overcome perceptions, cognitions, and feelings, and you will have no afflictions.

9. *Refining the Nature*

Putting your nature in order is like tuning a stringed instrument. If the string is too tight it will snap, and if it is too loose it will not respond. When you find a balance between tautness and slackness, the instrument can be tuned.

It is also like making a sword. If there is too much hard metal it will break, and if there is too much soft metal it will bend. When hard and soft metals are in balance, then the sword can be cast.

If you embody these two principles in refining your nature, it will naturally become sublime.

10. *Combining the Five Energies*

The five energies mass in the central chamber, the three bases gather on the peak, the blue dragon spouts red mist, the white tiger spews black smoke. Myriad spirits stand in rows, the hundred channels flow gently, the cinnabar sand shines brightly, the lead and mercury congeal clearly. For now the body is in the human world, but the spirit already roams in the heavens above.

11. *Merging Essence and Life*

Essence is spirit, life is energy. If essence sees life, it is like a bird taking to the wind, sailing lightly upward. This saves work and is easy to accomplish. This is what the *Classic on Yin Convergence* means when it says, "The control of a bird is in energy." People who cultivate reality should not fail to study this, and they should not divulge it to practitioners of the low arts, lest spiritual luminosities come down to admonish them. Essence and life are the basis of practice. Be very careful to refine them.

12. *The Way of Sages*

To enter the Way of sages it is necessary to struggle with determination for years on end, to accumulate achievement and build up practice, to be highly illumined, wise and understanding. Only thus can you enter the Way of sages. Then while your body lives in one room your essence fills the universe. All the holy hosts of heaven silently protect you, the infinite immortal adepts invisibly surround you. Your name is among those registered in the Violet City, and your rank is among the stages of immortals. While your body temporarily lodges in the material world, your mind is already illumined beyond things.

13. *Transcending the Three Realms*

The realm of desire, the realm of form, and the formless realm—these are the three realms. When the mind forgets thoughts, you transcend the realm of desire. When the mind transcends objects, you transcend the realm of form. Do not cling to the view of emptiness, and you transcend the formless realm. When you detach from these three realms, your spirit lives in the homeland of the immortal sages, your essence is in the realm of jadelike purity.

14. *The Method of Developing the Body*

The spiritual body is formless. It is neither empty nor existent. It has no past or future. It is neither short nor long. Use it, and it penetrates everywhere. Store it, and it is imperceptible, without a trace. If you attain this Tao, you can develop this. The more you develop it, the greater your achievements. Don't look back, don't cling to the world, and you'll go or stay naturally.

15. *Leaving the Ordinary World*

"Leaving the ordinary world" does not mean leaving it physically, it refers to a state of mind. The body is like a lotus root, the mind is like the lotus blossom. The root is in the mud, but the blossom is in the air. People who attain the Tao are physically in the ordinary world but mentally in the realm of sages. People today who want to avoid death forever and leave the ordinary world are imbeciles who do not understand the principle of the Tao.

Extracts from
Contemplative Literature

Introduction

This section presents readings from a variety of important works on the practical aspects of Taoism. The first selection is from *Records of the Source Teaching of the Pure Clarity of the Spiritual Jewel of the Exalted,* which is itself an anthology drawing on a number of different sources, containing extracts from both religious and alchemical forms of Taoism. This text is supposed to have originally come from an old Taoist-Confucian religious movement that may have started in the fourth century C.E.; later it was associated with the tradition of Lü Yen, or "Ancestor Lü," which is undoubtedly the source of its alchemical contents.

The second selection, *Stabilization and Observation of Spiritual Jewels from the Open Mystery*, is a short work on meditation derived from the *Ling-pao (Lingbao)*, or *Spiritual Jewels* scriptures, which form the section of the religious Taoist canon known as *Tung-hsüan (Dongxuan)*, or *Open Mystery*. It does not appear, however, to be a product of one of the religious orders based on the scriptures, but rather seems to be a concentration of practical teachings from the scriptures made by a later Complete Reality Taoist.

This would also appear to be the case with the next selection, *Essential Secrets for Visualization According to the Immortals' Ancient Books of Great Clarity*. The *Books of Great Clarity* are the *T'ai-ch'ing ching (Taiqingjing)*, ancient texts on alchemy dating from around the end of the Han dynasty, in the early third century C.E. The text presented here is undoubtedly a much later work aimed at distilling practical techniques from the ancient scriptures. The visualizations taught in this text represent a glimpse into what some Western scholars have called the "Inner Gods" school of Taoism because of the practice of visualizing supernal beings within oneself. There are many inner ceremonies like the one described here; in reality they are simply mind-body exercises like Chang Po-tuan's practice of "opening the passes" translated in the preceding section of this anthology. Generally speaking, the Complete Reality school stripped the ancient "Inner Gods" ceremonies of color and personification to arrive at more abstract forms of psychophysiological energetics. This text is interesting in that it demonstrates the connection between ancient and reformed versions of such practices.

The fourth selection of extracts is taken from *Transformational Writings* by T'an Ch'iao (Tan Qiao), a Taoist adept of the tenth century C.E. Written during the period of disunity and instability between the T'ang and Sung dynasties, this text carries on the ancient Taoist tradition of political and social criticism. It is also concerned with the psychological bases of human behavior and presents one of the earliest and most graphic discourses on the development of vitality, energy, and spirit.

The fifth selection is from a text called *Blue Flower Secret Letters,* or more fully, *On the Method of the Alchemy of the Inner Refinement of the Gold Treasure, According to the Blue Flower Secret Letters from the Golden Box of Jade Purity.* The author, Wang Pang-shu (Wang Bangshu), was an apprentice of the great Chang Po-tuan himself, founder of the Southern school of Complete Reality. This work is quoted at considerable length in Ch'en Yingning's commentary on the poems of the great Sun Pu-erh, translated in my *Immortal Sisters* (Boston: Shambhala Publications, 1989).

The sixth selection is extracted from *Records of Sayings of Banshan,* a collection of talks by a Taoist master, named after the mountain (Pan-shan/Banshan) where he taught. The "records of sayings" format, widely used by Complete Reality Taoists, is modeled on Ch'an Buddhist literary practice. This text appears to be from the late twelfth or mid-thirteenth century, and like many such Taoist collections has a strong Buddhist flavor.

The final three selections are taken from famous works of Complete Reality Taoist masters of the Yuan dynasty (1278–1368). *Compass Center Directions* by Ch'en Hsü-pai (Chen Xubai)) is even today one of the most highly esteemed alchemical texts. The extracts translated here are summary essays on three fundamentals of spiritual alchemy: the "mysterious female," the "medicinal substances," and the "firing process." *Overall Essentials of Alchemy* is one of the magna opera of Shang-yang-tzu (Shangyangzi), who is famed for his commentaries on alchemical classics such as *Triplex Unity* and *Understanding Reality*. The extract translated here deals with "seeing essence and attaining buddhahood," a Ch'an Buddhist theme, from the point of view of a Complete Reality Taoist. *Clarifying the Way,* by Wang Wei-i (Wang Weiyi), is an outstanding collection of didactic verse presenting an excellent summary of Taoist theory and praxis as understood in the Complete Reality tradition.

Records of the Source
Teaching of the Pure Clarity
of the Spiritual Jewel of the Exalted

THE FIVE ENERGIES RETURNING TO THE ORIGIN

The five energies are the true energies of five fundamental forces.
When they are correctly aligned they congeal into one.

When your body is not agitated, your vitality is stable, and its
energy returns to the origin.

When your mind is not agitated, your breath is stable, and its
energy returns to the origin.

When your nature is always tranquil, the higher soul is stored,
and its energy returns to the origin.

When emotions are forgotten, the lower soul is subdued, and its
energy returns to the origin.

When the physical elements are in harmony, the will is stable,
and its energy returns to the origin.

When these five forces are in their proper place and at peace,
they revert to their reality, which is the source of religion.

THE THREE PASSES

The three passes are the critical junctures of the three fundamentals:
vitality, energy, and spirit.

The body unmoving, refining vitality into energy, rising through
the coccyx, is called the first pass.

The mind unmoving, refining energy into spirit, stopping at midspine, is called the middle pass.

The intent unmoving, refining the spirit into spaciousness, rising to the back of the skull, is called the upper pass.

When body, mind, and intent merge into one, the vitality, energy, and spirit meet, without excitement or disharmony; this is the seed of the gold elixir.

THE PRIMORDIAL UNIFIED ENERGY

The point of true positive energy, which exists before the dichotomizing of the primordial, is the same as nothingness, the same as breathing. There is only coming and going, not dichotomy.

This is why it is said that the unified energy becomes dichotomized due to the disturbance caused by conditioned cognition.

To absorb and cultivate the primordial energy, suspend discursive thought and watch serenely; then you will see natural reality.

This may be done by keeping the mind on the point between the genitals and the navel, while poised between forgetfulness and mindfulness.

GOVERNING THE MIND

Practitioners should spy out the mind's habits, biases, prejudices, fixations, obsessions, and indulgences, so that eventually they can catch them and treat them accordingly. It will not do to be too easygoing; even slight faults should be eradicated, and even small virtues should be developed. In this way entanglements may be cut off, and one may become constantly aware of true eternity.

TIMES OF BODY AND MIND

The mind has five times, the body has seven. The five times of mind are as follows:

1. When there is more activity than stillness

2. When activity and stillness are equal

3. When there is more stillness than activity

4. When the mind is still if there is nothing to do, active when things come up

5. When mind merges with reality and does not stir even when stimulated

When cultivation reaches the fifth phase, one is finally at peace. The seven times of the body are as follows:

1. When activity accords with the time, and the demeanor is harmonious and joyful

2. When illnesses gradually disappear and the body is light and comfortable

3. When weaknesses and defects are repaired, and one is physically and mentally strong and healthy

4. When the body is refined into congealed energy

5. When the energy is refined into spirit and stabilized

6. When one is both physically and spiritually sublimated

7. When the spirit is refined so as to merge with the Tao

Stabilization and Observation of Spiritual Jewels from the Open Mystery

A Celestial noble stated to the Real Human assisting the unseen:

To practice the Tao, first be able to set things aside. Cut off contact with external things, so nothing involves or opposes the mind. After that, sit comfortably.

Inwardly observe arisings of mind. If you notice a thought arise, you should get rid of it, to bring about peace and quiet.

Next, even if you don't clearly have any craving or clinging, wandering thoughts should also be completely exterminated.

Work diligently, day and night, without giving up.

Just extinguish the stirring mind, don't annihilate the shining mind. Just stabilize the open mind, don't solidify the dwelling mind.

Don't lean on anything at all, and you'll always have presence of mind.

But still the mind is ordinarily impulsive and compulsive, so the next step, of making the mind rest, is very difficult. You may be unable to stop it, only halting it for a while, then losing it.

While you are struggling with the mind, the body goes with the current. Meditate sincerely for a long time, and you will harmonize it well; don't give up the work of a thousand lifetimes just because you can't collect your mind right away.

When you have attained a little inner quiet, then wherever you are and whatever you do, be attentive yet at peace. Whether there is something to do or nothing to do, if you are always as if mindless, then whether you are in a tranquil situation or in the midst of commotion, your mental focus will be unified. If you restrain your mind too intensely in too much of a hurry, this will also produce illness. Madness is a symptom of this.

If the mind does not move, then you should let it be, leaving relaxation and intensification to find their proper places.

Spontaneously adjust it appropriately all the time.

Controlled without fixation, liberated without excitement, unfazed by commotion, undisturbed by events—this is true stability.

Do not seek many affairs just because involvement in things does not bother you; don't purposely take to the hubbub just because commotion doesn't dismay you.

Make no thing your true home.

Let work be the traces of your response to the world.

When mind is like a mirror, it shows whatever is there.

Artful expedients only enable one to enter concentration trance. Whether insight emerges slowly or quickly is not up to people. Don't let yourself rush for it in trance; if you rush, you will damage your essence. When the essence of consciousness is damaged, there is no insight.

When concentration trance does not seek insight, but insight arises spontaneously, this is called true insight.

Insight unemployed, those of real knowledge appear ignorant, increasing sustenance to their concentration and insight, refining both without limit.

If thoughts or mental images in concentration are very sensitive to the wrong things, then weird vitalities, a hundred sprites, will appear according to the state of mind.

Celestial Nobles, Immortals, and Real People seen are auspicious signs. Just let the stable mind be open and uncovered above, vast and unfixated below.

Old habits dissolve day by day; new habits are not formed. Nothing gets in the way; you are free from the cage of the world.

Practice this for a long time, and you will naturally attain the Tao.

There are generally seven phases experienced by those who attain the Tao. The first is when the mind attains stability and easily notices sense influences.

The second is when existing complexes melt away everywhere, so body and mind become light and fresh.

The third is when they repair unnatural damage and restore their natural life span.

The fourth is when they extend their life span tens of thousands of years. They are then called Immortals.

The fifth is when they refine their physical bodies into energy. They are then called Real People.

The sixth is when they refine the energy into spirit. They are then called Spiritual People.

The seventh is when they refine the spirit to unite with the Tao. They are then called Perfected People.

As far as perceptive powers are concerned, they become clearer with every phase. When fulfillment of the ultimate Tao is reached, wisdom is then complete.

If you practice stabilizing mind and body for a long time but do not have any of these experiences, only at physical death will you be empty. If you call this awareness of wisdom, or call it attainment of the Tao, that is not really true.

Essential Secrets for Visualization According to the Immortals' Ancient Books of Great Clarity

If you want to know the secret of the Oneness of the Trinity and Unity within the body, every day when you have free time go into your room and collect your mind and body, gathering in your spirit and energy.

First visualize the point 1.3 inches below the navel as the lower field of elixir: in the sacred workshop in the alchemical field is a newborn infant, sitting upright, facing outward.

This infant is called the Mystic at the Bottom of the Valley.

This infant is also named Occult Valley, and styled Splendor of Original Creative Energy.

This is the producer of vitality and energy.

Next, imagine a scarlet-robed infant inside the Crimson Palace of the heart, named Elixir of the Midnight South, styled Stability of Central Light.

This is the producer of spirit.

Then concentrate on the spot one inch inward from the spot between the eyebrows. This is the Palace of Bright Halls. To the left is the Violet Chamber, to the right the Crimson Room. Above is the Palace of the Garden of Heaven.

Two inches inward from the spot between the brows is the Palace of the Secret Room. One inch above that palace is the Palace of Ultimate Reality.

Three inches inward from the spot between the brows is the upper field of elixir, the upper alchemical field. In the sacred workshop there is a baby dressed in scarlet, sitting upright. The baby's name is Imperial Officer Born of the Second Mystery, styled Leader of the Three Bases.

This one is the leader of the infants of the central and lower fields, who both ascend to the upper field to sit together as the Three Primal Lords.

Above this field of elixir is the Sacred Workshop of the Mystic Alchemy.

Four inches in from the point between the brows is the Palace of Liquid Pearl. One inch above this is the Palace of the Celestial Emperor.

An inch in from between the brows is called the Palace of the Jade Emperor of Perfect Tranquillity. Another name for this is the Valley of Heaven.

Also visualize an infant under your nose, dressed in a robe of five colors, sitting upright. This infant, entitled Honorable Lord of the Imperial Unity of the Great Clarity, occupies the connecting point of the active and passive energy channels; its name is Where Is the Father, its style is Extending Vitality with the Mother.

It rides on a cloud up to the point of perfect tranquillity on the top of the head, where it commands the statements of the *Jade Scripture of Great Clarity*.

Don't let it wander off; it is the leader of myriad spirits, who points out the stations of the hundred spirits in the body.

This is called the Unity of the Trinity. Whatever you are doing—walking, standing still, sitting down, or reclining—turn the attention inward and focus on the top of the head, not losing this focus of attention.

Escaping misfortunes, heading for good fortune, getting rid of a hundred ills, you will attain superior immortality.

Transformational Writings

NO CONSTANT MIND

If you put a board eight inches square on the ground and have someone stand on it, there is plenty of room. But if you put a board ten inches square on top of a pole and have someone sit on it, it is not big enough.

It is not a matter of something being big or small, it is a matter of the mind being empty or full. Therefore those who fuss about the hot weather get even hotter, and those who are afraid of the pain of curative moxa burning get sicker.

People do not have a constant state of mind; things do not have permanent natures.

MADNESS

Children playing with shadows do not realize the shadows are playing with them. Madmen vilifying images do not realize the images are vilifying them. Those who are running households do not realize their households are running them. Those who are ruling countries do not realize the countries are ruling them.

The enlightened chieftains of remote antiquity did not know their enlightenment would turn into the charisma of later leaders. Those charismatic leaders did not know their charisma would turn into the humanity and righteousness of subsequent rulers. The humane and righteous rulers did not know their humanity and righteousness would turn into the war of the imperial dynasties.

When the drunk carry the drunk and the fevered carry the fevered, there is all the more stumbling and sickness, with no turning back.

EMOTION

To appreciate your parents' kindness is not filiality. To rejoice at the favor of your superiors is not loyalty. Appreciation begins from not appreciating, rejoicing begins from not rejoicing. Much appreciation means much resentment, much rejoicing means much indignation.

Emotion in the heart is like poison in a substance, like fire latent in reeds—one ought to be aware of this. Therefore, as superior people do their work, they do not feel exalted when given status, do not feel aggrandized when honored, do not pay attention when treated familiarly, do not become suspicious when treated with aloofness, and cannot be abased. Thus they cannot be moved by emotions.

THE SEVEN RIP-OFFS

If you don't eat for one day, you feel tired. If you don't eat for two days, you get sick. If you don't eat for three days, you die. Of all the things people are concerned with, nothing is more urgent than food.

Yet the kings take away one part of that food, and the aristocrats take away another part. Soldiers and officers take away one part, and wars take away yet another. Artisans take a part, merchants take a part, Taoist and Buddhist clergy take a part.

When the harvest is good they take a part, and they take a part in lean years too. This is why people are already wearing burlap when the silk making has just finished, and people are already living on chestnuts when the harvest has just ended.

When kings control dissatisfaction by punishment, this leads to extreme dissatisfaction. According to the Tao of great people, to try to remedy injustice by law leads to extreme injustice. So how can those who take the food of the people repay them by making a fuss over benevolence and principle?

THE ENERGY OF SOUND

The sound of a harp produces a feeling of tranquillity. Sensual music produces rapture and abandon. The sound of scraping bricks sends shivers up the spine. The sound of drums makes the hair on the back of the neck stand up.

This is the way it is with the stimulation of feeling. If it is harmonious it evokes positive energy, which produces a benign influence that enlivens everything. If it is inharmonious it evokes negative energy, which produces a harsh influence that degrades everything.

The energy depends on the sound, the sound depends on the energy. When energy moves, sound is emitted; when sound comes forth, energy vibrates. When energy vibrates, influences are activated and things change. Therefore it is possible thereby to command wind and clouds, produce frost and hail, cause phoenixes to sing, get bears to dance, make friends with spiritual luminescences.

The science of the use of music is very great indeed.

TRANSFORMATIONS OF THE TAO

The fading away of the Tao is when emptiness turns into spirit, spirit turns into energy, and energy turns into form. When form is born, everything is thereby stultified.

The functioning of the Tao is when form turns into energy, energy turns into spirit, and spirit turns into emptiness. When emptiness is clear, everything thereby flows freely.

Therefore ancient sages investigated the beginnings of free flow and stultification, found the source of evolution, forgot form to cultivate energy, forgot energy to cultivate spirit, and forgot spirit to cultivate emptiness.

Emptiness is truly free-flowing communion. This is called the great sameness. Thus when stored it becomes the original vitality, when used it becomes myriad consciousnesses, when relinquished it becomes the absolute one, when let go it becomes the absolute purity.

So as water and fire wane and wax in the body, "wind and clouds" come forth in the eyes, ears, nose, and mouth. True energy pervades the body, and through the seasons there is no cold or heat. When pure positive energy flows, people have no death or birth. This is called the Tao of spiritual transformation.

When emptiness turns into spirit, spirit turns into energy, energy turns into form, and form turns into vitality, vitality turns into attention. Attention turns into social gestures, and social gestures turn into elevation and humbling. Elevation and humbling turn into high and low positions, and high and low turn into discrimination. Discrimination turns into official status, and status turns into cars. Cars turn into mansions, mansions turn into palaces. Palaces turn into banquet halls, banquet halls turn into extravagance. Extravagance turns into acquisitiveness, acquisitiveness turns into fraud. Fraud turns into punishment, punishment turns into rebellion. Rebellion turns into armament, armament turns into strife and plunder, strife and plunder turn into defeat and destruction.

When this comes, its momentum cannot be stopped. When it goes, its power cannot be removed.

Therefore great people swim in it by virtue of the Tao, hunt it by benevolence and justice, trap it by laws and manners. Thus do they preserve their countries and gain their prosperity.

So if there is anything untrue in the virtue, anything incomplete in the benevolence and justice, anything insufficient in the laws and manners, this is teaching people to be crafty deceivers, causing the people to be loose and dishonest, making the people rebellious, driving the people to theft and banditry. When those above are unconscious of their own degeneracy and those below are unaware of their own sickness, how can they be saved?

Emptiness turns into spirit, spirit turns into energy, energy turns into blood, blood turns into form, form turns into infant, infant turns into child, child turns into youth, youth turns into adult, the adult ages, the aged die, the dead revert to emptiness. Emptiness then again turns into spirit, spirit again turns into energy, and energy again turns into myriad beings. Transformation after transformation goes on unceasingly, following an endless cycle.

Beings do not wish to be born, they have no choice but to be born. Beings do not wish to die, they have no choice but to die. Those who realize this principle empty themselves and have compassion for others. Their spirits can thereby avoid change, their forms can thereby be unborn.

When emptiness turns to spirit, spirit turns to energy, and energy turns to form, form and energy ride each other to produce sound. Even though the ears do not listen for sound, sound spontaneously enters the ears. Even though a valley does not respond with echoes, echoes naturally fill it.

The ear is a small opening, a valley is a large opening. Mountains and lowlands make small valleys, heaven and earth are a large valley. When one opening resounds, myriad openings all resound. When one valley hears, myriad valleys all hear.

Sound conducts energy, energy conducts spirit, spirit conducts emptiness. Emptiness houses spirit, spirit houses energy, energy houses sound. They conduct each other and house each other. This reaches everywhere, even to the flying about of the autumn mosquitoes, the buzzing around of the green flies. This is how we know this.

To perceive even the slightest thought, to hear even the whispered word—this is possible only for great people. This potential of great people cannot be seen by heaven and earth, cannot be known by yin and yang, cannot be perceived by ghosts and spirits. Why is that? It is the doing of the virtue of the Tao, and of benevolence and justice.

Blue Flower Secret Letters

Mind is the house of spirit. It is the source of all wonders and the director of all beings. Essence is in it, life is in it. People studying the Way should first understand the mind; everything else comes after that.

When Chang Po-tuan came back from western China to the mountains where he used to live, he built a house in the midst of the greenery. It was completely desolate, yet he was happy, as if he had attained something.

When a traveler reported in town that Chang had come back to the mountains from exile, a whole crowd of followers went to his house. Weeping and bowing, they said to him, "Are you all right, Teacher? You have been traveling for ten years now, and over difficult and dangerous terrain; yet you do not seem to be haggard or worn. Is this because of some art that you have?"

Master Chang said, "I'll tell you the reason why people get worn out. Who makes them that way? It is the mind. A hundred matters collect in the mind; before one thought is finished, another thought continues it. There is not a moment of leisure all day long. When sleeping at night, the mind does rest a little, but the spirit isn't there.

"I have no art but the ability to settle the mind. The reason spirits and ghosts can read our minds is simply that we have

156

thoughts. If there are no thoughts in the mind, then the awareness of spirits cannot know it. Not only do the spirits not know my mind; I myself do not even know it is mind. This is the basis of steadying the mind."

A disciple asked, "Then should alchemists quiet the mind or not?"

The master replied, "If you can quiet the mind, then the gold pill can be produced at once; but it is hard."

The disciple said, "When you talk to people about alchemy, the way of the gold pill, you cause people to get ideas in their minds. Ideas in the mind are the directors of creation and evolution. So can the mind indeed be quieted?"

The master answered, "Why does the mind move? It is silent and unstirring, yet sensitive and effective; this is the function of our minds. The North Star does not move; the movement is that of the surrounding stars only. The surrounding stars cannot but move; their movement is relative to the North Star, which is as a hub around which they turn. The existence of movement in the midst of the immovable is the alchemist's use of mind. To remain mindful of the immovable in the midst of the movement is sensitive use of mind. To remain permanently immobile is to be like earth or wood. The mind is in the center; seven openings belong to it, all of them inexhaustible in their marvelous functions."

Records of Sayings of Banshan

Practitioners should apply effort and use energy to burn away the habits and biased ideas that have accumulated in their minds.

Having done this and relinquished what is difficult to relinquish, when the limit of the body arrives they will be able to let go of it immediately.

Whatever is in the mind is unreal; when you clear it all away, you will be unobstructed by vexations. As for external things, nothing is worth keeping the mind on. Things come and go before your eyes, but they are like mosquitoes or gnats; brush them off, and you'll be comfortable.

In olden times there was a Taoist who told his teacher that he had gotten rid of the fire of ignorance.

His teacher said that once one has gotten rid of the fire of ignorance, the mind does not stir.

Later the teacher secretly sent someone to test that Taoist. Arriving at his hermitage at nightfall and finding the gate already closed, he knocked at the gate and shouted. As the Taoist answered from inside, his voice already showed a tone of asperity; when he grudgingly opened the door, he was visibly disturbed by the man's coarse behavior.

When they got to the hall, the man bounded in without removing his shoes, and sat down unceremoniously.

At this point the Taoist became very angry and began to scold the man roundly. The man laughed and said, "I have not acted this way on my own initiative. The teacher had me come here to test your unstirring mind. But even without a test your condition is obvious. So there's no further need for a test."

That Taoist was very much ashamed. He had no reply.

Generally speaking, though practitioners may have some accomplishment, they should not be presumptuous and arrogant about it, for they will unexpectedly be found wanting. If they have really reached dispassion, they will have no sense of self-satisfaction. If they feel any pride, this itself proves they are lacking. Furthermore, even if one has reached immovability, there is still something beyond this.

There are many kinds of visions practitioners may have in stillness; all of them are productions of the discriminatory consciousness, which appear due to stillness in order to seduce the mind.

As an ancient said, appearances are illusions; even the desire to get rid of them means the discriminatory consciousness is still there. It will then manifest hallucinations to disturb the mind. If the mind remains unmoved and sees as if not seeing, being like open space, not dwelling on anything, these visions will naturally disappear.

The Tao is everywhere; the thing is to be able to use it in yourself in a way appropriate to the time. This is all there is to it, but still people's minds are tangled up in objects, and this seriously hinders them. Not knowing what is fundamental, they pursue superficialities. Few people turn back from superficial pursuits; though they may study, they don't seek the real. Instead they concoct supernatural visions.

People engaged in self-cultivation should avoid discussing others' strengths and weaknesses or right and wrong, as well as the ups and downs of society and all worldly affairs.

Do not speak or think about what does not concern you—as soon as you start making judgments, you have obscured your self.

If you concentrate on refining your mind, you should always search out your own faults. Why should you be concerned with others' personal affairs?

But since all people usually have some good points, you should emulate them and avoid people's bad points. Beyond this, don't be concerned, and you will gradually reach peace.

Conditions have their own order, which doesn't come from human effort; one should accord with what is natural, calmly awaiting direction. Inner work and outer activity are all in one's own mind; if one is able to apply effort and has accomplishment in oneself, whether one acts or not, in any case one is self-possessed.

If the teaching is inactive in public, one should hide and conquer the mind to commune with the celestial; once the teaching goes into action publicly, outward effort corresponds. If it is in accord with the celestial and corresponds to human needs, effort and activity should be carried out as much as possible. Success depends on the firmness and stability of the mind.

The subtleties and practices transmitted by enlightened teachers accorded with the celestial intent; they did not cling to a fragment and consider it the whole Tao.

Seen in terms of their traces, the ancients were not the same in behavior or practice; but the subtle basis, the spiritual source, has never differed.

It is like the function of the mind being seeing in the eyes, hearing in the ears, speaking in the mouth, thinking in the brain, grasping in the hands, walking in the feet—the functions are not the same, but the substance of mind is not different.

The secret message of real teachers is beyond doctrine, specially transmitted. Speech and thought have no access to it. This is the subtlety of the secret communication of the teaching of real people.

Compass Center Directions

THE MYSTERIOUS FEMALE

Understanding Reality says, "If you want to attain the eternal immortality of the valley spirit, you must set the foundation on the mysterious female. Once the true vitality has returned to the room of yellow gold, the globe of spiritual light never parts."

One opening in the body is called the mysterious female: it receives energy, whereby it gives birth to substance. It is the spiritual capital, where the three bases aggregate without further distinction. Vitality, spirit, and the higher and lower souls meet in this opening, which is the root of the restoration of the gold elixir, the place where spiritual immortals congeal the sacred embryo.

People of old called this the Stem of the Ultimate, the Handle of the Primal, the Source of Open Emptiness, the Root of Undifferentiated Wholeness, the Valley of Cosmic Space, the Source of Evolution, the Opening Back to the Root, the Passway to Restoration of Life, the Point of True Unity, the Yellow Room in the Center, the Capital of the Fundamental, the Altar of Preserving Unity, the Crescent Moon Furnace, the Red Sand Cauldron, the Lair of the Dragon and Tiger, the House of the Go-Between, the Lead Furnace, the Earth Pot, the Spiritual Water, the Flower Pond, the Divine Unity, the Chamber of the Spirit, the Pedestal of

Awareness, the Crimson Palace. All of these terms refer to one point.

But if you look for it in the body, it is not the mouth, not the nose, not the heart, not the genitals, nor the liver, not the lungs, not the spleen, not the stomach, not the umbilical sphere, not the coccyx, not the bladder, not the perineum, not the aperture between the kidneys and genitals, not the point 1.3 inches below the navel, not the point between the eyebrows, not the center of the brain, not the lower abdomen.

So then where is it? My secret is called the unified attention in the center of the compass; if it is not scattered, it forms the embryonic immortal. The corresponding statement of the *Triplex Unity* says, "Real people plunge into the abyss and float around keeping to the center of the compass." This is the place.

Lao-tzu said, "Much talk runs out of reason; it is better to keep to the center." It is right in the center, the region where fire and water interact, precisely in the middle of the heaven and earth within the body. The empty opening where the systems of the eight channels and nine apertures interlink is a tiny pearl hanging in space. It is not based on physical form, but arises from understanding the Way.

"It seems to exist, yet seems not to exist; it seems to be there, yet seems not to be there." It has no inside or outside, but there is a universe in the center: the pervasive principle of the center abides in the proper position. An ancient document says, "Pure and unified, hold to the center." A scripture on human salvation says, "The center orders the five energies and combines the hundred spirits."

Ch'ung-yang called this "finding out the beginning of receiving the energy that produces the body." Chang Po-tuan said, "I urge you to find out the point where your body is produced." This is where the basic energy comes from, and this is where the true breath comes from. Therefore Yu-chan also called it the place where thoughts stir. If alchemists do not understand this opening, then the true breath will not stay and spiritual evolution has no foundation.

Furthermore, this opening develops in the primal but is contacted temporally. When the primal and temporal energies are totally merged into an undifferentiated whole, in the midst of the unknown depths there is a vitality, in the midst of ecstatic abstraction there is a thing. The thing is not an ordinary thing, the vitality is not ordinary vitality. It is by this that the sky is clear, by this that the earth is steady, by this that humans are conscious.

Master T'an said, "Finding the gate of the vast energy is the way to return to the root; knowing the pouch of the original spirit is the way to hide your light, like an oyster keeping a pearl inside, like a stone concealing jade."

All of these are authentic teachings. However, this opening has no sides, and no inside or outside; if you seek it through forms and images of the physical body, that is making a big mistake. Therefore it is said, "Do not cling to nondoing, do not formalize action, do not get stuck in visualization, do not get attached to holding concentration."

The symbols used by sages appear in the alchemical classics. Some call [the mysterious female] an elevation in the center of the mystery, shaped like a jar, closed and sealed, with the spirit operating within. Some say at first it is shaped like a black and white hen's egg an inch in diameter, then after ten months it sheds that enclosure. Some say it is white as plain silk, continuous like a ring, 1.2 inches across, enclosing the pure essence of the body.

These expressions clearly point out the essential aspect of the mysterious pass, revealing the mechanism of creative evolution. If students do not find out the underlying mystery, when they meditate they concentrate on it as a jar, think of it as an egg, visualize it as a ring. Depicting such forms, thus they cling to them as actually there, and their spirits enter into illusion. Is this not a serious error?

If you want to know the opening of the mysterious pass, the gateway of the mysterious female, the spiritual immortals have only pointed to the foundation of creative evolution. Yu-chan said, "It seems to exist, but does not; setting aside your own body, where does it rest?" The substance, function, and balance therein, however, are fundamentally not different. It is like using symbols from the *Book of Change* to represent heaven and earth, sun and moon.

The *Triplex Unity* says, "Conjoining with the undifferentiated, setting up the foundation in the balance pan, working to nurture the basis, solidify the spirit to form the body." Thus spirit and energy can be drawn upon; the higher and lower souls do not become scattered and confused. Turning the light of awareness around to reflect back, you then return; never for a moment astray, you are always here.

A poem says, "Working on the basis you realize nothingness, then grasp the original spirit and dwell within. Breathing out and breathing in without interruption, the complete embryo forms and combines with the original beginning." The teaching of the mysterious female is completely contained in this.

To discuss this further, Heng-lin said, "When the mysterious pass opens up, all of a sudden the essential pathway of the three passes lightly moves, and spiritual water spontaneously flows." He also said, "Below the heart, above the genitals, between the liver and lungs, the center is not the intestines or the stomach; one energy naturally circulates."

Now when we speak of the opening of the mysterious pass, the gateway of the mysterious female, it is right in the center of the heaven and earth within the human body; here is our connection with creation. I have reflected on these explanations; they are generally clear, but still cannot be considered direct indications. Heaven does not begrudge the Way, but circulates it in the human world.

Lao-tzu was so compassionate that he certainly would not insist on withholding this, so I dare to reveal the celestial mechanism, pointing out the great meaning of the mysterious pass as it really is, passing it on in spite of the tradition of secrecy, so that bone and flesh may join, and practitioners of immortalism may understand mentally and spiritually on reading this and put it into practice within themselves, matching each statement in experience.

Wherever this book is, spiritual beings protect it. If your karma is heavy, your blessings are slight, and you have no affinity with the Way, then even if you happen to encounter this teaching and read it, you will disregard and disbelieve it. Then it will mean no more to you than writing means to the blind or music to the deaf. It is the mystery of mysteries—how can such people know it?

An esoteric statement on it says, "A body an inch across, it combines heaven, earth, and humanity. It is vaguely in the area above the genitals and below the heart. This is called the mysterious pass. It cannot be held by mindfulness, it cannot be sought by mindlessness. If you try to hold to it by mindfulness, after all it does not exist; if you try to seek it by mindlessness, after all you see its nonexistence."

Then what should one do? If you use your will undividedly, then you solidify the spirit. Just clarify the mind, cut off rumination, tune the breathing until it is even, and maintain a calm, constant awareness. Do not allow yourself to become oblivious or distracted. Watch for your energy to become peaceful and harmonious; real people enter concentration herein.

In concentration you observe your inner state: when attention reaches it, evidence of it appears, and you notice a breath arising from the center of the compass, flowing continuously, steady yet lively. Sustain this earnestly, listen to it mentally. The six sense faculties become calm and steady, the womb breathing stabilizes; neither stopping nor counting it, you let it be as it is. When stillness climaxes, you breathe out, like fish in a spring pond; when movement climaxes, you breathe in, like insects going into hibernation.

As the creative energy opens and closes, the subtlety therein is inexhaustible. After a while of this, you should forget energy and merge with spirit, returning completely to undifferentiated wholeness. Reaching utter emptiness, keeping completely quiet, the mind does not stir, thoughts do not come and go, and profound calm is permanently stabilized. This is what they call "real people breathing from their heels." The use of the word *heels* means that the breathing is very deep. This is the time when spirit and energy interact.

This is what I referred to earlier as the source of the original energy and the true breath. Where this attention reaches, you see creative evolution; where this breath arises is the mysterious pass. It is not high or low, not left or right, not in front or in back, not on one side or another, but precisely in the center of the heaven and earth in one's body. This is exactly the point: culling is herein, intercourse is herein, refining is herein, bathing is herein, incubation is herein, formation of the embryo is herein, release from the matrix is herein, spiritual transformation is all herein.

If I do not clearly explain this now, students will surely indulge in guesswork based on erroneous ideas, either going too far or not far enough. The classic *Understanding Reality* says, "Even if you are intellectually brilliant, if you have not met an enlightened guide, do not indulge in guesswork." It is just because the alchemical classics do not have personal transmission that they give you no place to form the spiritual embryo.

But this opening expands with yang and contracts with yin; it basically has no form of its own. When attention reaches, then it opens. Its opening and closing have their times. In one hundred days you set up the foundation, developing the matrix of energy, until "light arises in the empty room," whereupon you spontaneously see it. This is the procedure the Yellow Emperor followed when he "spent three months in introspection."

The area below the navel, where the bowels are, is called hell, or the directorate of the ninefold darkness. It is where negative filth accumulates, so true positive energy does not abide there. For this reason various methods visualize this area as the pass of darkness. It is certainly not the place to practice refinement. Students should think about this truthfully.

THE MEDICINAL SUBSTANCES

An ancient song says, "If you ask what our body is based on, it is not apart from vitality, energy, and the primal spirit. I now explain the principle of the birth of the body; a tiny dark pearl is the obvious parent."

Spirit, energy, and vitality are the three higher medicines. The essential secret of the "seven reversion and nine restoration" is to refine vitality into energy, refine energy into spirit, and refine spirit to merge with the Way.

There are many different names for the medicines, all of them metaphors: red lead, black mercury, wood liquid, metal vitality, crimson sand, liquid silver, white gold, black lead, the metal man, the go-between, the fire woman, the water man, the blue tortoise, the red snake, the fire dragon, the water tiger, white snow, yellow sprouts, the gold raven, the jade rabbit, the horse of heaven, the ox of earth, sunrays and moonbeams, the celestial soul, the earthly soul, the lead in the homeland of water, the mercury in the metal cauldron, metal in water, wood in fire, yang within yin, yin within yang, white within black, the female within the male.

So what are the medicinal substances? The essential point in cultivating the alchemical elixir is in the mysterious female. If you want to establish the mysterious female, first make the root stable. The basis of the root is the original vitality. Since it is a transformation of the original energy, therefore vitality and energy are one. When you make them abide by means of the original spirit, then the three aggregate into one.

Heng-lin said, "Myriad beings are born and then die. The original spirit dies and then is born. Put spirit back into energy, and the alchemy takes place naturally."

Shih Ch'ien-wu said, "Energy is a medicine that adds to your years; mind is the spirit employing the energy. If you know the master activating energy, you have become a wizard."

If vitality is depleted, energy is exhausted. When energy is exhausted, spirit wanders. The Book of Change says, "When vitality and energy materialize and the wandering soul therefore changes, if you want to return to the root, wouldn't that be hard?" Yu-ch'i-tzu said, "When you take the original energy in which the original vitality has not yet been converted and transmute it into spirit, then the spirit is luminous and transformation unfathomable."

What we call spirit refers to a medicinal substance in the body, not to something external. However, there is a source where the medicine is produced, there is a time to gather the medicine, there is a rule for manufacturing the medicine, there is a creative process in which to put the medicine, and there is a firing work by which to refine the medicine.

In the past I heard about this from my teacher, who said, "The homeland of the southwest is called the yellow court: there is something in abstraction, there is vitality in profound darkness. Distinctly clear, the uniformly flavored metal within water: just set your attention on the flower pond to look for it." This tells of the source of the medicine.

"Lower your eyelids, close the senses, stop reverberations, detach from the body, part with knowledge, and you are near to sitting forgetting. I urge you to spend the days silent, like a dunce, and refine a wish-fulfilling jewel." This tells of the time for gathering the medicine.

"The rootless spiritual herb prior to heaven and earth: measure it out with undivided attention to produce the ultimate treasure. The Great Way is not apart from the heart; working carefully and closely, there is practical discipline." This tells of the rule for manufacturing the medicine.

"No mind in the mind, no thoughts in the thoughts, concentrate the attention on the center of the compass and unify the energy." Also, "Breath after breath, continuity unbroken, in every action, and whenever sitting, it becomes increasingly clear." This is the creative process into which the medicine is put.

"The medicinal substances of clarity and calm are made into a pill by close attention; twenty-four hours a day, the fire of no thought cooks. Always keep the water in the gold cauldron warm; don't let the fire in the jade furnace cool." This tells of the firing work by which to refine the medicine.

In sum, the mysterious female is the source of yin and yang, the house of spirit and energy. Spirit and energy are the medicines of essence and life, the root of womb breathing, the ancestor of respiration, the way to make the roots deep and the stem firm. The "womb" is the place where the spirit is stored, the breathing is the basis of evolving the embryo. The embryo is produced by the breathing, the breathing is stabilized by the embryo. Without the breath, the embryo does not form; without the spirit, the breathing has no master.

Before people are born, there is a vast emptiness; a sign of future development first appears when father and mother have intercourse. When that one point first congeals, it is purely essence and life; after three months, the mysterious female is established therein. Once the mysterious female is established, a link is formed like the stem of a melon; the infant is in the womb, unconsciously focused on the energy of the mother. When the mother breathes out it also breathes out, and when the mother breathes in it also breathes in. In all movements, inside and outside sense each other, unconsciously, unknowingly, without understanding. The energy of heaven an undifferentiated whole, the energy of earth an undifferentiated whole, there is just a single breath there. Then when the time comes and the fetus is developed, heaven and earth overturn: the human being is startled, the amniotic sac breaks. It is like losing one's footing while walking atop an enormous mountain: the baby is ejected head down and feet up, then gives a great cry. Now the womb breathing is forgotten, so following essence and sense cannot go together.

How much greater is the alienation when confusion floods the mind, craft amuses the eye, emotional attachment leads feelings, and desire changes nature. When the rich natural reality is dispersed and turns into myriad things, it is all because of this. The breath of the womb is no longer maintained.

Spiritual immortals teach people to refine the vitality so as to return to the basis and revert to the beginning, recreating the internal organs and reestablishing the physical body, producing substance from no substance, forming the spiritual embryo. The secret of this is in the saying, "Concentrating energy, making it supple, can you be like an infant?" Remove accretions, stop thoughts, quiet the mind, and keep unified: external imaginations not entering, internal imaginations not coming out, all day long there is an undifferentiated wholeness, like being in the mother's belly.

When the spirit is settled, thereby it combines with energy;

when the energy is harmonious, thereby it joins with spirit. When spirit is one with energy, it stabilizes; when energy is one with spirit, it abides in a state of silent rest, detached in the homeland of nothing whatsoever. The celestial mind, oblivious of all else, concentrates attention on one opening, the way a hen incubates her eggs, like a fish in water. Exhaling all the way to the root, inhaling all the way to the stem, continuously on the brink of existence, again you maintain focus on the breath within the womb.

When you maintain focus without focusing on anything, the true breath spontaneously stays, imperceptible, as if it weren't there. Although mindful, you do not keep anything in mind, but dwell in profound abstraction, only aware of a single consciousness in the center of cosmic space, which is the master of creative evolution.

When the right time comes, the subtle design will become self-evident. Lightly moving, silently active, you subtly use attention to steady energy, and respond to the pivotal mechanism of creative evolution. Then sense and essence naturally merge, vitality and spirit naturally rise and descend. All of a sudden a tiny point falls into the center of the yellow court. This is the mechanism of gathering real knowledge and putting it into conscious knowledge, which is forming a day's elixir in one day.

The classic *Verses on Restoring Life* says, "Last night the undifferentiated fell to the earth; the varied array of myriad forms is totally unknown." At this time, the body is completely merged with space, and one does not know of spirit being energy or of energy being spirit. This creative evolution is not a visualization; it is all a natural process. It is so without our knowing why it is so. Once the medicine is produced, the fire then emerges.

Generally speaking, when the medicine is produced, if small it can be used to match the creative evolution of real knowledge and conscious knowledge; if great it can be used to assimilate to the function of heaven and earth.

The teaching of the gold elixir has now been completely divulged. It cannot be discussed in the same terms as minor tangential techniques. If you don't believe me and try to establish a foundation without the mysterious female, seek medicinal substances apart from spirit and energy, arbitrarily carry out a firing process without knowing the natural womb breath, abandon the root and pursue the branches, follow illusion and lose reality, then heaven will foil your plans, and there is nothing I can do about it.

THE FIRING PROCESS

An old song says, "The sages transmitted the medicines, but did not transmit the firing. The people who know the firing process have always been few."

What does it mean to say that it has not been transmitted? It is not that it has not been transmitted because it is secret. When gathering, it is called medicine; within the medicine there is fire. When refining, it is called fire; within the fire there is medicine. If you know the medicine and get the fire, then you see the elixir form in concentration; there are naturally those who know without it being transmitted. This is what is meant by the poem that says, "The medicinal substances are yin within yang; the firing process is yang within yin: if you understand the meaning of yin and yang, the firing process is clear all at once."

People of later times who are confused about the alchemical classics and unable to understand immediately then want to find out what the fire is and what the process is when they hear such terms as the twenty-four energies, the seventy-two periods, the twenty-eight stations, the sixty-four hexagrams, the twelve fields, the meeting of sun and moon, the rise and fall of the ocean tide, the trance of eternal life, the positive cultural and the negative martial. Exhausting their minds all their lives, sticking to various descriptions, even if they get the real medicinal substances they are unaware and will not refine them.

What they do not know is that the real firing has no process, the great medicine is not weighed. Yu-chan said, "The fire is symbolic of mind. Mind is spirit; spirit is the fire. Energy is medicine. Refine the medicine with the fire and you form the elixir. This means operating energy by means of spirit, thus to attain the Way."

The explanation is so clear and so direct, but if you do not already have the bones of an immortal you will scorn it as empty words and stumble right past. This is very lamentable.

However, the essential point of verbally transmitted secrets of the firing process should above all be sought in true breathing. This is because breathing comes from mind; when the mind is quiet, the breathing is harmonious. When each breath returns to the root, that is the matrix of the gold pill. This is what is meant by the *Heart Seal Scripture* when it says, "The returning breeze mixes the compound, the hundred days' work is effective." This is also what is meant by *Guide to Putting in the Medicine* when it says, "Rouse the breeze to operate the fire; in the yellow room they form the ultimate treasure." It is also what is meant by the saying of old master Hai-chan, "Opening and closing creativity and receptivity is the handle of evolution, refining the real sun and moon in one furnace."

What does this mean? "Real People plunge into the abyss and float around keeping to the center of the compass." It is necessary to use spirit to operate energy and use energy to settle the breathing. Like the opening and closing of a bellows, the rising and descending of yin and yang, exhalation and inhalation are allowed their natural spontaneity. Concentrating energy and making it supple, covering up your light and keeping silent, practice this with subtle continuity whatever you are doing, like a woman carrying a child in her womb, like an oyster developing a pearl. Gradually gathering, gradually refining, gradually solidifying, gradually crystallizing, when the work becomes pure unity is attained.

Further adjustments should be made between movement and stillness: do not give rise to thoughts, for when thoughts arise the fire flames; and do not let attention scatter, for when attention scatters the fire cools. Just make it so that it is neither excessive nor insufficient, and find the mean between grasping and letting go. When spirit embraces energy and energy embraces spirit, the unified attention, in a state of profound harmony, enfolds the undifferentiated whole. This is what is called the seed of the fire continuing, so that the alchemical cauldron is always warm. There is not a breath of interruption, not a hair of deviation.

When you cultivate refinement in this way for half an hour, that is half an hour's cycle. When you cultivate refinement in this way for an hour, that is an hour's cycle. When you cultivate refinement in this way for a day, that is a day's cycle. When you refine this for a hundred days, that is called setting up the foundation. When you have cultivated refinement for ten months, this is called the embryonic immortal.

Even when positive energy arises in the ocean of the primal, fire arises within water, heaven and earth revolve, and the creative and receptive repeat, none of this is apart from a single breath. The same is true of what we call bathing, incubation, advance and withdrawal, extracting and adding: therein one intimately accords with the celestial mechanism, subtly tallying with creative evolution, yet without admitting any of one's own power therein.

Therefore it is said, "Although the firing has a process, it does not need time; the mechanism is known to oneself." There is no rule about midnight and noon, morning and evening; there are no divisions of the lunar cycle, no distinctions of winter and summer solstice, no separation of yang fire and yin convergence, no doctrine of the twenty-four hours being just one time, no secret of three hundred days being in half a day. It is also not in the teaching of concentrating years into months into days into hours. If you talk in terms of time, then it can be practiced twenty-four hours a day, whenever the attention is there. If you talk in terms of its subtlety, then the seasons and intervals of a whole year are inherently there within a half hour's work.

Just settle spirit and breath, letting them be natural. This is my teacher's clear explanation. Night and day, through difficulty and darkness, emulate nature; why struggle to watch the firing process? This is my teacher's certain exposition. This is all there is to the saying that the sages transmitted the medicine but not the firing. Here is a poem:

Why should students necessarily
bother to seek a teacher?
Just this book divulges
the celestial mechanism.
Even if you wear out iron sandals
there is no place to search:
once you've got it,
you expend no effort at all.

Overall Essentials of Alchemy

ON "SEEING ESSENCE AND ATTAINING BUDDHAHOOD"

A disciple asked Shang-yang-tzu, "It is certainly true that 'there are not two Ways in the world.' The Way of Lao-tzu is the Way of alchemy, the Way of alchemy is the Way of essence and life. But what Bodhidharma [the founder of Ch'an Buddhism] brought from India is 'directly pointing to the human mind for perception of its essence and attainment of buddhahood.' Is this beyond alchemy?"

Shang-yang-tzu said, "The Way of Bodhidharma is identical to the Way of alchemy. People of the world differ in terms of the keenness or dullness of their faculties and capacities, so the buddhas and masters set up names expediently out of compassion. Among students of later times, the intelligent went too far while the ignorant didn't go far enough.

"Why do I say this? Intellectuals do not understand the one great matter in the reality that is right at their feet: it shines through eternity, free of all entrapment, able to kill and able to give life. Once this point is obscured, people run off wherever their feet take them; this is call going too far.

"The ignorant, on the other hand, have not heard that there is a 'true human with no status in this mass of flesh' carrying the great matter. If this point is obscure, it is foolish to try to see essence

175

and attain buddhahood by reciting scriptures, fasting, chanting sacred names, or sitting still. This I call not going far enough."

The disciple asked, "Is seeing essence itself attainment of buddhahood?"

The master answered, "Great Master Fu said, 'Even if you go through eight hundred eons, after all you fall into voidness and perish.' Seeing essence is like attaining the Way. When you hear the Way you need to carry it out, so 'when the best people hear the Way, they carry it out diligently.' Seeing essence calls for cultivation, so the Buddha practiced cultivation in the Himalayas before realizing the state of buddhahood. Without learning and practice, how can seeing essence be considered attainment of buddhahood?"

The disciple asked, "It is said that all living beings have buddhanature, and it is also said that intellectual understanding and knowledge constitute effective clarity and cognitive awareness. How can these two attain buddhahood?"

The master said, "The nature of intellectual understanding and knowledge cannot attain buddhahood; only the essential nature of living beings can attain buddhahood."

The disciple asked, "This is different from what I have heard. May I ask, is the nature of living beings the nature of the self?"

The master answered, "It is."

The disciple asked, "What is it?"

The master said, "Intellectual understanding and knowledge are of the nature of obstructions caused by the action of affirmation and denial. The nature of living beings is the nature of creation and evolution, the nature of all conscious life. People simply don't know the nature of living beings, so they cannot escape birth and death, and thus miss out on nirvana.

"The nature of intellectual understanding and knowledge arises in the six senses; it is daily bound up in sentiment and emotion, without rest. The nature of living beings is right at our feet, immutable being as is, with great freedom. An ancient worthy said, 'Hell is not painful compared to the tremendous misery of failing to understand the great matter.'

"Do people of the world realize the nature of living beings is itself the true buddha-nature? When you realize this true buddha-nature, you know it exists of itself within; it is not carved of wood or molded of clay. Therefore, it is said, 'The real Buddha sits within.' When you reach this point, only then is it 'seeing essence and attaining buddhahood.' Therefore it is said, 'Mind is itself Buddha.'

"If you do not realize the true Buddha within is our own essential nature, and instead take the nature of intellectual understanding and knowledge to be Buddha, this is like taking a stranger for your own child, a big mistake; this is why it is said 'Mind is not Buddha.'

"Once you have realized that your own real nature is the real Buddha within, then this nature, this buddha, is still a temporary compound of elements; this is why it is said, 'It is not mind, not Buddha.' If you realize clearly that your own nature is your own real Buddha, you use this for cultivation and attainment; this is why it is said, 'See essence and attain buddhahood.' "

Clarifying the Way

There are no words for the subtle primal principle—whatever you may say is all conditioned. Students produce a welter of differing views and do not find out the state before birth.

The enlightening process is uncontrived, in accord with nature—there is no immortality outside naturalness. Always keep one thought, remaining on the middle way, not asking about the primordial or temporal.

It is better to comprehend essence before life, for when essence is clear there are no demons in comprehending life. If you want to know where essence and life rest secure—before ideation sprouts you're one with the universal harmony.

Although the science of life can be transmitted, the science of essence cannot be handed on. The ignorant who practice blindly are truly pitiful. If you don't get personal instruction from an adept, all your psychological manipulations will instead bring on error.

The essential subtlety of our path is in sincerity alone—without sincerity you have nothing, and the Tao cannot be approached.

When utterly silent and unstirring, there is no sensation—in the midst of trance you see original reality.

When human desires have not sprouted, the celestial design is there. As soon as thoughts stir, ghosts and spirits know. Don't ignore even subtle hidden thoughts—be strict and extra cautious. Practice this in everyday life—it won't work if you stray.

Good and evil both arise in the moment of a thought. Let a single thought slip, and you're obstructed by a thousand barriers. If you know there is no good and no evil, you are calm and serene, standing aloof like a great mountain.

The Tao is always to be practiced in the midst of daily life. Stop talking about lofty wonders and the empty void. Just carry out the human Tao, and there will be no shame in your heart. When you fulfill your nature, you'll know heaven and earth are the same.

The myriad affairs of the human world all come from mind. The mind is basically formless—where will you look for it? Understand before a single thought is born, and then you finally see the real mind.

The moment thoughts go awry they become afflictions. When the mind is empty, objects are empty of themselves. Empty yet not empty, one is perfectly aware, gazing clearly, unobstructed, through the great void.

All things are empty, but essence isn't void. Set to work inside of empty voidness—when you reach the point where nothing can be established, gold light fills the room and you see the mystic pearl.

Before you know true emptiness, do not speak of emptiness. If you cling to emptiness, you will easily lose the inner self. Do you want to know the true state within emptiness? It is all before the differentiation of the primordial unity.

To learn the Tao you must know birth and death. If you don't know birth and death, it is vain to seek immortality. When you know where you are born, then you know death. Free to leave or stay, you leave it up to nature.

Originally there is no death and no birth—the moment a thought goes astray, you see myriad forms. If you know where thoughts arise and vanish, the solitary orb of the bright moon illumines the central courtyard.

Spiritual practice requires that you know the true self. All those who do not know the true self fall into the void. If you can awaken to real eternity, then you attain the Tao—transcending the world, you manifest supernatural powers.

Chang San-feng

Introduction

Chang San-feng is one of the greatest figures of later Taoist history and legend, believed to be master of all the arts and arcana of the Way. He is particularly famous as the alleged originator of the popular exercise system known as *t'ai-chi-ch'üan* (*taijiquan*). Like Ancestor Lü, Chang San-feng is also believed to have attained immortality in more than a purely spiritual sense, and to have reappeared in the world after his supposed physical death. The works attributed to him, again like those of Ancestor Lü, are also evidently mixed with later additions and in some cases may be viewed as generic products of a school rather than works of an individual author. The Chang San-feng literature shows an amalgamation of Southern and Northern schools of Complete Reality Taoism, as well as traces of older Taoist sects practicing magical arts.

It is very difficult to assign exact dates to Chang San-feng. One account says he lived from about 1391 to 1459, but he is also said to have lived during the Yuan dynasty (1278–1368); some even claim he was born in the Sung dynasty (960–1278). A Taoist master said to be Chang San-feng is known to have been summoned to court by an emperor of the Ming dynasty in the fifteenth century, and some Western scholars regard the record of this event in the dynastic history to be the only hard data on him. No one really knows, however, who Chang San-feng was, or even how many Chang San-fengs there were. All that is certain is that there is a considerable body of writings attributed to him, containing a wealth of interesting and practical material.

This anthology presents several of Chang's works. The first selection is a commentary on Ancestor Lü's seminal work, *The Hundred-Character Tablet*. This piece shows a strong trace of the psychophysical yoga practice associated with the Southern school of Complete Reality. The next selection is a set of essays on the teachings of Wang Che, founder of the Northern school, presenting an excellent summary of the principles and practices of that tradition of meditation. This is followed by *Words on the Way*, a collection of extracts from Chang's own talks on meditation, which combine approaches characteristic of both Southern and Northern schools. The last three selections from Chang's works to be presented here are his fascinating essays on moral and psychological understanding: "Loving People," "On Medicine," and "On Human Characters."

Commentary on Ancestor Lü's
Hundred-Character Tablet

THE TEXT

Nurturing energy, forget words and guard it.
Conquer the mind, do nondoing.
In activity and quietude, know the source progenitor.
There is no thing; whom else do you seek?
Real constancy should respond to people;
In responding to people, it is essential not to get confused.
When you don't get confused, your nature is naturally stable;
When your nature is stable, energy naturally returns.
When energy returns, Elixir spontaneously crystallizes,
In the pot pairing water and fire.
Yin and yang arise, alternating over and over again,
Everywhere producing the sound of thunder.
White clouds assemble on the summit,
Sweet dew bathes the polar mountain.
Having drunk the wine of longevity,
You wander free; who can know you?
You sit and listen to the stringless tune,
You clearly understand the mechanism of creation.
The whole of these twenty verses
is a ladder straight to heaven.

COMMENTARY

Nurturing energy, forget words and guard it.

Practitioners should first nurture energy. The method of nurturing energy is in forgetting words and keeping unified. Forget words, and energy is not dispersed; keep unified, and the spirit does not go away. The secret is to quietly hold the spirit steady.

Conquer the mind, do nondoing.

Ordinarily people's minds move and shift ceaselessly. If practitioners want to quiet down their minds, it is important to control their eyes. The eyes are the door of the mind, and should be nearly closed. Use the mind on all things like a sword. Think of worldly things as of no benefit to you; then both craving and irritation will disappear, without any attempt to get rid of clinging.

The secret is to look through the eyes at the nose, look through the nose at the navel, align above and below, keep mind and breath on each other; now keep your attention on the Mysterious Pass, and you can overcome thought.

In activity and quietude, know the source progenitor.

Activity and quietude are yin and yang; the Source Progenitor is the place where the body is born. Practitioners should know that prior to Birth is the Mysterious Female.

This is the place where the upper and lower parts of the body, the celestial and earthly parts of the being, and all the psychological elements of human nature are all gathered together. This is made of the point of spiritual light that is prior to the separation of Heaven and Earth, and is what is called the Absolute, or the Great Ultimate.

This is the vague area below the heart and above the genitals where thoughts ceaselessly arise. This is the Source Progenitor, or Progenitor of the Clan.

In this context, activity and quietude mean tuning and harmonizing of the true breath, or true energy, and securely aligning the truly fundamental in its proper position in your life.

It is said that when you breathe out you contact the Root of Heaven and experience a sense of openness, and when you breathe in you contact the Root of Earth and experience a sense of solidity. Breathing out is associated with the fluidity of the dragon, breathing in is associated with the strength of the tiger.

As you go on breathing in this frame of mind, with these associations, alternating between movement and stillness, it is important that the focus of your mind does not shift.

Let the true breath come and go, a subtle continuum on the brink of existence. Tune the breathing until you get breath without breathing; become one with it, and then the spirit can be solidified and the elixir can be made.

There is no thing; whom else do you seek?

If you can nurture energy, forget words, and conquer body and mind, spirit returns to the lair of energy; the attention focuses on the Center of the Compass, merged with unified energy, like a hen sitting on her eggs, like a dragon nurturing a pearl.

Keep your mind on this all the time, without a moment's distraction, and after a long time, when the work becomes deep, there naturally appears a tiny pearl that shines like the sun, silently turning into the light of awareness of the original spirit, beyond conceptual measurement.

Real constancy should respond to people; in responding to people, it is essential not to get confused.

This Tao is the Way of real constancy and true eternity. It is easy to get confused by things when dealing with situations, so when you come in contact with people, it will not do to get confused by what happens.

If you do not respond to people, then you are empty and silent, an open absence; when they come to you, you ought to respond, then let the thing pass when it's past. Be clear, upright, and magnanimous, and you won't be confused. Your true nature will then be clear and serene, while your original spirit will solidify and crystallize.

The secret is to pay attention everywhere you mistake nondoing and fall into vacuity.

When you don't get confused, your nature is naturally stable; when your nature is stable, energy naturally returns.

Ordinary people's natures are fiery, emotional, exaggerated one way or another, inconstant. Any sort of stimulus will activate random mental images in them, so it is hard to quiet their natures.

It is necessary to be truly careful of anger and be truly sparing with desire. Physical calm is called refining vitality; refine your vitality, and "the tiger hisses," the original spirit solidifies. Mental calm is called refining energy; refine your energy, and "the dragon sings," the original energy remains safeguarded. Steadiness of attention is called refining spirit; refine your spirit, and the two energies combine, the three originals merge, and the original energy spontaneously returns.

The three originals are original vitality, energy, and spirit. The two energies are yin and yang. When you deal with people without confusion, then the original spirit naturally returns, and the fundamental nature is there of itself.

When our fundamental nature as conscious beings is present, then the primal energy in the body naturally returns. Then it is not hard to "return to life, go back to the root."

The secret is to turn the attention around to illumine the source of consciousness, the whole unified mind remaining within, inward thoughts not coming out, outward thoughts not coming in.

When energy returns, elixir spontaneously crystallizes in the pot pairing water and fire.

When practitioners are not confused by objects and events, then energy naturally returns. Thereby they see the two energies rising and descending in the center of their bodies, yin and yang pairing in the Alchemical Crucible. Suddenly they feel a thread of hot energy in their genitals, rising up into the heart. Sense comes back to the essence of consciousness, like husband and wife joining in blissful rapture.

The two energies interact to form the substance of the elixir; water and fire mix in the lair of energy. The cycle goes on and on, so that the spirit drives the energy and the energy maintains the body. Then one does not need a variety of exercises or arts to live long naturally.

The secret is that the three treasures—ears, eyes, and mouth—be closed off and not allowed to exercise their powers. "Real People dive deep into the abyss, and travel floating, keeping within the Compass." Do this until the energy in the elixir field is full, and this forms the Medicinal Spoon, the linkage between the macrocosm and microcosm.

Yin and yang arise, alternating over and over again, everywhere producing the sound of thunder.

When the work gets to this point, the spirit does not run outside, the energy does not leak out. The spirit returns to the lair of energy, water and fire have already mixed; increase the intensity of your effort, to "reach the ultimate of emptiness, and keep careful tranquillity." Then the body is peaceful in the Middle of Unfathomable Darkness, the mind is clear in the Homeland of Nothing Whatsoever.

Then the true breath spontaneously stills, all the body's nerve channels spontaneously stop. Sun and moon halt, the stars do not revolve in the sky.

At the Extreme Limit, stillness gives rise to movement. Suddenly there is a point of spiritual light the size of a grain of rice. This is the indication of the production of the medicine.

A blazing light passes through the kidneys like boiling water; the bladder is like fire burning; in the belly there are sounds like a roaring gale and pealing thunder. This is represented by the *I Ching* sign "Return," and is when the Root of Heaven appears.

When the Root of Heaven appears, it stabilizes mastery of mind; help this with the spirit, and the energy is like fire applied to metal, passing up through the coccyx. Lightly convey the energy, silently raise it, a ball of gentle energy, like the reverberation of thunder, bringing it up to the center of the brain, whence it spurts out all over the body. This is represented by the *I Ching* sign "Meeting."

From the Moon Cave, which is the cessation of intense effort when the energy has filled the brain to the forehead and center of the brows, there leaks light from the origin of being.

Then at the Extreme Limit, movement gives rise to yin, which has transformed into a psychic water, like a sweet dew. Inside one there is the pearl of spiritual awareness, which has settled in the Yellow Courtyard in the center of the self, transmuting mercurial consciousness so that it becomes stable, characteristic of the sage.

Go through the developmental process of the whole cycle once, purifying and refining consciousness, and the elixir will naturally crystallize.

White clouds assemble on the summit, sweet dew bathes the Polar Mountain.

When you get to this stage, the medicine has been obtained. The two energies interlock to form the medicinal spoon, which is the unification of higher and lower wills, and the nerve centers and synapses of the body and brain open up. Fire descends, water rises, and unified energy circulates all over: from within the Extreme Limit (tai-ji) it stirs the Root of Heaven, passes the Dark Valley Pass, rises up through the vertebrae until it reaches the Pass of the Valley of Heaven. In the Moon Cave, yin is born, fragrant, sweet, delicious; it goes down the Multistoried Tower without stopping. This is called sweet dew bathing the Polar Mountain.

The secret is when the mouth is filled with saliva after a period of stillness followed by rising and circulating of energy. Visualize the saliva as sweet dew, or ambrosia, what the Buddhists call the elixir of immortality, and as you swallow it, mentally send it down into the Alchemical Cauldron, where it solidifies the original energy and thus nurtures it.

Having drunk the wine of longevity, you wander free; who can know you?

When development of energy reaches this degree, the bone joints are already open, and the spiritual "water" ceaselessly circulates up and down, flowing all around, coming and going without stopping; taking it in time and again, it is called the wine of longevity.

The secret is that the flowing pearl, the essence of consciousness, bathes and nurtures the spiritual nature; people who practice this know unknowing.

You sit and listen to the stringless tune, you clearly understand the mechanism of creation.

When your work reaches here, you hear the sound of the music of the immortals, and there are also the tones of bells and drums. The five energies assemble at the source, the three flowers gather on the peak; that means the true sense of real knowledge of the true essence of consciousness is present in the will, and the vitality, energy, and spirit have been refined and united. It is a state like when a raven comes to roost in the evening. The mind field is open and clear, knowledge and wisdom spontaneously grow, and one clearly understands the writings of the three teachings, tacitly realizes one's roots in former lives, foreknows what bodes good and ill for the future; the whole world is as though in one's palm. You see for myriad miles and have the subtle psychic faculties available to complete human beings. This is real being.

Discourses on the
Teachings of Wang Che

ON SITTING

Wang Che, the real human like multiplied sunlight, said that since
your body becomes fatigued when you sit for a long time, it is
unreasonable to do this, and it can even cause illness. As long as
the mind does not stick to things you can be imperturbable. This
is the correct foundation of true stability.

Using this for stabilization, the mind and energy are harmonized,
becoming lighter and clearer the longer this is practiced. Using
this as a test, you can tell right from wrong.

If you can extinguish each arousal of mind, you will annihilate
conscious cognition and enter into the steadiness of forgetting. If
you let the mind get aroused and do not collect or control it, then
you are no different from an ordinary person. If you only cut off the
sense of good and bad, and your mind is aimless, floating and
roaming around arbitrarily, depending on self-stabilization, you are
just fooling yourself in vain. If you engage in all sorts of activities
and claim your mind is not influenced by them, this is very good
talk but quite wrong in practice. True learners are especially wary
of this.

Now if you put a stop to delusions but do not extinguish
awareness, keep calm but do not stick to voidness, practicing this

with consistency, you will spontaneously attain true vision. In case you have doubts about something, go ahead and think it over, so that the matter can be settled and what is in doubt can be understood. This too is a correct basis for producing wisdom. Once you have understood, then stop thinking—if you go on thinking, you will harm essence by intellect, damaging the basis because of the offshoot. Though intellect may bring you distinction for a time, ultimately it will cause defect in the work of eternity.

All toilsome, rambling, and random thoughts are to be dismissed as soon as you become aware of them. If you hear slander or praise, or anything good or bad, brush it all off right away; don't take it into your mind. If you take it in, your mind will be full, and there will be no room for the Tao. Whatever you see and hear, see and hear it as if you did not see or hear. Then right and wrong, good and bad will not enter your mind. When the mind does not take in externals, this is called emptying the mind. When the mind does not pursue externals, this is called pacifying the mind. When the mind is peaceful and empty, the Tao comes of itself to dwell therein.

EMPTYING THE MIND

A classic says if people can empty the mind and remain empty, without desiring the Tao, the Tao comes of itself. Once the inner mind does not dwell fixedly on anything, outward action too is uncontrived. This is neither pure nor defiled, so there is nowhere for praise and censure to arise. It is neither knowledge nor ignorance, so gain and loss have no way to cause disturbance.

In truth, one accords with the mean as the constant; provisionally, one adapts to the time. At least one avoids entanglements; this is its wisdom. If you exercise thought and act insistently at an inappropriate time, on an inappropriate matter, and claim you are unattached, this is not real study. Why? The mind is like an eye— if even a tiny hair gets in an eye, the eye is uncomfortable. Similarly, if even a small matter concerns the mind, the mind will be disturbed. Once afflicted by disturbance, it is hard to concentrate.

What is essential to practice the Tao is to get rid of afflictions. If afflictions are not removed, it is impossible to attain stability. This is like the case of a fertile field, which cannot produce good crops as long as the weeds are not cleared away. Cravings and ruminations are the weeds of the mind; if you do not clear them away, concentration and wisdom do not develop.

The mind is used to resting on objects and not used to independence. If it is not placed on anything for a while, it finds it difficult to be at ease. Even if it is peaceful for a while, it again reverts to distraction, now aroused, now quiet. If you purposely cause it to be undisturbed, taming it perfectly over a long period of time, it will naturally become peaceful and at ease.

Day and night, no matter what you are doing, you should attentively settle the mind. If you are not yet able to attain peace, then you should calmly nurture it, not letting anything vex you; then you will gain a little peace and relaxation, and so can be naturally comfortable. Gradually taming the mind, it will become increasingly clear and deep.

Oxen and horses are domestic animals, but if you let them go free and do not restrain them, they will naturally become wild and will not submit to the harness. Hawks and falcons are wild birds, but if they are tied up by people and are always perched on the wrist, they naturally become tame. So it is with the mind; if you let it run wild and do not restrain it, it will grow increasingly coarse—how then will you be able to perceive that which is subtle?

BEING UNAFFECTED

Some say, "Those who practice the Tao are in the midst of things, but their minds are unaffected. Though involved in action, their spirits are undisturbed. There is nothing that they do not do, yet never are they perturbed. Now if one only avoids activity and takes to calm, seeking stability apart from action, struggling to suppress and control, then whether there is movement or stillness, one single-mindedly sticks to keeping stationary. This produces the twin illnesses of grasping and rejection, totally unawares. Is it not a mistake to consider an external fixation to be an essential step on the Way?"

The answer to this is that what we consider great is the totality of things, and what we call the Way is penetration of things. To be in the midst of things without being affected, to deal with affairs without being disturbed, is truly great, truly wonderful. But there is something as yet unclear in the view expressed in this question. What is that? It is only seeing the result without understanding the process. Just as an enormous tree grows from a tiny sprout, the stabilization of the spirit and attainment of enlightenment comes about through accumulated practice. It is useless to speak only of the qualities of sages without knowing why they have such qualities.

SIMPLIFYING AFFAIRS

For people practicing the Way, nothing compares to simplifying affairs. Know what is essential, discern relative importance, understand what to leave and what to take. Whatever is not essential and not important, one should omit. For example, luxurious food and clothing, social distinction, and material riches are all extraneous likes of psychological desire, not good medicines that enhance life. When people pursue them, they bring about their own destruction. What could be more confused?

GENUINE OBSERVATION

Genuine observation is the prescience of the wise, the perceptivity of the able. Every meal, every nap, is a potential source of gain or loss; every act, every word, can be a basis of calamity or fortune. Skillfully holding the branch is not as good as clumsily preserving the root. Observing the root and knowing the branches is not a feeling of competitive haste. Collecting the mind and simplifying affairs, day by day one reduces contrivance. When the body is calm and the mind uncluttered, only then can one observe the subtle.

Nonetheless, the body that practices the Way must be sustained by food and clothing. There are some matters that cannot be neglected, some things that cannot be abandoned. These you should accept with an open mind and manage with clear eyes. Don't consider them obstacles, lest your mind become anxious. If you become vexed and anxious over things, mental illness has already acted up—how could that be called peace of mind?

Social relations and the necessities of life are a boat for us—if we want to cross the sea, we need the aid of a boat. How could we neglect food and clothing before we have yet crossed over? That which is unsubstantial is really not worth striving for, but in the process of freeing ourselves from that which is insubstantial we cannot get rid of it all at once.

Yet even though we work and strive, we should not think of gain and loss. Let the mind be always calm and steady, whether or not there is anything of concern. Seek the same as other people, but do not be greedy like other people; get what others get, but do not hoard like others do. Without greed, there is no anxiety; not hoarding, there is no loss. One is then like others in outward appearance, but the inner mind is always different from that of worldlings.

These are basic essentials of speech and action, which should be rigorously practiced.

THE ILLS OF MATERIALISM

If there is an illness that is hard to get rid of even when one has cut off entanglements and simplified affairs, one should observe it objectively. If one is seriously affected by materialism, one should realize that infection by materialism is entirely due to thoughts. If thoughts do not arise, there is no concern with material things.

One should know that when thoughts of material things are not projected outwardly, the materialistic mind is forgotten inwardly. Forgetting thoughts, the mind is empty—who plays host to material things? A scripture says that forms are only imaginations, and imaginations are all empty. Why be concerned with forms?

If you see other people doing evil and conceive aversion to them, that is like seeing people destroy themselves, stretching out their necks to the sword to kill themselves. They are doing evil on their own, and it is no business of yours. So why detest them? This is one's own mental illness. Not only should you not detest those who do evil, you should dislike those who do good. Why? Because they are obstructing the Way.

One's deeds are done by oneself, but destiny is bestowed by heaven. The relation of deeds to destiny is like shadows and echoes following form and sound. What is unavoidable should not be resented. Only the wise accurately perceive and accurately know this; they are pleased with heaven and aware of destiny. Therefore they do not grieve over the miseries of poverty and sickness. A classic says, "Heaven and earth cannot change their operation, yin and yang cannot avert their misfortunes." In these terms, this is true destiny—how can we resent it?

When a valiant warrior encounters brigands, he charges ahead brandishing his sword, routing the enemy. Once his achievement is accomplished, his rewards last all his life. Now when poverty and illness afflict our bodies, they are brigands; to immediately straighten the mind is to be a valiant warrior. When the burden of mental affliction is dispelled, this is victory in battle; tranquillity and eternal happiness are the rewards.

Whenever painful things oppress our minds, if we do not oppose them, we will become burdened with anxiety. This is like someone who does not do battle with brigands, but turns tail and runs, only to be punished for flight. To give up happiness and take to misery— how can this be pitied?

If you are afflicted by poverty and illness, consider this pain to proceed from having a body. Where can affliction abide? As a classic says, "When I have no body, how can I have any affliction?"

GREAT STABILITY

Great stability is the consummation of leaving mundanity, the elementary foundation of arrival at the Tao, the accomplishment of cultivation of tranquillity, the completion of maintaining calm. The body is like a dead tree, the mind is like dead ashes. Neither grasping nor rejecting, it is the arrival of utter quiescence. There is no consciousness of stabilization, yet there is total stability; therefore it is called great stability.

Chuang-tzu said, "Those whose abode is great stability emanate the light of heaven." The abode is the mind, the light of heaven is wisdom. When emptiness and tranquillity reach the extreme, then the Tao is present and wisdom arises. Wisdom comes from fundamental essence and is not a personal possession; therefore it is called the light of heaven.

It is due to pollution and confusion by greed and craving that people become dull and muddled. When people are confused, wisdom does not arise.

Once wisdom has arisen, one should treasure it and not let intellectualism damage stability. It is not that it is hard to produce wisdom; what is hard is to have wisdom but not use it. Since ancient times there have been many people who have forgotten their bodies, but few who have forgotten their names; to have wisdom but not use it is to forget one's name. Few people in the world reach this, so it is considered difficult.

If the highly placed can avoid arrogance and the wealthy can avoid extravagance, this is considered freedom from vulgar faults, and is a way to preserve nobility and wealth. If one is stable and does not stir, is wise but does not use it, one thereby attains profound experience of true eternity.

Chuang-tzu said, "To know the Tao is easy; not to speak of it is hard. To know but not say is that whereby one becomes divine; to know and speak of it is that whereby one becomes human. People of old were divine, not human." He also said, "Those who cultivated the Tao in ancient times used calmness to nurture knowledge. Knowledge arose in them, but they didn't make anything of it. This is called using knowledge to nurture calm." Knowledge and calm nurture each other and emerge from the fundamental essence in harmony with universal principle.

Calmness and knowledge are stability and wisdom; harmony and universal principle are the Tao and its power. Having knowledge but not using it, one is peaceful and calm; when this builds up for a long time, it spontaneously develops one's Tao power. One will naturally reach a point where one is not startled even by thunder and lightning so powerful as to split a mountain, not frightened even by swords clashing right in front of one's face. One sees fame and fortune are fleeting, and knows the cycle of birth and death is like a running sore. If the will is exercised undividedly, then it solidifies the spirit; the intangible subtlety of the mind will be inconceivable.

ATTAINING THE TAO

The Tao is something miraculous. Spiritual, it has an essence; empty, it has no form. It is unfathomable whether we follow after it or go forth to meet it. It cannot be found in shadow or echo. No one knows why it is as it is. Supreme sages attained it in antiquity; it has been transmitted to the present by subtle means.

The Tao has a profound power that gradually transforms the body and the spirit. The body is mastered along the way, becoming united with the spirit. One who has attained this is called a spiritual person. The essence of spirit is open and fluid; its substance never changes or disappears. Because the body is mastered through the Tao, it has no birth or death. In concealment, the body is the same as spirit; revealed, the spirit is the same as energy. This is how it is possible to walk on water and fire without harm, to cast no shadow in the sunlight or moonlight. Whether to remain alive or disappear is up to you at this point; there is no gap between leaving the world and entering the world.

If even the body, which is material, can reach intangible sublimation, how much the more so can spiritual knowledge, which becomes more far-reaching as it grows deeper. *The Classic on the Living Spirit* says, "When the body and spirit are united, that becomes the true body." *The Scripture on Rising in the West* also says, "Body and mind join, thus making it possible to last forever."

There are, however, differences in depth of power along the way of open nonreification. If the power is profound, it affects the body as well, but if it is shallow it affects only the mind. One whose body is affected is a spiritual person; one whose mind is affected only gains intelligent awareness and cannot escape physical death. Why? Intelligence is a function of the mind; when used too much, the mind is fatigued. When one first gains a little wisdom, one is joyful and becomes loquacious; spirit and energy leak out, so no spiritual light bathes the body, ultimately resulting in early death. Therefore the Tao is hard to complete. This is what the classics call liberation from the corpse.

Therefore great people hide their light and conceal their brilliance; this is how they gain complete fulfillment. Stabilizing the spirit, taking good care of energy, they study the Tao unminding. When the spirit merges with the Tao, this is called attainment of the Tao. A classic says, "Those who assimilate themselves to the Tao are also absorbed by the Tao."

In the mountains there is a kind of jade that keeps plants and trees from withering. Similarly, if people embrace the Tao it will keep their physical bodies strong. By steeping oneself in the Tao for a long time, one can transform substance so that it is the same as spirit, refine the body into something subtle, and merge with the Tao. Then the illumination of knowledge is boundless, and the body is infinitely transcendent. One makes the totality of matter and emptiness one's function, one sets aside creation in achieving realization, one adapts from reality without convention—this is the power of the Tao.

SITTING FORGETTING: ESSENTIALS AND AUXILIARIES

If you want to practice the way to attain reality, first get rid of warped behavior. After disconnecting your mind from external things, inwardly observe correct awareness. When you notice a thought arise, you should immediately extinguish it. Extinguishing thoughts as they arise, strive to effect calm quietude.

Next, even though you may not have obvious fixations, still floating random thoughts are also to be completely eradicated.

Working diligently day and night, never wavering for a second, just extinguish the stirring mind, do not extinguish the shining mind; just stabilize the open mind, do not stabilize the dwelling mind. Do not rest on anything, yet have the mind always present.

This method is inconceivably subtle, and its benefits are very profound. It is possible only for those who already have affinity with the Tao and whose faith is undivided. If you have set your heart on the supreme Tao, and your faith is firm and in earnest, first accept three precepts, then act in accord with these three precepts with consistent heedfulness, and you will attain the true Tao.

These three precepts are as follows: one, simplify involvements; two, remove desire; three, quiet the mind. If you diligently practice these three precepts without slacking or backsliding, then the Tao will come of itself, without any intention of seeking the Tao on your part. A classic says, "If people can always be clear and pure, the whole universe will come to them." Speaking from this point of view, should we not have faith in this quintessential method?

But the contentiousness of the ordinary mind is firmly ingrained through long habit, and it is very difficult to stop the mind by these precepts. One may be unable to stop it, or one may still it temporarily and then lose that stillness. Battling with it, now failing, now succeeding, one pours with sweat. With continued practice over a long, long time, eventually it is possible to tame the mind. Do not give up this work, which has far-reaching consequences, just because you are temporarily unable to collect the mind.

Once you have gained a bit of tranquillity, then you must consciously stabilize it at all times, whatever you are doing, even in the midst of activity and turmoil. Whether you have anything to do or not, always be as if unminding. Whether in the midst of quietude or in the midst of clamor, let your will be undivided.

If you try to control the mind too intensely, this will produce illness, a symptom of which is fits of madness. If the mind does not move, then you should let it be, so that relaxation and intensity find their balance. Constantly tuning yourself, controlled yet without fixation, free yet without indulgence, you can be in the midst of clamor without aversion, you can handle affairs without vexation. This is true stability.

This does not mean you seek many affairs because you can handle them without vexation, or that you take to clamor because you can be in its midst undisturbed. Unconcern is the real home; having concerns is responsive manifestation. This may be likened to a mirror, which reflects things that come before it. Skillfully exercising expedient means, still one can enter stability.

Whether insight emerges slowly or rapidly is not up to the person. Do not be in a hurry to seek insight in concentration. If you seek insight, you will injure your essence. If you injure your essence, you will have no insight. When insight arises spontaneously without seeking, this is true wisdom. Being wise but not exercising it, true knowledge appears ignorant, thus increasingly fostering stability and wisdom, so that both are endlessly perfected.

If you think and imagine in the midst of concentration, you will experience much distraction and bedevilment, which appear according to your state of mind. Just cause there to be unlimited openness above the concentrated mind and vast buoyancy below the concentrated mind. Then past problems will vanish day by day, and new habits will not be formed, so there will be no binding obstruction, and you will shed the net of sense objects. Practice this for a long time, and you will naturally attain the Tao.

In people who attain the Tao, there are five times and seven signs of mind and body. The five mental times are: (1) when movement predominates over stillness, (2) when movement and stillness are equal, (3) when stillness predominates over movement, (4) when there is stillness in leisure and movement in work, and (5) when the mind merges with the Tao and is not stirred by impacts. When the mind reaches this last state, one finally attains peace and comfort; defilements are obliterated, and there are no more anxieties.

The seven physical signs are: (1) action is timely, and the countenance is peaceful and joyful; (2) chronic ailments disappear, so body and mind are light and fresh; (3) untimely wastage is compensated, so that one returns to the original and is restored to life; (4) the life span is extended thousands of years—this is called being an immortal; (5) the body is refined into energy—this is called being a real human; (6) the energy is refined into spirit—this is called being a spiritual person, and (7) the spirit is refined to merge with the Tao—this is called being a complete human.

If people practice concentration for a long time, but their minds and bodies show no evidence of the five times and seven signs, and their lives are short and their bodies are polluted, when they pass away physically they return to the void. They may consider themselves wise, and even claim to have attained the Tao, but it is not really so.

VERSES ON SITTING FORGETTING

Always be silent, and basic energy won't be hurt;
minimize thought, and the lamp of wisdom shines within.
Avoid anger, then the spirit is peaceful and realized;
subdue vexations, and the mind is clear and cool.
Without seeking, there is no flattery or cajolery;
without fixation, one can change adaptively.
If you are not greedy, then you are rich;
if you are not presumptuous, why fear rulers?
When tasting is ended, the spiritual spring descends of itself;
when the energy is settled, true breath grows daily.
In terms of feeling, the body dies and the spirit travels;
in terms of imagination, one leaves the corpse in dreams.
When energy leaks, the body returns to the earth of the grave;
when thought leaks, the spirit heads for the realm of death.
When the mind dies, only then can the spirit live;
when the earthly soul passes away, the celestial soul is strong.
It's hard to investigate the subtle principles of all things;
responsive adaptation is not apart from true constancy.
Supreme vitality submerges into ecstasy;
great form merges with immensity.
Adaptations of the Way are like the evolution of beings;

even ghosts and spirits cannot fathom this activity.
Not drinking, not eating, not sleeping;
this is called the sitting forgetting of real people.

Wang Che, ancestor of the Complete Reality school, said, "When the mind forgets thoughts, it transcends the realm of desire. When the mind forgets objects, it transcends the realm of form. When the mind does not cling to emptiness, it transcends the formless realm. Detached from these three realms, the spirit abides in the homeland of immortals and sages, the essence exists in the domain of pure openness."

Words on the Way

"Freezing the spirit, tune the breath; tuning the breath, freeze the spirit." This is the starting work. This should be done single-mindedly, continuing from step to step.

Freezing the spirit means gathering in the clarified mind. As long as the mind is not yet clear, the eyes should not be closed in meditation. It is first necessary to exert oneself to restore clarity, coolness, and serenity; then one may concentrate on the pocket of energy in the body. This is called freezing the spirit.

Once you have begun to freeze the spirit, after that it is like you are sitting on a high mountain gazing down at the foothills and rivers, like a lamp illuminating the sky, lighting up every recondite obscurity. This is what is called freezing the spirit in space.

Tuning the breath is not difficult. Once the spirit of mind is quiet, breathe naturally; I just keep this naturalness, and also focus attention downward. This is tuning the breath.

Tuning the breath is tuning the breath centered on the base of the torso, joining with the energy in the mind, breath and energy meeting in the pocket of energy in the abdomen. The mind staying below the navel is called freezing the spirit; the energy returning below the navel is called tuning the breath.

When spirit and breathing stay together, keeping their clarity and naturalness is called "not forgetting," going along with their clarity and naturalness is called "not forcing." Not forgetting, not forcing, quietly, gently, the breath is vigorous and the mind is free.

Then apply the principle of using space as the place to store the mind, using dark silence as the abode to rest the spirit; clarify them again and again, until suddenly the spirit and breath are both forgotten, spirit and energy merge. Then unexpectedly the celestial energy will arise ecstatically, and you will be as though intoxicated.

The real experience is when the Mysterious Pass appears. Generally one finds in the alchemical teachings the words *primordial, real,* and *original.* All of these emerge from the crucible of yin and yang, all of them are produced after profound mystic silence. In attaining this, like the first opening up of primal unity, all the sages and real people are alike; after this one can figure out the alchemical classics.

There are many people who study the Way for months without making any progress at all, because their minds aren't really on the Way. If your mind is on the Way, there will naturally be no things on your mind; if you are serious about the Way, you will naturally be lighthearted about things; and if you are engrossed in the Way, you will naturally be aloof from things.

Preserving the essence of consciousness, you don't become fragmented and distracted; nurturing the spirit, you don't become torpid or inattentive. How can you then be disturbed by idle thoughts? When reason prevails over desire, you live; when desire prevails over reason, you perish.

Plunge the mind into the profound abyss, and the spirit does not wander outside. When the mind is dragged by things, fire stirs within; and when fire stirs within, it destabilizes the vitality.

The Way is entered from the center. There is a center in the body, and a center that is not in the body. The work should be done in two stages, the first of which is to seek the center in the body.

Master Chu (Zhu) said, "Keep to the center, prevent wandering off." Keeping to the center calls for turning the attention inward to concentrate on a sphere 1.3 inches below the navel, neither clinging fast to it nor departing from it, with neither obsession nor indifference. This is seeking the center within the body.

Second is to seek the center that is not in the body. *The Classic on Central Equilibrium* speaks of "before emotions arise" as the center. In this time before arising, be careful in your innermost mind of the unperceived, and naturally the essence of consciousness will be stabilized and the spirit will be clear.

When the spirit is clear, the energy is keen; when you attain this you see your original being. This is seeking the center that is not in the body.

Using the center within the body to seek the center not in the body, after that human desires are easy to clear up, and the celestial design again becomes clear. The sages and saints, immortals and buddhas of all times, have taken this to be the first stage of the work.

Traveling around and sitting still are certainly not in themselves the Tao. But if you don't travel around in cities and mountains, you should have your energy travel around the passes and openings throughout your body; that will do. If you do not sit under withered trees or in cold halls, you should have your spirit sit in the subtle opening within the body; that will do.

Study of the Way is based on the alchemical foundation. Once the alchemical foundation is stabilized, then you can return home and work to support your family. After having fulfilled your familial and social duties, then you go into the mountains and look for a teacher, to complete the Great Way. Those who abandon their homes and leave their wives are simply wasting their days and are not worth talking about.

Loving People

Humans are the most intelligent of living beings. Because they are intelligent, we should love their life.

Don't connive to encompass people's downfall, don't injure people with weapons, don't poison people with chemicals.

Don't oppress people with authority and power.

Actions that are harmful to people are eventually punished in some way or another, outwardly or inwardly. Ultimately it is impossible to escape the consequences of deeds.

People like talking birds, they like beautiful and fragrant plants, they like tame animals, they like pet fish—are not other people as important as these creatures?

Just look at the way people despise each other and treat each other cruelly, even as they multiply and congregate.

Whatever you do, you should think of caring for people's reputations and fostering their reputations, caring for people's merits and fostering their merits, caring for people's work and fostering their work, caring for people's benefit and fostering their benefit.

Fostering the good name of others is the way to foster your own good name. Fostering the merits of others is the way to foster your own merit. Fostering the work of others is the way to foster your own work. Fostering the benefit of others is the way to foster your own benefit. It is all love.

In fostering people's reputation and merit, work and benefit, don't conceal the loyalty of loyal people, don't usurp the achievements of meritorious people. Don't slander the virtuous, don't cast aspersions on the chastity of virgins.

Don't envy the able, don't borrow the ability of others either. Don't resent the talented, don't be blind to people's talents either.

Don't conceal goodness, and don't appropriate the goodness of others. Don't elevate evil, don't imitate the evil of others.

Don't secretly inhibit the advancement of others, don't ruin the flourishing activities of others, don't foil the good deeds of others, don't destroy the good plans of others.

Don't lessen the life or wealth of others, don't fool with others' goods.

Don't help evil people usurp the position of good people, don't collaborate with petty people in seducing the offspring of good families.

Don't defame the worthy. Don't defraud the destitute. Don't separate parents and children, don't come between relatives. Don't destroy others' marriages. Don't slight the handicapped.

Save people from difficulty, help them in times of need. Take pity on those who are alone. Forgive people's faults. Help people when they are sick or suffering, feed and clothe them when they are hungry and cold.

Support your relatives and help out your neighbors. Have compassion for the orphaned and widowed, respect the aged and care for the poor. All this is love for people.

Heaven gives birth to the millions as a ground for kind people to exercise kindness, as a place for good people to accumulate goodness; as a result they can broaden their minds to protect and take care of large numbers of people.

Those with wealth and status who love people will surely enrich their descendants; the poor and lowly who love people will surely be able to attain success.

For Heaven helps the good, God enriches people. Therefore to those who want to know the way to deal with the world, I suggest, Love People.

On Medicine

Medical science can make a nation lively, and it can also make a nation ill. Medicine can give people life, and it can also kill people. It is necessary to be careful about its application.

Therein are principles whose study is endless, whose practice is inexhaustible. There are principal and auxiliary medicines, there are diseases of lack and excess, old and new; all doctors can talk about these things, but few really know them.

The finer the learning of sages becomes, the humbler they are; the loftier their virtue becomes, the more modest they are. This is the way physicians should be too. They should not slight themselves, mislead themselves, or deceive themselves. Those who deceive themselves deceive others, those who mislead themselves mislead others, those who slight themselves slight others. The fault devolves on oneself.

Therefore, in this field it is easy to establish good works, yet it is also easy to err; it is hard to accumulate blessings, but it is not hard to invite disaster. Those who wish for accomplishment without error, fortune without calamity, must diligently discipline themselves.

The principles of pulse taking are subtle; those of shallow learning hardly know them. I urge physicians to first ask the patients about the development of their maladies, and not test medicines on them. I urge the sick seeing a doctor to first understand basic reason, and not risk your life to test the doctor. To use one's life to test the doctor is the fault of the patient; to test medicines on people is the fault of the doctor.

Also, physicians should take care of emergencies without concern for elevating their reputations, and should help the wretched without calculating how much they will get paid. If they can clearly perceive the symptoms, then they can proceed with treatment; if not, they should wait for the more expert. Then they will build up the virtues of calmness and truthfulness.

I also urge those who study the social sciences to include extensive and thorough study of medical arts and sciences in their curricula. Don't keep them secret, and don't get them wrong. Use this knowledge for your own benefit and for the benefit of others. People should not take medical science lightly.

On Human Characters

You should understand the distinctions between human characters that appear to be similar.

There are upright, mentally healthy people who keep to themselves, are independent and aloof from the crowd, whom others consider conceited, but I consider strong.

There are people who are modest, avoid ostentation, are in control of themselves, and appear no different from ordinary folk, whom others consider conformists, but I consider to be in harmony.

There are people who are serene and free, following natural reality, whom others consider lazy, but I consider at peace.

There are people who are ebullient and spontaneous, going along with the natural order, whom others consider eccentric, but I consider masterful.

There are people who are careful in their behavior and strict in their manner, whom others consider haughty, but I consider rigorous.

There are people who conduct themselves simply and have very stable personalities, whom others consider uncultured, but I consider unspoiled.

There are people who clearly distinguish between duty and gain, and have no selfishness, whom others consider too conservative, but I consider uncompromising.

There are people whose hearts are transcendent and detached from objects, whom others consider one-sided, but I consider high-minded.

There are people who are mild, complacent, and unlettered, whom others consider vulgar, but I consider genteel.

There are people who concentrate on purity and do not know scriptures or ceremonies, whom others consider ignorant, but I consider awakened.

There are people who are not changed by food and drink, are not bothered by heat and cold, whom others consider strange, but I consider immortal.

Whether people are sages or not may be difficult to distinguish, as there may be resemblance without real sameness. It is necessary to observe carefully.

Liu I-ming

Introduction

Liu I-ming was one of the greatest Taoists of the Ch'ing dynasty (1644–1911). He seems to have been born around the year 1737, and lived until at least 1826. His lifetime coincided with the middle stage of the modern Western rape of China, and the British scheme to create mass opium addiction in China had already been well established with great commercial success by the time he passed away. The institutionalized forms of Taoism, Buddhism, and Confucianism were corrupt and ineffectual, thus contributing to the general demoralization of Chinese culture and society.

Liu I-ming left home in search of truth at the age of eighteen after a Taoist cured him of what appeared to be a fatal illness. After years of fruitless search, he met an enlightened teacher who completely changed his outlook on spiritual studies. According to his own account, however, he left the company of this teacher too soon and was not able to resolve lingering doubts for another twelve years, when he met a second adept who helped him make a final breakthrough. Liu did not begin writing until he was in his sixties, vowing to reveal the secrets of the alchemical classics. The superb quality of his illuminated and illuminating commentaries and essays is already well known to Western readers through English translations of his explanations of the *I Ching, Understanding Reality,* and the *Four-Hundred-Character Treatise on the Gold Elixir.* This volume presents Liu's comments on three more great classics of practical Taoism: the *Classic on Yin Convergence, The Hundred-Character Tablet,* and *Journey to the West.*

The *Classic on Yin Convergence* is believed to be a very ancient text, traditionally attributed to the Yellow Emperor, a Taoist culture hero who is supposed to have lived in the middle of the third millennium B.C.E. Like other ancient texts, it is punctuated, read, and interpreted in a number of different ways by different commentators. Its importance in Complete Reality Taoist learning is indicated in Chang Po-tuan's *Understanding Reality,* where it is ranked with the *Tao-te Ching:* "The precious words of the *Yin Convergence* exceed three hundred, the spiritual words of the *Tao-te Ching* are fully five thousand: the superior immortals of past and present have all arrived at the true explanation herein."

In his commentary on *Understanding Reality,* Liu I-ming writes, "The two books *Yin Convergence* and *Tao-te Ching* are basic books for practice of Tao: they divulge the mechanism of creation and evolution of the universe, and reveal the opening of yin and yang, enlivening and killing. From ancient times to the present the adepts have all investigated the true principles in these two classics and arrived at the real explanation, whereby they have comprehended essence and life. This book, *Understanding Reality,* is also composed based on the *Yin Convergence* and *Tao-te Ching;* if students can understand this book, they will also be able to understand the meanings of the *Yin Convergence* and the *Tao-te Ching.*"

Liu I-ming also wrote commentaries on certain works of Ancestor Lü, the grand master of the original school of Complete Reality. *The Hundred-Character Tablet* has already been introduced in the present anthology both in the section on Ancestor Lü and in the commentary attributed to Chang San-feng. It will be noticed that Liu reads the text in a somewhat different manner, and his explanations reflect a very pure form of Complete Reality Taoism as practiced in the Northern school. A comparison of the commentaries by Chang and Liu not only provides an in-depth study of the original classic of Ancestor Lü, it also illustrates the main line of difference in later developments of his school.

The last selection from Liu I-ming's commentaries to be presented here is a set of extracts from his writings on *Journey to the West*, which has itself been translated into English as a "folk novel" and does not seem to be generally recognized as an esoteric map of human development except among certain Buddhists and Taoists. Liu attributes the original work to the thirteenth-century Taoist master Ch'ang-ch'un (Changqun), one of the great disciples of Wang Che, founder of the Northern school of Complete Reality.

Secular scholars vehemently deny this attribution, claiming it derives from confusion with another book called *Journey to the West* recounting Ch'ang-ch'un's expedition to Mongolia. The two works are so different, however, as to render this theory absurd. What is more likely is that scholars who believed the work to be a "folk novel" did not understand the inner content, which treats the most complex and sophisticated forms of Buddhism and Taoism. For centuries the stories of *Journey to the West* were current as a cycle of dramas, which were ultimately rewritten into the present form of a novel by Wu Ch'eng-en (Wu Chengen) in the sixteenth century. Currently available English translations are based on the "folk novel" theory of the work, and do not reflect sensitivity to the technical inner meanings. In a set of remarkable essays, Liu I-ming explains how the text appears to the initiate.

Commentary on the Classic
On Yin Convergence

TEXT

I.

Observe the way of Heaven, practice the action of Heaven.
  That is all.

Nature has five robbers; those who see them thrive.

The five robbers are in the mind; they carry on their activities
  in heaven. The universe is in the hand; myriad
  transformations take place in the body.

The celestial nature is humanity; the human mind is
  mechanical.

Setting up the celestial way is to stabilize humanity.

When heaven radiates killing potential, it moves the stars and
  shifts the constellations. When earth radiates killing
  potential, serpents cause trouble. When humans radiate
  killing potential, heaven and earth overturn. When heaven
  and humanity act in concert, myriad developments have
  their basis stabilized.

There are clever and dull natures, which can be subdued and
  put away.

The aberrations of the nine openings are in the three essentials,
  which can be active or still.

When fire arises in wood, disaster takes place with ineluctable

force. When treachery arises in a country, the time is
disturbed with ineluctable destructiveness. Those who know
this and practice refinement are those known as sages.

2.

Heaven gives life, heaven kills: this is the principle of the Tao.

Heaven and earth rob myriad things, myriad things rob
people, people rob myriad things. When the three robbers
are as they should be, heaven, earth, and humanity are at
peace. Therefore it is said, eat at the right time and the
body will be in order; act at the right moment and all
events will be peaceful.

People know the spirit as psychological, they do not know why
the nonpsychological is spiritual.

Sun and moon have measurements, great and small have
definition. The work of sages is born therefrom, spiritual
illumination emerges therefrom. When you take over the
mechanism, no one in the world can see you, no one can
know you. When developed people get this, they are
steadfast in poverty; when undeveloped people get this, they
take life lightly.

3.

The blind can hear well, the deaf can see well. Cut off one
wellspring, that of profiteering, and it is ten times better
than mobilizing the army. Introspect three times day and
night, and it is ten thousand times better than mobilizing
the army.

The mind is given birth to by things, the mind is killed by
things; the mechanism is in the eyes.

Heaven has no kindness, but great kindness arises from it.
With swift thunder and strong wind, all beings become
active. The nature of ultimate happiness is to be
unrestricted; the nature of ultimate peace is to be pure.

Heaven is ultimately private, but its function is ultimately
public.

Control and creation are in energy.

Birth is the root of death, death is the root of birth. Benefit comes from harm, harm comes from benefit.

Ignorant people consider the designs and patterns of heaven and earth holy. I consider the designs and patterns of times and beings wise.

People assume sages are ignorant. I assume sages are not ignorant. People expect wonders of sages. I expect sages not to be weird.

Sinking into water, going into fire, bring destruction on oneself.

The natural Tao is calm, so heaven, earth, and myriad beings are born. The Tao of heaven and earth is penetrating, so yin and yang prevail. Yin and yang push each other onward, and myriad changes go along.

Sages know the natural Tao cannot be violated; they follow it to master it. The Tao of supreme tranquillity cannot be aligned with the calendar, so they have an extraordinary vessel. This gives birth to myriad forms, the eight trigrams, the numerical cycles, the workings of spirits, the secrets of ghosts. The art of mutual supercession of yin and yang clearly progresses beyond forms.

COMMENTARY

Yin is darkness, silence, that no one can see, no one can know; it means solitary vision, solitary knowledge.

Convergence is meshing; it means a pair joining so that they become as one.

A *Classic* is a pathway, a road, a constant; it means a perennial path in life, something lasting and unchanging.

The Classic on Yin Convergence deals with the Way in which the light of the spirit is used subconsciously to mesh tacitly with creative evolution.

When they mesh tacitly with creative evolution, then people are united with heaven. Their action and stillness are both celestial workings, and the people are each a Heaven.

The three sections of this classic elucidate the three words *Yin, Convergence, Classic*; if you understand these three words, you can figure out the general meaning of the three sections of the classic.

I.

Observe the way of Heaven, practice the action of Heaven. That is all.

The Way of essence and life is one; it is the Way of Heaven. The Way of Heaven is simply the Way of yin and yang. If practitioners of the Way know the inner subtleties of the Way of Heaven, and through silent exercise of the light of the spirit take of the energy of yin and yang, and take over the authority of Creation, it is possible thereby to live long and not die; it is possible thereby to have no birth and no death.

What is most important is in being able to observe and to practice. What is observation? Observation means to investigate things and get to know about them. Observation means to make very deep and detailed study. Observation means mental knowledge and spiritual understanding. Observation means turning the attention within to see what's behind consciousness. Observation means not hiding anything from yourself or fooling yourself.

And what is practice? Practice means concentrating the mind and focusing the will. Practice means not going too far and not falling short. Practice means effort in personal action. Practice means getting stronger with perseverance. Practice means consistency from beginning to end.

To observe the nondoing effect of the Way of Heaven is sudden enlightenment, and is the means of realization of the essence of life. To take up the learning of the Doing of the action of Heaven is gradual cultivation, and is the means of realization of the life of essence.

By being able to observe and practice, you use the Way of yin and yang to become free from yin and yang; by means of things of the world you transcend the world. That is to say, you recognize that all there is, is change, and while intimately understanding vicissitudes of change you stand somehow apart from them, ultimately free.

When essence and life are both realized, mind and phenomena are both forgotten; transcending the universe, there is eternal subsistence.

The two expressions "observing the Way of Heaven" and "practicing the action of Heaven" are themselves a celestial ladder that can enable people to become enlightened immortals, a great road for saints and sages. Everything outside of this is a sidetrack, seductive but misleading talk. That is why the text says, "That is all."

Nature has five robbers; those who see them thrive.

The five robbers are represented by metal, wood, water, fire, and earth. Nature uses these five forces of yin and yang to produce beings, making their forms from energy.

People are born and grow through reception of this energy. But when yang peaks it gives rise to yin; the primal goes into the temporal, and the five forces cannot combine harmoniously.

This means that the five forces plunder one another of energy, each isolated in its own character. For wood, metal is a robber; for metal, fire is a robber; for fire, water is a robber; for water, earth is a robber; for earth, wood is a robber. These are what are called the five robbers of Nature.

These five robbers are used by people every day without their being aware of it. Because they go along with their energy they are born and die, die and are born, being born and dying endlessly.

If you can see them, you operate Creation in reverse, and reverse the five forces. Metal originally overcomes wood, wood thereby becomes vessels. Wood originally overcomes earth, earth thereby produces luxuriant growth. Earth originally overcomes water, water is thereby stopped from flowing uncontrollably. Water originally overcomes fire, fire is thereby stopped from heating up. Fire originally overcomes metal, metal thereby produces a glow. Within overcoming there is production; the five robbers turn into five treasures; the one energy, whole, returns to the source and goes back to the root.

*The five robbers are in the mind; they carry on their activities in heaven.
The universe is in the hand; myriad transformations take place in the body.*

People are born with the energy of the five forces, so they have the
energy of the five forces in their bodies. The mind is the host of the
body, the body is the house of the mind. When the five robbers are
in the body, really they are in the mind.

The mind, however, is divided into the human mind and the
Tao mind. When you do things by means of the human mind, the
five robbers become active as emotions and desires. When you do
things by means of the Tao mind, the five robbers turn into
benevolence, justice, courtesy, wisdom, and truthfulness.

If you can observe Heaven, understand the waxing and waning
of the five forces, and use the Tao mind to function, then every step
you take comes from Heaven, not from humanity. Great though
the universe may be, it is as though in the palm of your hand;
many though the myriad transformations be, they are not outside
your body. Can it not be difficult to assemble the five forces,
combine the four forms, and thereby realize essence and life?

*The celestial nature is humanity; the human mind is mechanical. Setting
up the celestial way is to stabilize humanity.*

Celestial nature is the nature bestowed by Heaven, which is the
nature of true being-as-is. What is called the true mind follows the
laws of God without consciously knowing. This is how people can
be people.

The human mind is the nature of temperament, the nature of
cognitive consciousness. What is meant when it is said that the
human mind is mechanical is that it gives rise to feelings when it
sees things, "raising waves along with the wind." People have birth
and death based on this.

The celestial nature is the working of Heaven, which is the Way
of Heaven; the human mind is the working of humans, which is
the way of humans. Those who keep the working of Heaven survive,
while those who follow human mechanicalness perish.

Only great sages observe the Way of Heaven and practice the

action of Heaven, standing in the center, without any bias, tranquil and unmoving yet sensitive and effective. They cultivate the true nature and transform the psychological nature; they keep the Way of Heaven and stabilize the human mind, not letting any foreign energies adulterate their hearts.

When heaven radiates killing potential, it moves the stars and shifts the constellations. When earth radiates killing potential, serpents cause trouble. When humans radiate killing potential, heaven and earth overturn. When heaven and humanity act in concert, myriad developments have their basis stabilized.

The killing potential is the harsh yin energy through which things are damaged. But without yin it is impossible to give rise to yang; but for killing, it is impossible to maintain life.

Therefore, once the killing potential of heaven comes forth, it goes through a cycle and then begins again; the stars and constellations move through the sky. Once the killing potential of the earth comes forth, stripping away of the primordial reaches its climax and the primordial returns; when stillness culminates, there is movement again.

Human beings also contain a heaven and earth, and also have yin and yang. If they can emulate heaven and earth in operating the killing potential, then the five forces are overturned, and heaven and earth commingle in tranquillity. What does this mean? If the human mind and the celestial mind combine, the overturning of yin and yang takes place in a short time; when celestial timing and human affairs are unified, then the basis of all developments is stabilized.

There are clever and dull natures, which can be subdued and put away.

People are physically formed from yin and yang energies, and are endowed with innate knowledge and innate capacity, which form their natures. Natures are all good, but energies may be clear or muddled. Those whose endowment of energy is clear are therefore clever, while those whose energy is muddled are therefore dull.

226

Those who are clever by nature are often crafty, while those who are dull by nature are often greedy and foolish. Whether people are clever or dull by nature is a matter of temper; when the human mentality is in charge of affairs, this is not the original celestial nature. The path of cultivating reality is to gather the primal to convert the temporal, so that cleverness and dullness are both subdued and put away, and not used.

The aberrations of the nine openings are in the three essentials, which can be active or still.

The nine openings are openings in the human body; the three essentials are the ears, eyes, and mouth. The nine openings of the human body are all receptors for aberrating influences, but among them it is only the ears, eyes, and mouth that are the main inlets which summon aberrating influences. When the ears listen to sounds, the vitality is shaken; when the eyes look at forms, the spirit runs; when the mouth talks a lot, the energy disperses. Once vitality, energy, and spirit are damaged, then the whole body deteriorates, and life is lost.

If you can curb looking and listening, and speak little, you close those main inlets, and let your mind be open and empty. With inward thoughts not coming out and outward thoughts not entering in, the three great medicines of vitality, energy, and spirit will congeal and no longer disperse. Then the nine openings can be active or still, and their activity or stillness is the working of heaven, without human artifice. So what more aberrant energy could there be that would not dissolve?

When fire arises in wood, disaster takes place with ineluctable force. When treachery arises in a country, the time is disturbed with ineluctable destructiveness. Those who know this and practice refinement are those known as sages.

Fire symbolizes the insane mind, wood symbolizes human nature. Treachery symbolizes hidden ills, a country symbolizes the body.

Wood originally produces fire; when fire breaks out, it is disastrous for the wood itself, as the wood is burned. Similarly, insanity comes from the mind; when insanity breaks out, it is disastrous for the mind itself, as human nature becomes deranged.

When there is treachery in a country, acts of treachery destroy the country, and the nation perishes. Ills are hidden in the body; when negative energies are strong, they destroy the body, and life is lost.

When body and mind are burdened, nature and life go along. Under these conditions, wise are they who know how to inwardly practice secret refinement, observe the Tao of Heaven, take up the action of heaven, conquer body and mind, preserve nature and life, and not be constrained by temporal forces.

2.

Heaven gives life, heaven kills: this is the principle of the Tao.

The Tao of Heaven is just yin and yang. Yang is responsible for giving life, yin is responsible for killing. There can be no yang without yin, no life without death. Therefore in spring there is birth, in summer there is growth; in autumn there is the harvest, in winter there is storage. The four seasons form an order, going through their cycle again and again, going on like this throughout the ages.

Heaven and earth rob myriad things, myriad things rob people, people rob myriad things. When the three robbers are as they should be, heaven, earth, and humanity are at peace. Therefore it is said, eat at the right time and the body will be in order; act at the right moment and all events will be peaceful.

Heaven begins all things, earth gives birth to all things. But once they give life to them, they also kill them. This is how heaven and earth rob all things. There are myriad things in the world; people give rise to feelings when they see objects, and when they indulge in feelings and desires, they use up their spirit and energy. The young become old, the old become feeble, the feeble die. This is how things rob people.

Human beings are the most intelligent of beings, and even

though things can steal energy from people, yet people consume the vitalities and flowers of myriad things, and are born and grow dependent upon the energies of myriad things. This is how people rob myriad things.

Great practitioners of deliberate cultivation are able to usurp the energy of myriad things for their own use, and they can take the energy things are taking from them, and they can take the energy heaven and earth are taking from things. When these three take-overs are unified this way, there is life in the midst of death, and the three robbers are as they should be.

When the three plunderers are as they should be, people are united with the qualities of heaven and earth, acting in concert with them, harmoniously, so they are all at peace.

Once heaven, earth, and humanity are at peace, the energy of the Tao is always present, so myriad things cannot constrain one, creation cannot contain one.

But the secret of this robbery involves work of one time, which must not be done too soon or too late, must not be forced or anticipated. It will not do to be excessive, nor to be inadequate. When real knowledge comes, conscious knowledge receives it; the other comes, and the self attends it. When yang returns, it is received with yin.

The most important element is not losing the timing and not mistaking the right moments. That is why it is said that when you eat at the right time your body will be in order, and when you act at the right moment events will be calm.

Eating at the right time means taking advantage of times to absorb primordial energy. Acting at the right moment means taking opportunities to seize control of life and death.

When eating is timely, acquired energy is digested and all parts of the body are in order, enabling one to preserve the physical body intact. When action is opportune, primordial energy returns and all events are peaceful, enabling one to extend one's years.

Time and opportunity are hard to talk about. If you want to know this time, it is the celestial timing, and this moment of opportunity is the celestial working. If you do not have a deep understanding of creation and change, and do not clearly penetrate the complementarity of opposites, how can you know this?

> Enjoying the radiance of the moon on the fifteenth of the eighth month,
> this is precisely when the vitality of gold is fully matured.
> If you come to where one yang just starts to arise,
> see to promoting the fire without delay.

People know the spirit as psychological, they do not know why the nonpsychological is spiritual.

Students in every age have taken the luminous awareness of the discriminating mind to be the original, fundamental spirit. This is why people cling to emptiness or stick to forms, attracted to all sorts of marvels and wonders, and grow old without attainment, with only death to look forward to. They don't realize that this intellectual spirit is an acquired spirit, not the primal spirit.

So what is spiritual but really not psychological is the primal spirit. It is not material, not void, ultimately nonexistent yet including ultimate existence, ultimately empty yet including ultimate fulfillment. This is the nonpsychological spirit, which is really most spiritual.

Nevertheless, people of the world know only the acquired spirit as the spirit, and gladly enter into routine existence; they do not know the primal nonpsychological spirit can preserve essence and life. They do not even suspect that myriad things steal their energy without their realizing it.

Sun and moon have measurements, great and small have definition. The work of sages is born therefrom, spiritual illumination emerges therefrom. When you take over the mechanism, no one in the world can see you, no one can know you. When developed people get this, they are steadfast in poverty; when undeveloped people get this, they take life lightly.

The reason people can take the energies of heaven, earth, and myriad beings is that heaven, earth, and myriad beings have fixed measurements. Heaven, earth, and myriad beings cannot take energy from people insofar as the Tao of sages has no shape or form.

For example, the sun and moon are high above, but they have measurable courses that can be figured out. In the case of the sun, there is the yearly cycle with the four seasons, which can be observed. In the case of the moon, there is the monthly cycle of waxing and waning, which can be seen.

The great is yang, and the small is yin. When yang culminates, it gives rise to yin; when yin culminates, it gives rise to yang. When the great goes, the small comes, and when the small goes the great comes: the cycle of yin and yang is a fixed, unchanging course.

People who arrive at the Tao figure out the waxing and waning of the creative evolution of yin and yang; they apply effort and soon cull the primal undifferentiated energy for the matrix of the elixir, taking the measurements of filling and emptying of heaven and earth for the foundation of life. In the primordial they are not opposed by nature, and in the temporal they serve the timing of nature.

The work of sages arises from this, spiritual illumination emerges from this. The takeover of the mechanism of nature involved in this work and this illumination is unfathomable even to ghosts and spirits, to say nothing of people. How can anyone see it or know it?

No one but wise and virtuous people can know this path; only those who are strong enough to transcend all things can carry it out. If people are really developed through true practice of the Tao, forgetting the words when they get the meaning, being wise yet appearing ignorant, being expert yet appearing inept, they will not be willing to reveal their excellence until they have perfected essence and life; they will remain steadfast in poverty, appearing to have no knowledge.

As for undeveloped people of slight virtue, if they happen to get a taste of this richness, they will be self-satisfied and complacent. They will not value essence and life. They will think they have what they don't, think they are fulfilled when they are empty, think all is well when in fact they are restricted. So they will go wrong and will not only fail to benefit but will even be harmed.

3.

The blind can hear well, the deaf can see well. Cut off one wellspring, that of profiteering, and it is ten times better than mobilizing the army. Introspect three times day and night, and it is ten thousand times better than mobilizing the army.

The blind are good at hearing what is not easy to hear, because their eyes see nothing and their spirit is stored in their ears, so their hearing is clear. The deaf are good at seeing what is not easy to see, because their ears hear nothing and their energy works in their eyes, so their seeing is clear.

Those who understand this observe that when the eyes are closed the ears are sharp, and when the ears are shut the eyes are clear. How much the more so when you subdue the primal energy, give up the artificial and cultivate the real, maintain truthfulness and depart from falsehood; do this, and there is no doubt that you can attain long life.

The Scripture of Purity and Clarity says, "The reason people do not attain the Tao is because they have errant minds. Once they have errant minds, this disturbs their spirit, and their spirit then clings to things. Once they cling to things, they give rise to greedy craving, and this greedy craving is an affliction. When afflictions and errant imaginations torment body and mind, people are defiled and disgraced; they flow in the waves of birth and death, always sunk in an ocean of suffering, having forever lost the true Tao."

Errant imagination that leads to greedy craving is what the *Classic on Yin Convergence* calls the "one wellspring of profiteering." If people can cut off this one wellspring, then everything is empty, and all rumination ceases; this is ten times better than exercises, here referred to as "mobilizing the army." And if you can reflect on yourself over and over, keeping what is truthful and getting rid of what is false, working by day and reflecting by night, being careful all the time without lapse, gradually returning to the state of ultimate good without evil, this is ten thousand times better than "mobilizing the army" of exercises.

The reason for this is that the effect of the army can change only the face and not the heart. It can give people rules and regulations, but it cannot give people skill. If you cut off greed for gain, reflect upon yourself, rectify the mind, do your work, and be careful of what you have not perceived, how can the power of the army reach this?

A sage said, "If for one day you can master yourself and return to considerate behavior, the whole world will return to humanity." Do you think humanity depends on yourself or on others? This is indeed the subtle point of this passage.

The mind is given birth to by things, the mind is killed by things; the mechanism is in the eyes.

The mind is like the master of the house, the eyes are like doors. The original true mind is open and clear, with no sense of self, person, or thing. It is one with the great void; how can it have birth or death?

The existence of birth and death is only in terms of the physical organ associated with mind.

Mind cannot be seen but through things; when you see things, then you see the mind. When there is nothing there, the mind does not appear. This master may come alive, and may die. Things give birth to it, things kill it.

What enables things to give life to or kill the mind is just a matter of opening up the doors and letting thieves assemble. This is because when the eyes see something, the mind senses it. This is how the mechanism of the birth and death of mind is actually in the eyes.

If people can turn back their gaze to illumine inwardly, then external things have no way to get in, so where can birth and death come from?

Heaven has no kindness, but great kindness arises from it. With swift thunder and strong wind, all beings become active. The nature of ultimate happiness is to be unrestricted; the nature of ultimate peace is to be pure.

Heaven is most high, and myriad beings are most low; heaven is so far from beings that it seems as if it had no kindness toward beings.

What we don't realize is that there is really a great kindness that arises from where there is no kindness. The energy of heaven drums and makes thunder, blows and makes wind: when swift thunder stirs them, myriad beings come to life; when strong wind blows on them, myriad beings flourish. Coming to life and flourishing, myriad beings are all unconscious of the reason why they act, since it comes from nature. This is no kindness producing great kindness; what does heaven mind?

So those who are ultimately happy cannot be cramped by anything. Nothing holds them back. For them there is always more than enough. Those who are ultimately peaceful cannot be moved by anything. They have no greed, no attachment. They are always pure. When the happy have no desire for freedom and are spontaneously free, when the peaceful have no desire for purity and are spontaneously pure, this is like heaven having no kindness yet having great kindness. Desireless action is spiritual.

Heaven is ultimately private, but its function is ultimately public. Control and creation are in energy.

The path of heaven goes on where there are no images, operates where there are no forms. It is unique, and in that sense completely private. On the other hand, since the four seasons go on and all beings are born, the function of heaven is in that sense completely public.

When we try to figure out the inner subtlety, it seems that the flow of one energy controls and creates all beings. That is, what orders beings and what makes beings is in one energy.

When the energy rises, all beings are born and grow along with it. When the energy descends, all beings withdraw with it into storage. Birth, growth, withdrawal, storage—it is all one energy.

Seize control of this, and one root disperses into myriad differences, myriad differences resolve into one root. It is private yet public, public yet private, neither public nor private, both public and private.

The flow of the one energy is a cycle that has no beginning, one bursting with life.

Birth is the root of death, death is the root of birth. Benefit comes from harm, harm comes from benefit.

The celestial Tao giving birth to beings is the function of one energy rising and descending. When the energy rises, that is yang; when it descends, that is yin. Yang is birth, benefit; yin is death, harm. When there is birth, there must be death, and when there is death, there must be birth. So birth has death as its root, death has birth as its root. When there is benefit, there must be harm, and when there is harm, there must be benefit. So benefit arises in harm, and harm arises in benefit.

If people seek birth in death, then they will live forever and not die. If people can seek benefit in harm, then they will have benefit and no harm.

In leaving one to enter the other, it is imperative to be careful.

Ignorant people consider the designs and patterns of heaven and earth holy. I consider the designs and patterns of times and beings wise.

Ignorant people do not know that birth and death, benefit and harm, are the secret of the cycle of creation of heaven and earth. They just consider the designs and patterns of heaven and earth to be sacred. I say that the designs of heaven have forms and the patterns of earth have shapes. Manifest outwardly, they are perceptible. Therefore they are obviously not adequate to identify with the sacredness of heaven and earth.

As for the designs and patterns of times and beings, these have no forms or shapes. They are the courses of the operation of the spirit. Concealed within, they are imperceptible. This is what makes heaven and earth wise.

Beings have a time to be born and a time to die. When they are born, it is the time that gives birth to them, so they cannot but be born. When it is time to die, it is the time that kills them, so they cannot but die.

Birth is benefit, death is harm. Born and dying, dying and born, benefit and harm, harm and benefit—it is time that carries this on, and it is the operation of the course of the spirit of heaven and earth.

The course of the spirit of heaven and earth cannot be seen, except through the medium of beings. Observing how the birth and death of beings have their times, one can know the wisdom of the path of the spirit of heaven and earth.

People assume sages are ignorant. I assume sages are not ignorant. People expect wonders of sages. I expect sages not to be weird.

"The science of essence and life begins with doing, which people can hardly see; then when one reaches nondoing, everybody finally knows." Therefore the highest sages who cultivated reality since ancient times, when they were involved in doing, would dismiss intellectual brilliance, hide their light, and cultivate obscurity.

They took over the pass of heaven, turned the handle of the Northern Star, culled medicine from the realm of abstract darkness, carried out the great firing process where there is no conscious knowledge. They entrusted their wills to open nonreification, and their spiritual light operated silently. Even heaven, earth, ghosts, and spirits could not fathom them. Other people could not fathom them at all.

People did not know the profound inner wonder there, and sometimes thought the sages were ignoramuses. They did not know that a good merchant hides his wealth well and appears to have nothing while really being full. There seems to be something going on that is not ignorance.

When in nondoing, the sages softened their light and assimilated to the world, building up accomplishment and cultivating virtue, going to the limits and returning with knowledge, responding a hundredfold to a sincere approach, spiritual communications great and far-reaching, knowledge and wisdom boundless.

Yet people sometimes expected wonders of the sages, not knowing that true constancy responds to beings and really is not strange behavior.

The fact that sages are not ignorant is like the wisdom of the designs and patterns of times and beings. The fact that sages are not strange is like the nonsanctity of the designs and patterns of heaven and earth.

236

Sages are those who can participate in the evolution of heaven and earth, and their virtues are combined with heaven and earth.

Sinking into water, going into fire, bring destruction on oneself.

People's stinginess, greed, and sentimental attachments are like deep water. The energies of alcohol, sex, and material goods are like a pit of fire. Ordinary people do not investigate the Tao of evolution of heaven and earth, do not study the science of essence and life accomplished by sages, but abandon themselves to ruin. Taking the false for real, taking pain for pleasure, they sink into deep water without knowing it, they go into a pit of fire without realizing it. When one brings destruction on oneself, whose fault is it?

The natural Tao is calm, so heaven, earth, and myriad beings are born. The Tao of heaven and earth is penetrating, so yin and yang prevail. Yin and yang push each other onward, and myriad changes go along.

The great Tao is formless, yet produces and develops heaven and earth. The great Tao is nameless, yet it matures and nurtures myriad beings. It is the formless, nameless, natural, perfectly calm Tao. But calm is the foundation of activity. When calmness is ultimate, it goes into action, whereupon heaven and earth and all beings are born.

Once it has given birth to heaven and earth, the natural Tao is inherent in heaven and earth, as their guiding Way. Therefore the Tao of heaven and earth is penetrating. Gradual penetration also means naturalness, with movement not apart from stillness and stillness not apart from movement. Movement and stillness are rooted in each other, so "yin and yang prevail."

Movement and activity are yang, stillness and calm are yin. Movement ends in stillness, stillness ends in movement. When yin culminates it produces yang, when yang culminates it produces yin. Yin and yang push each other onward, the four seasons form an order, and myriad beings are born and develop, change and pass on, all going along.

Do you think the creator minds any of this? Because the natural Tao has no form, is formless yet can change and evolve, therefore change and evolution are endless.

Sages know the natural Tao cannot be violated; they follow it to master it. The Tao of supreme tranquillity cannot be aligned with the calendar, so they have an extraordinary vessel. This gives birth to myriad forms, the eight trigrams, the numerical cycles, the workings of spirits, the secrets of ghosts. The art of mutual supercession of yin and yang clearly progresses beyond forms.

Sages are those who share in the qualities of heaven and earth. Because they share in the qualities of heaven and earth, they do not deviate from the natural Tao of heaven and earth. They follow it to master it, adapting progressively with the same function as heaven and earth.

What does this mean? The natural Tao is not material, not void. It is ultimate nonbeing that contains ultimate being, ultimate emptiness that contains ultimate fulfillment. It includes both being and nonbeing, works with both emptiness and fullness.

Therefore when we talk about it in terms of nonbeing, it is an open, empty energy that cannot be perceived. As a path, it is supreme tranquillity. When tranquillity reaches as far as it can go, something in it is beyond the range of any system of order.

Whatever can be aligned with a system of order has form. What cannot be aligned with a system of order is formless. Supreme tranquillity is formless—how can systems of order accord with it? This is what a famous poem refers to in these words: "There is something before heaven and earth; nameless, it is originally completely silent."

When we talk about it in terms of being, it is beyond the ken of creation, encompassing everything. As a vessel, it is most extraordinary. To say that a vessel is extraordinary here means that it is a spiritual vessel. The term spiritual is used to speak of the most subtle of all things.

Commentary on Ancestor Lü's Hundred-Character Tablet

Nurturing energy, forget talk and fixation.
Conquer the mind, do nondoing.
In activity and quietude, know the source progenitor.
There is no thing; whom else do you seek?
Real constancy should respond to people;
in responding to people, it is essential not to get confused.
When you don't get confused, your nature is naturally stable;
when your nature is stable, energy naturally returns.
When energy returns, elixir spontaneously crystallizes,
in the pot pairing water and fire.
Yin and yang arise, alternating over and over again,
everywhere producing the sound of thunder.
White clouds assemble on the summit,
sweet dew bathes the polar mountain.
Having drunk the wine of longevity,
you wander free; who can know you?
You sit and listen to the stringless tune,
you clearly understand the mechanism of creation.
The whole of these twenty verses
is a ladder straight to heaven.

COMMENTARY

Nurturing energy, forget talk and fixation.

The science of essential life begins and ends with nurturing the primordial open nonreified true one energy. There is nothing else. When you gather medicine you are gathering this. When you refine drugs you are refining this. When you restore elixir you are restoring this. When you free the pill from the matrix, you are freeing this. When you ingest the pill, you are ingesting this. When you form the embryo, you are forming this. When you free the spiritual child from the womb, you are freeing this. When you use special arts to extend life, you are extending this. When you use the Tao to preserve your body, you are preserving this. When you start by doing, what is doing is this. When you end up not doing, what is not doing is this. When you live long, what lasts is this. When there is no birth, what is absent is this.

An ancient classic says, "Know the one, and all matters are concluded." These words can comprehend a thousand classics, ten thousand books.

But this energy is neither material nor immaterial, it has no shape or form. It cannot be known cognitively, it cannot be perceived consciously. When you look at it you do not see it, when you listen to it you do not hear it, when you try to grasp it you cannot find it. It is profoundly abstruse, beyond all description.

This has, nevertheless, been represented by the symbol of a circle, and called by various names. Confucians call it the absolute, Taoists call it the gold pill, Buddhists call it complete awareness.

But basically there is nothing in it that can be put into words. What is there to fix upon? Anything that can be put into words and fixed upon is not the primal open nonreified energy, but must be acquired energy that is emanated and absorbed.

Primal energy never decomposes, while the existence of acquired energy depends on the phantasmic physical body.

People who have not gotten the true meaning of tradition do not know what the primal energy is, and mistake energy in an acquired form for primal energy. Some say it is in the ocean of breath, some say it is in the elixir fields, some say it is in the yellow court, some say it is in the active and passive channels, some say it is between the kidneys and genitals, some regulate their breathing to equalize energy, some stop breathing and settle into the womb breath to store energy, some convey energy up their spines into their heads then down into their midsections to amass energy.

Some hold it still, some move it. There are various different practices people imagine will form the pill of the elixir of immortality. Let us ask, where does this formed energy eventually congeal and crystallize, and into what form? Will it congeal into a mass of energy?

I have seen many cases of people who keep their attention fixed upon points in their heads suffering from brain leakage. Those who keep their attention fixed on points in their lower torso often suffer leakage below. Those who keep their attention fixed on the solar plexus area often get bloated. Those who keep their attention fixed on the forehead lose their eyesight. Those who try to keep a blank mind develop symptoms of epilepsy. They want to seek long life, but instead they hasten death.

It is a pity they do not know the primal open nonreified energy enwraps heaven and earth, produces and develops all beings. It is so great that it has no outside, so fine it has no inside. Release it and it fills the universe, wrap it up and it withdraws into storage in secrecy. It can only be known, it cannot be said. It can only be nurtured, it cannot be fixed upon.

When there is no talk and no fixation, words and fixations are both forgotten. Nurturing without trying to nurture, one enters into absorption in nurturing energy.

The Great Way is alive. It is not stuck in the realms of being or nothingness. To be stuck in the realm of being means to be attached to appearances. To be stuck in the realm of nothingness means to be attached to emptiness. Neither attachment to appearances nor emptiness is the Way of the creative flow of heaven and earth. Nor are they the sages' Way of true emptiness and subtle being.

Since we are talking about nurturing energy, there must be

something nurtured, so we don't fall into emptiness. Since we forget words and fixations, there can be no specific location, no fixed position, so we don't cling to appearances.

When not clinging to emptiness and not clinging to appearances, there must be a source of nurture that is not empty and not apparent. Nurture that is neither empty nor formal is quiet and still yet sensitive and effective, sensitive and effective yet quiet and still. Herein lies the way to nurture energy.

Conquer the mind, do nondoing.

When the text says to nurture energy, without talk or fixation, it seems like it means doing nothing whatsoever. After people are born, their primal energy becomes full; when yang peaks, it must turn to yin. Only sages can preserve their primal energy intact without losing it. As for mediocre and lesser people, the primal energy disappears into latency as soon as it encounters acquired energy.

As acquired energy takes over affairs, yang gradually wanes and yin gradually grows. The sense organs and data of time immemorial emerge, the individual temperament and constitution go into action, the spirit becomes distorted, and external influences cause confusion. At this time, the whole body is in the sphere of yin— what is the yang vitality? Even if you want to nurture energy, there is no way to do it.

The founding teacher's *Yellow Crane Ode* says that those of superior qualities use the Tao to preserve their bodies, which is before pure yang has been broken, while those of inferior qualities use arts to prolong life, which only works after water and fire have been paired.

Using the Tao to preserve the body is something done by nondoing, using arts to prolong life is something done by doing. In people of superior qualities the primal energy has not lost its pure yang body: keep to the center, embrace the one, and it is possible to preserve that original real body. In mediocre and lesser people, the primal energy has already been damaged, yang has been overthrown by yin: it is necessary to steal yin and yang, take over creation, and first stabilize the foundation of life, entering nondoing by way of doing, before it is possible to attain realization.

Furthermore, as an ancient immortal said, to restore the elixir is very easy, to refine the self is very hard. The classic *Spring Pervading the Garden* also says, "The restored elixir is in people; first they must refine themselves and await the right time."

The accomplishment of self-refinement starts with conquering the mind. But to conquer the mind it is necessary to know the mind. There is a distinction in the mind between the human mind and the Tao mind, a difference between the true mind and the artificial mind.

The Tao mind is the original true mind that obeys the laws of the universe without consciously knowing it. The human mind is the artificial mind of acquired consciousness, cognition, feelings, and desires.

The true mind enhances people's essence and life, the artificial mind damages people's essence and life.

To conquer the mind means to conquer the artificiality of the human mind.

But conquering the human mind is not a matter of fixating on the mind, emptying the mind, or forcibly steadying the mind. It is necessary to go along with its natural state. As the classic *Understanding Reality* says, "Go along with desires, gradually guiding them." This is the secret of conquering the mind.

This is why the text says, "Conquer the mind, do nondoing." When it says "do," it means the mind must be conquered; when it says "nondoing," it means not to conquer it by force. Conquering without trying to conquer, not trying to conquer yet conquering, within active action there is nonaction, within effortless effort you exert effort.

This is because the stubborn human mind has piled up habits until they have become a nature, and if you try too quickly to control it, this is using the mind to control the mind, which will just make you mind more, affirming the habit nature all the more. Instead of succeeding in controlling the mind, this will create mental illness. This is what the *Classic on Yin Convergence* means when it says, "When fire arises in wood, disaster takes place with ineluctable force."

Therefore conquering the mind requires application of the effects of gradual cultivation. The work of gradual cultivation does not injure anyone else, does benefit to oneself, doing yet not doing.

Active or quiet, know the source progenitor.
There is no thing—whom else do you seek?

The primal true one energy is the generative energy that gives birth to heaven, earth, and human beings. It contains all patterns, and is present at all times. This is what is called the source progenitor of essence and life. Those who keep aware of this are sages, those who ignore it are ordinary people.

But this energy becomes concealed when it is submerged under acquired conditioning. It may appear every now and then, but people are so preoccupied with getting something, if only respect, and they are so agog with personal whims, that they miss it even when it is right in front of their faces—now it's there, now it's gone.

If you want to look for this energy, first you need to recognize the Tao mind, because the primal energy is stored in the Tao mind. The Tao mind is the substance, the primal energy is the function. They have different names, but their source is the same. The Tao mind is the source progenitor of cultivation of the Tao.

The Tao mind is the master, the human mind is the servant. To know the source progenitor is to have the master employ the servant. The servant listens to the directions of the master and is docile without being forcibly overcome. Each action, each rest, is all the operation of the Tao mind. The human mind itself turns into the Tao mind. Inwardly there are no errant thoughts, outwardly no arbitrary concerns. Inside and outside are peaceful and quiet. External energies cannot penetrate. This is the realm of no-thing.

If you can reach the realm of no-thing, you find it empty and clear. There is nothing but the Tao mind. Whom else do you seek?

Real constancy should respond to people;
in responding to people, it is essential not to get confused.

Once you know the source progenitor and are in a state of no-thing, then realization can be constant. When realization can be constant, external artificialities cannot damage it.

However, the path of real constancy is not a matter of avoiding society or leaving the ordinary world. It is also not a matter of sitting quietly and stopping thoughts. Your feet must walk on the real ground: practicing the path strongly with your whole body, refining it in the furnace of creation, only then is it real and constant.

If you know the real but do not know how to act on the real, even if you can attain the state of no-thing, you will be like a wooden sculpture or a clay statue. Even though there is no-thing outside, you cannot avoid having something inside. This is what is called closing the door, trapping the burglar—the artificial cannot leave, the real will get hurt. How is it possible to be really constant?

Therefore the text says that real constancy should respond to people, and in responding to people it is essential not to get confused. Real constancy responding to people here means the real responding to the artificial. In responding to people it is essential not to get confused, in that we use the artificial to cultivate the real.

This is because the real is hidden in the artificial, the artificial is not outside the real. Without the artificial, we cannot attain realization; without the real, we cannot transform the artificial.

It is just a matter of always being responsive yet always being calm, stealing the mechanism of life from within the mechanism of death, steering a boat calmly through the waves, high and dry. If you can be unconfused, this is true constancy. If you can be truly constant, you may respond to people all day without ever having responded. As you are in the realm of no-thing and are not moved by anything, what can obstruct response?

When not confused, nature is spontaneously stable.

When you respond to people without confusion, the reality of the Tao mind is constantly present. When the reality of the Tao mind is constantly present, the artificiality of the human mind does not arise. When the artificiality of the human mind does not arise, then the temperamental nature does not act up. When the temperamental nature does not act up, the innate nature is clear and bright, like a crystal tower. Unaffected, unattached, unmoving, unwavering, it is spontaneously stable.

The effect of stabilization of nature depends on the work of responding to people without confusion. Get confused, and the human mind does things—the true nature is obscured and artificial nature acts up. Do not get confused, and the Tao mind does things—the artificial nature is transformed, and the true nature is revealed.

The path of stabilizing nature is all a matter of not getting confused. In his *Yellow Crane Ode,* Lü Yen says, "Cultivate transcendental truths based on worldly truths." Fine words indeed.

When nature is stable, energy spontaneously returns.

Nature is inner design. In heaven it is principle, in humans it is nature. Therefore that nature is called celestial nature. Energy is life. In heaven it is energy, in people it is life. Therefore that life is called celestial life.

When people are first born, principle and energy are not separate, nature and life are not separate. Principle and energy are one individual, nature and life are one thing. It is by mixing with the temporal that principle and energy lose continuity and nature and life become separate.

If you can stabilize your nature and not be moved by external influences, true energy will spontaneously return. Where there was no life there will again be life. Nature and life will be one as before, principle and energy are basically not at odds. This is what is called fulfilling nature and attaining life.

The restoration of energy is all a matter of stabilization of nature. If you can be stable in nature, then energy will spontaneously return. It cannot be forced.

When energy returns, the pill spontaneously crystallizes.

The pill is something round and bright. It is formed through the combination of two energies, yin and yang. When one's nature is stabilized, and all thoughts have stopped, this is called true calm and true openness.

When calm reaches the extreme, there is movement. When openness reaches the extreme, it produces light. The primal energy comes from within open nonreification, and in a trice it congeals into a pill.

Generally speaking, the essence of restoration of the elixir pill is in the return of energy, the essence of the return of energy is in stabilization of nature, the essence of stabilization of nature is in not getting confused, the essence of not getting confused is in conquering the mind, and the essence of conquering the mind is in knowing the source progenitor.

When you know the source progenitor, you conquer the mind and respond to others without being confused by others. Your nature is spontaneously stabilized, energy spontaneously returns, and the elixir pill spontaneously crystallizes.

The spontaneity in each case comes from responding to others without confusion. Responding to others without confusion is the work of refining the self. As it is said, when refinement of the self is complete, the restored elixir spontaneously crystallizes.

The Song of Understanding the Tao says, "Before refining the restored elixir, first refine nature. Before cultivating the great medicine, for now cultivate the mind. When your nature is settled, naturally news of the elixir arrives. When the mind is calm, sprouts of the herb grow."

Restoring the elixir is very easy, refining the self is very hard. If self-refinement does not reach the point where there is no self, one's nature will not be settled and one's mind will not be calm. How can the elixir be restored?

But to refine oneself it is necessary to know the source progenitor; otherwise don't do the practice. Old San-feng said, "When you set up the foundation, you need to use the bellows. When you refine your self, you must have true lead." True lead is the source progenitor. If you do not meet a real teacher who can tell you all about the great medicine of true lead, who would dare to set to work?

In the pot, pair water and fire.

When energy returns and the elixir pill crystallizes, the true seed is in your hands. But you have only restored the original face you were born with. This is called restored elixir, and it is called minor restored elixir. This elixir has still not been forged by true water and fire. It is still raw elixir, not yet mature. It cannot yet be ingested to save life. This elixir must be refined into something that is purely positive before it can extend your years and enhance your life.

The *I Ching* trigram for water is yin outside and yang inside. The yang inside it is real, creative energy in correct balance. This is the spiritual water of primal true unity. The trigram for fire is yang outside and yin inside. The yin inside it is real, receptivity in correct balance. This is the true fire of primal open awareness.

This water and fire are the water and fire of spaciousness and spontaneity, not any sort of water or fire with shape or form. Use this water and fire to boil spiritual medicine, twenty-four hours a day. Don't let there be any interruptions. Don't forget about it, but don't try to urge it along either. "Continuously on the brink of existence, use it without urgency." This is what is meant by the statement in the *Guide to Putting in the Medicine,* "Beware lest the water dry up or the fire go cold."

As for the expression "pair in the pot," natural water and fire need not be sought externally. The luminosity of the spirit works silently, not leaking any information on the processes that go on in vast profound secrecy—the quality of the medicinal ingredients, the advance and withdrawal of the firing, the adjustments according to the time.

The birth of yin and yang repeats,
Producing a peal of thunder everywhere.

The work of cooking and refining with water and fire is that work known as "difficulty in the morning, darkness at night." Difficulty in the morning means advancing the yang fire, darkness at night means working the yin convergence.

When it is time for yang, then promote yang. When it is time for yin, then operate yin. Yin to yang, yang to yin, yin and yang hold together, themselves producing repetition.

What repeats is found in ecstasy. In the dark of the unknown there is change. Repeating this over and over again, yin and yang completely transform. The sprouts of primal awareness grow firm and mature; gradually practice leads to sudden realization. All at once from the furnace of creation there spurts out a pill of pure positive energy, like a peal of thunder in the sky, waking up dreamers.

White clouds gather over the peak,
Sweet dew showers the polar mountain.

When the positive energy pill pops out of the crucible, swallow it, and it will act on your individual weak mercuriality, like a cat catching a mouse. White clouds gathering over the peak means that a gentle, clear energy rises, and the five energies gather at the source. Sweet dew showering the polar mountain means spiritual water from the flower pond descends, and health is recovered from all illnesses.

The polar mountain is right in the middle of heaven and earth. Thus it is a symbol for the existence of one reality in the center of the human being. The one reality in the center is the spiritual embryo, which is also called yellow sprouts. This is the meaning of a famous line by Lü Yen, "Thunder in the earth stirs movement; there is rain on the top of the mountain, needed to wash the yellow sprouts emerging from the earth."

Drinking the wine of long life by myself,
I roam free, unknown to anyone.

When the spiritual embryo congeals, spiritual water flows, irrigating the elixir field. The substanceless spontaneously produces substance, the formless produces form. All forced effort is useless.

That is why he says, "Drinking the wine of long life by myself, I roam free, unknown to anyone."

When he says he drinks by himself unknown to anyone, this is because the matter of eternal life and freedom is a matter of taking over the operation of the universe, inviolate to nature in the primordial, in the service of the time of nature in the temporal. This is unfathomable even to the spiritual awarenesses of heaven and earth, to say nothing of other people.

Sitting listening to the stringless tune,
One clearly comprehends the mechanism of creation.

Chuang-tzu said, "Concentrate vitality and spirit, and you live long; forget vitality and spirit, and you are unborn." Long life is the path of perfecting life by doing. Being unborn is the path of perfecting essence by nondoing.

The path of perfecting essence is the work of "nine years facing a wall." The work of facing a wall is the work of "ten months of incubation."

When we say nine years, it does not mean there really is a period of nine years. It is just that nine is the number of pure yang. So it has the meaning of the nine-restoration of the gold liquid, when mundane is exhausted and the celestial is pure. This is what is meant by the saying that as long as the slightest mundanity is left one does not become immortal.

As for the notion of ten months, this is also a symbol. The formation of the spiritual embryo and its emergence from the matrix of mundanity is likened to the course of human pregnancy, which lasts ten lunar months.

The work of ten months of incubation is to prevent danger carefully. All things are empty, no external energy is allowed to enter the embryo. One is like a massive wall, seeing nothing at all.

The ten months of incubation and nine years of facing a wall have the same meaning. They are not different things. Both are merely symbolic representations used by the ancients.

Because of this incubation facing a wall, the author speaks of sitting listening to the stringless tune. Sitting does not mean physically sitting, it means the mind is quiet and the intellect is still. It is the sitting of imperturbability.

A string tune has sound, the stringless tune has no sound. Having no sound means emptiness. Since there is no sound, what is there to listen to? Listening means emptiness is not empty, not empty yet empty. It is not senseless emptiness but true openness.

Sitting listening means leaving the one-sidedness of wishful thinking, and not being attached to it at all. Listening to the stringless tune means listening without listening. Having detached from the listener, one also is unattached to the sound.

The Buddhist *Diamond Scripture* says, "Those who see me in form, those who seek me in sound, are on a false path, and cannot see the enlightened." This is the truly open original face, which is the great method for freeing the spiritual potential, the true secret for perfecting the spiritual body.

To sum up, the work of nondoing is expressed in the word *sitting*. Sitting means stopping in the right place and inwardly observing the mind, outwardly observing the body, and at a distance observing things. You see the mind as having no such mind, the body as having no such form, and things as having no such things.

Once you understand these three, you see only emptiness, and emptiness does not empty anything. There is not even any absence of nothingness. Once there is not even any absence of nothingness, this is called seeing all the way through space, uniquely revealing the whole body, unborn and undying. This at last is complete attainment.

Living is the means of escaping the illusory body, and it is the path of the restorative elixir that stabilizes life. It creates being from nothingness. Being unborn is the means of escaping the spiritual body and realizing the source of the essence of consciousness, the path of the great elixir. It transforms from being into nonbeing.

Living and being unborn are mechanisms of creation. Those who know this science start by creating being from nonbeing to live long, then finally return from being to nonbeing to be unborn. Neither being nor nonbeing is final, essence and life are cultivated simultaneously. They clearly understand the mechanism of the evolution of heaven and earth, and are one with heaven and earth.

Commentary on
Journey to the West

The book known as *Journey to the West* is about the universal Way that has been handed on by word of mouth from sage to sage, verified mind to mind. Ch'ang-ch'un, the originator of the *Journey to the West* cycle, dared to say what the ancients did not dare to say, revealing the celestial mechanism.

So what the book is about is what is most important. Wherever this book is, there are celestial spirits guarding it. If you are going to read it, you should clean your hands, light incense, and read it with sincere respect. When you feel fatigued, then close the book and put it away in a safe place. Don't be careless.

Only those who know this are ready to read *Journey to the West*.

The use of words in *Journey to the West* is a lot like that of Zen devices; the points to notice are all outside the words. Sometimes they are concealed in ordinary folk sayings, sometimes they are represented in mountains, rivers, or human characters. Sometimes false and true are distinguished by a laugh or a joke; sometimes real and artificial are differentiated by a single word or letter. Sometimes the artificial is used to bring out the real, sometimes the story follows the true to get rid of the false. There are a thousand changes, myriad transformations, all unpredictable, extremely difficult to fathom. People who study this book need to look very deeply into its subtleties, and not "scratch the itch from outside the shoe" on the literary level.

Only those who know this are ready to read *Journey to the West*.

Journey to the West is a book of spiritual immortalists, not a book of intellectuals. The books of intellectuals talk about the ways of the world, appearing real but actually false; the books of spiritual immortalists talk about the celestial Way, appearing false but actually real. The books of intellectuals prize literary embellishment without making much of a statement; the books of spiritual immortalists prize verbal simplicity, using meaningful but simple statements of profound principles.

Only those who know this are ready to read *Journey to the West*.

Journey to the West is permeated with the principle of the unity of Buddhism, Confucianism, and Taoism. In terms of Buddhism, it corresponds to the *Diamond Cutter* and *Lotus of Truth* scriptures; in terms of Confucianism, it corresponds to the "River" and "Lo" diagrams and *I Ching*; in terms of Taoism, it corresponds to the *Triplex Unity* and *Understanding Reality*.

The *Journey to the West* uses the theme of the journey to India to obtain Buddhist scriptures as a means of elucidating the secrets of the *Diamond Cutter* and *Lotus of Truth*. It uses the theme of alchemy to open up the mysteries of the *Triplex Unity* and *Understanding Reality*. It uses the Chinese monk and his companions to expound the meanings of the "River" and "Lo" diagrams and the *I Ching*.

Only those who know this are ready to read *Journey to the West*.

In *Journey to the West*, each topic has its meaning, each chapter has its meaning, each phrase has its meaning, each word has its meaning. Real people do not speak or write to no purpose. The reader must pay attention line to line, phrase to phrase, not letting a single word pass by lightly.

Only those who know this are ready to read *Journey to the West*.

Journey to the West thoroughly explains both social realities and ultimate realities; it explains the times of nature and the affairs of humanity. When it comes to methods of learning Tao, self-cultivation, and dealing with society, *Journey to the West* explains them all. This is the most extraordinary Taoist book of all time.

Only those who know this are ready to read *Journey to the West*.

In *Journey to the West* is to be found the method for overturning life and death, the way to take over Creation, which in the primal state is obeyed even by Nature, while in temporal manifestations serves the timing of Nature. This is not any sort of mental fixation, nor is it quietism. Those who would learn it should not fixate on the unruly mind or the physical body; they should find the real ineffable truth out from where there is no form or image. Only then can they avoid wasting effort.

Only those who know this are ready to read *Journey to the West*.

The Great Tao or Way of the *Journey to the West* is the learning of primordial open nonreification, it is not an artificial, acquired, formal art. First set aside interest in occult arts, and then study to find out what is really true.

Only those who know this are ready to read *Journey to the West*.

The main issues in the *Journey to the West* may span one or two chapters, three of four chapters, even five or six chapters. The main idea of what is being said is in the capping verse of each issue, presented clearly in a poem. If the main idea passes you by, it will be as if there were no head, no brain; not only will the subtle meanings be hard to penetrate, even the words will be difficult to read. The reader must clearly discern the context, the thread of the story, the vein of what is being said, and then read over again what follows, so that they can understand its proper place.

Only those who know this are ready to read *Journey to the West*.

Twentieth-Century Taoists

Introduction

Taoism in twentieth-century China is like that of earlier times in that there is no monolithic uniformity in either outer form or inner content and quality. There are many varieties of theory and practice, including many sectarian developments and tangential cults. It is for this reason that Completely Real Taoists traditionally encourage prospective students to acquaint themselves thoroughly with the theoretical bases of the study before seeking a teacher; for without this groundwork the seeker is at a disadvantage when it comes to discerning the real from the false.

The following extracts from sayings and writings of twentieth-century Taoists are selected to illustrate certain matters relevant to the central concern of this anthology, and are by no means intended either as a survey of modern Taoism or as a recommendation of any particular individual or mode of practice as a personal guide. They are taken from *Fang-tao yu-lu*, (*Records of Sayings from Inquiries into the Way*), a collection of reports on the ideas and practices of contemporary Taoists, compiled by Li Luo-ch'iu, whose gracious permission to translate from this work was kindly obtained for me by my friend Liu Shih-i.

Most of what the modern Taoists have to say will already be familiar to the reader from the classical and neoclassical sources translated in the present anthology. Perhaps the most noticeable peculiarity of modern Taoist meditation method as represented here, in comparison with early Complete Reality Taoism, is the prevalence of preoccupation with the so-called openings, or apertures, sensitive points in the body where meditators may concentrate their attention.

While this method is in fact of ancient origin in both meditation and healing lore, the modern concern with it seems to be largely a relic of the Ming dynasty, when psychophysiological techniques of producing altered states of consciousness surged in popularity to eclipse the more subtle metaphysical and spiritual practice of pure Complete Reality Taoism. Nevertheless, as in the case of the great Ch'ing dynasty Taoist Liu I-ming, there are still those who openly criticize cults based on "focusing on apertures" in "quiet sitting" and warn of the possibility of harmful side effects resulting from obsessive practice of such exercises.

The collection from which the extracts herein are translated was first published in 1966. The following sketches of the individuals whose talks are recorded are excerpted from Li Luo-ch'iu's introductions. No representations are made here in this anthology as to their present existence or whereabouts.

Wang Hsien-ch'ing was born in the early 1880s; took a degree in law from Shanghai Graduate School of Law, but in 1940 he immersed himself in the study of ancient books. One day while reading the Taoist classic *Chuang-tzu* he had a realization that led him to give up *t'ai-chi-ch'üan* and turn to the practice of quiet sitting. In 1955 he published a book on nurturing life that won great acclaim among followers of Taoism. As an illustration of manifest effects of Wang's practice, Li Luo-ch'iu recounts how Wang was arrested and tortured by the Japanese Constitutional Police (*Kempei*) in 1944, during the war of resistance. As a result of injuries suffered, Wang's leg had to be amputated. In spite of the fact that he was already over sixty years old, he made a complete recovery from the operation in little more than a month, without taking either acupuncture or drugs to alleviate pain.

Ch'en Tun-pu, born into a well-to-do family, spent his time and resources pursuing practical research into Taoism. At one point in his life he became gravely ill and in desperation tried a kind of inner alchemy that he had learned about, the method transmitted in the controverisal late Ming dynasty Wu-Liu school. Cured by this method, he subsequently became a loyal devotee of this peculiar school, which is generally considered unorthodox by those not of its ranks.

Virtually no information about Wu Tseng-lin is given except his occupation as a professor of physical education at "a certain college." Not much is told of Yuan-hua-tzu either, other than the facts that he had an M.D. from an American university and practiced medicine in Shanghai and Taiwan, and was said to be particularly skilled in treating ailments of the elderly.

Wang Hua-chen is also rather obscure, although it is known that he was postmaster at various branches of the postal service in different areas. Li Luo-ch'iu notes that he talked with Wang once, then found he had disappeared when he went to see him a second time.

Ku-yang-tzu and Ma Ho-yang were cousins, both of whom had researched Taoism since youth and were well known in the Taoist world. Ku-yang-tzu was also an accomplished artist in the traditional mode.

Ko Chung-ho first practiced Taoism in a cloister for several years. Later he went to Iran at the request of a friend to manage a textile factory. Li Luo-ch'iu notes that his latest information on Ko was that he had gone into the mountains in a foreign country to concentrate on spiritual practice.

Hsiao T'ien-shih learned to read the classics from his father when he was a boy and took up martial arts when he got older. At one point he became seriously ill, nearly succumbing twice. He was given up by doctors in both Chinese and Western traditions, but was healed by the arts of a Buddhist monk. Becoming a follower of the monk, he began to practice Ch'an meditation; later he also practiced Taoist work on the advice of his teacher. Subsequently he studied the main schools of Taoism. After World War II he went into journalism, where he became well known. Moving to Taiwan after the Communist revolution, Hsiao immersed himself in Buddhism and Taoism, and became active in the publication of Taoist texts.

Little is said of Fu Hua-i, except that he was a physician and authored a popular book called *Ta-t'ung chih Tao,* or *The Way of Great Sameness.*

Wang Hsien-ch'ing

LIVING MIDNIGHT

The real living midnight is like this: when you are sitting quietly, body and mind are both free, and the whole being is supple and relaxed; empty and silent, merged into one whole, you are not aware of the existence of heaven, earth, people, or yourself—you only sense a great physical and mental stability and a springlike warmth. This is the arising of positive energy, and it is called the real living midnight. When you experience this, it is imperative to let it be as it is naturally and not become overjoyed, lest the experience disappear and your work regress.

FOCUSING ON OPENINGS

In the initial work of quiet sitting, focusing on openings is an important method. Here is a list of those that frequently appear in alchemical literature:

Nirvana (top of the head)
Hall of Brightness (between the eyebrows)
Root of the Mountain (between the eyes)
Tip of the Ruler (point of the nose)

Tongue Tip (the tip of the tongue lightly touches where the teeth and upper palate join, and pure attention is kept on this point)

Yellow Court (this is a point about three or four feet from the body, directly in front of the navel; when pure attention is concentrated lightly on this spot, this is called mental focus on the Yellow Court)

Upper Field (at the point of intersection between a line going straight back from the point between the eyebrows and a vertical line from the top of the head, this is also called the Nirvana Chamber)

Central Field (below the heart and above the navel)

Lower Field (the Ocean of Energy, this is the lower abdomen below the navel)

Welling Spring (the center of the front part of the soles of the feet)

There is no generalizing as to which of these various openings is right and which is wrong, but some practitioners past and present have focused on one opening while some have focused on others. If you can be light, relaxed, and natural, focusing without focusing, then whatever opening you focus on can produce effects without the usual drawbacks.

The method of quiet sitting for women involves concentration on the hollow between the breasts when sitting. It is best, however, to concentrate without concentrating; it will not do to cling fixedly. When thoughts stop and the mind is tuned, there is a return to empty silence. Also, lightly massage the nipples to promote circulation, and you will naturally reach a marvelous state.

Ch'en Tun-pu

AUXILIARY TECHNIQUES

Although methods of attaining bliss and the minor arts of auxiliary techniques cannot produce real attainment of the Way, nevertheless they are helpful in matters of human health.

HALLUCINATIONS

Various kinds of hallucinations may occur when sitting quietly. If you can view them as if you did not see them, and listen to them as if you did not hear them, then truth will remain while the hallucinations spontaneously vanish.

Wu Tseng-lin

FOCUSING ON OPENINGS

When sitting quietly, if you focus on an opening your progress is slow, while if you do not focus on an opening your progress is rapid. If you do not focus on an opening, however, it is still necessary to maintain a subtle unified awareness, lest you fall into insensible emptiness.

What we call focus of the spirit on the lower field simply refers to the area below the navel; it does not mean concentrating on a specific point measured in feet or inches. If you focus too intensely on a certain spot, this fixation will cause illness.

Where pure attention subtly dwells is "gazing into an opening." First you focus on an artificial opening, and eventually when your work deepens the true opening spontaneously appears.

If you must focus on an opening, then focus on the region above the navel and below the heart, the so-called central elixir field. In comparison to the lower elixir field, it seems to produce effects more easily and have less of the typical drawbacks.

Yuan-hua-tzu

NATURALNESS

Lao-tzu said, "The Way is patterned on nature." It cannot be forced, and does not need arrangement. Those who cultivate realization should not deviate from this iron rule of naturalness from beginning to end.

To want to open the passes immediately upon entering into mystic studies is a common affliction of beginners. The more they want to open the passes, the more the passes resist opening. As it is said, "If you want speed, you will not arrive." This does not apply only to the Way.

FOCUSING ON OPENINGS

The exercise of focusing on an opening is like having a post to tether a horse; it is easy to get started. As for meditation without focusing on an opening, even though it is most wonderful, nevertheless random thoughts fly about, and without a tethering post beginners have an extremely difficult time conquering thoughts. If your will is strong, however, you can conquer any thoughts; so it is simply a matter of the quality of individual effort.

THE MYSTERIOUS PASS

The first step of the essential work is in seeing "the opening of the mysterious pass."

When the first step of the work is done properly, then the mysterious pass opens up of itself. The mysterious pass is a higher experience that takes place after spirit and energy have united. You will know what that experience is like yourself when the time arrives. If we talk about it, it is easy to get attached to descriptions; and if you cling to descriptions, the mysterious pass will never open up.

In his *Treatise on Clarifying Confusion,* Pai Yu-chan says, "If you can be silent and still, free from thought even in the midst of thought, your meditation pure and unadulterated, turning into a single whole, silent all day long, like a hen incubating her eggs, then your spirit will return and your energy will come back, and you will spontaneously see the opening of the mysterious pass." This explains the proceses of the work of revealing the mysterious pass most concisely and clearly. Please study it closely.

NORTHERN AND SOUTHERN SCHOOLS

The Southern school lays predominant emphasis on mastery of life, while the Northern branch lays predominant emphasis on mastery of essence. The Southern school seeks spirit from the "other," while the practice of the Northern branch depends on oneself. The effects of the Southern school are rapid, the effects of the Northern branch are slow. In general, although the Southern and Northern schools have their own special emphases, yet when it comes to mastery they are one.

Wang Hua-chen

SUDDEN AND GRADUAL

In immortalism there is a distinction between sudden and gradual. The sudden method is direct transcendence in a single step; the whole process is no more than "keeping to the center" and "returning to openness." The transformations are very few.

In the gradual method, there is stage after stage, so it is imperative to progress gradually, in an orderly manner; it is impossible to approach at a single bound.

THE SOUTHERN SCHOOL

Anyone who clings to one thing and does not know how to adapt is not a true follower of the Southern school. After people have reached the age of sixty, their original energy has deteriorated, so that "their remaining years are like a lamp in the wind." Because they are pressed for time, without the immediately effective Southern school there is no way to treat their emergency and save them from the ravages of old age.

The intercourse of yin and yang is inconceivable. The work of the Southern school can easily cause illness if it is not carried out properly. It can cause debility and even death, so it is imperative to be careful.

To practice the Southern school, the first requirement is a high level of knowledge and wisdom; the second requirement is a firm will. This is because the usual human condition is to be moved by experiences; unless you are a powerful person, how can you "stop your horse at the edge of the cliff"?

Ku-yang-tzu

A SUPERIOR METHOD OF MEDITATION

Not focusing on an opening, not tuning the breath, being utterly empty and silent, not giving rise to a single thought—this is a superior form of meditation.

CURING AND PREVENTING SICKNESS

Medicine has no effect on sicknesses that are caused by practicing Taoist exercises. Only the practice of quiet concentration known as "returning to emptiness" can cure them.

In the beginning, when random thoughts occur in profusion, then it is appropriate to focus intently on an opening. When your mind has cleared and thoughts have diminished, then you should gradually let go and relax. Only by using these techniques alternately can you avoid becoming attached to forms and thus producing sickness.

RECOGNIZING TEACHERS

Practitioners should first study alchemical classics thoroughly, then use the classics to resolve their doubts and use the classics to evaluate their experiences. Then they can soon discern who are illumined teachers.

THE MYSTERIOUS PASS

Sitting quietly, when you reach the point where there is no person, no self, and you forget all about your body, then you are not far from the mysterious pass.

ATTAINING THE ONE

"Attain the one, and all tasks are done." Oneness means that all differences return to one root. The one root is where there is no opposition of yin and yang. This can be attained only by emptiness, and can be preserved only by emptiness.

ENERGETICS

Energetics (*ch'i-kung* or *qigong*) that are forced and violent would seem to be contrary to the Way. Energetics that are spontaneous and natural are not opposed to the Way.

EXERCISES AND EXPERIENCES

Whether you are doing external exercises or the exercise of stopping thought and forgetting impulses, all experiences, regardless of whether inside the body or outside the body, should be left alone and not made into objects of concern. Otherwise you will cling to their characteristics, and by clinging will either regress on the Way or develop a sickness.

Ma Ho-yang

SEEKING TEACHERS

There is nothing to seeking teachers but complete sincerity. As it is said, "Where complete sincerity reaches, even metal and stone open up for it." How could anyone wish to be given the ultimate Way without moving true teachers to act?

FOUR STEPS

Ancestor Lü once indicated to students that practice of the Way is encompassed within the following four steps:

1. Forgetting the body to nurture energy—this is getting the medicine.
2. Forgetting energy to solidify spirit—this is crystallizing the elixir.
3. Forgetting spirit to return to emptiness—this is projecting the spirit.
4. Forgetting emptiness to return to reality—this is refining emptiness.

RETURNING TO THE SOURCE

Cultivation of the Way is returning to the root, going back to the source. The root source is the original state; the original state is the pristine state wherein human essence and life have not yet divided.

ESSENTIAL NATURE

What is essential nature? To talk about essential nature, it is necessary to discuss mind first. To talk about mind, it is necessary to discuss thought first. If people revolve along with their thoughts, then they can never escape the rise and fall of repetitious routines. So we can see that the first sprouting of a single thought is the dividing line between the sage and the ordinary mortal.

THE MYSTERIOUS PASS

The point where thoughts stop is "the single opening of the mysterious pass." The union of spirit and energy, from which creative evolution is born, can also be called the mysterious pass. Obtaining the medicine, crystallizing the elixir, restoring the elixir, release from the matrix, and spiritual transformation—all are intimately connected with the mysterious pass. After the Way is realized, there is nowhere that is not the mysterious pass: the flow of the streams, the blooming of the flowers, the chattering of the birds, and the humming of the insects—all are natural revelations of the mysterious pass.

Ko Chung-ho

CONCENTRATION ON OPENINGS

When you sit quietly, whatever opening you focus upon, it is good to do so in a light, relaxed, natural manner. If you cling to it too fixedly, over a long period of time blood and energy will pool and stagnate, easily producing strange illnesses.

SUITABLE METHOD

If you are comfortable and peaceful when sitting, this proves that the method is suitable to your own body and mind, so you can continue to practice it. If you feel discomfort, or in extreme cases pain, then you should consider the method carefully, switch to another one, or ask for correction from someone of high illumination, so that you may cultivate practice without negative side effects.

Hsiao T'ien-shih

In the practice of the Southern school, some start from energetics, some start from quiet sitting. One cannot be lax about the successive steps—setting up the foundation, culling the medicine, restoring the elixir, forming the embryo, incubation—so unless one lives with a teacher one cannot be directed and corrected in a timely fashion.

The experiences of those who study the Southern school are individually different; the transmissions from teacher to teacher are not the same.

The Northern branch's practice of clarity and calm may be less powerful, and its results may come slower, but if it is continued and built up little by little, there is no doubt that it can also result in attainment of the Way.

Nine out of ten Taoists practicing meditation focus on openings, but a work called *The True Explanation of Immortalism* says that the meditation of the school of Wenshih, "The Literary Founder," is most simple and easy, not focusing on any opening at all. However, it may be hard for any but those of the highest faculties to enter into it.

The higher form of meditation according to the Green City

school, not focusing on any opening, may be somewhat difficult to get started in, and may be somewhat slow to produce results, but when the power of the practice is realized, it certainly has the marvelous function of "myriad openings opening at once."

The path of the school of the Literary Founder is entirely rooted in open emptiness and based on nurturing essence. Openness means formlessness, emptiness means nonattachment. Thereby it is possible for vitality and energy to unite, for mind and essence to unite, for body and spirit to unite, thus to transcend to the realm of sages all at once.

But it is very hard to get into the practice of this school's great path of open emptiness. It is all a matter of cultivating the true positive energy in oneself so as to connect to the true positive energy of the universe. At first there seem to be no boundaries, there seems to be no place to stand. Actually it is necessary only to keep on doing the work; then you can naturally understand how there is fulfillment in openness and reality in emptiness.

The Green City school is based on the dual cultivation of the Southern school. It closely resembles the school of Chang San-feng, but with even more of the essential marrow of the school of the Literary Founder. The founder was Ch'ing-ch'eng Chang-jen, the Master of Green City.

All cultivation done is based on openness and rooted in emptiness. If you can realize it and experience it through open emptiness, you can awaken forever at once and attain permanent attainment at once. At first there seems to be no way to get started, but once you enter the gate and get the secret, you can immediately transcend and directly enter; broad as the ocean and open as the sky, wherever you are you get through.

The Green City school has its source in the method indicated by Lao-tzu's "ultimate emptiness" and "complete quiet." When utterly empty you are aware, and when completely quiet you are clear. All functions, spiritual powers, and mystical states are produced from emptiness, quiet, awareness, and clarity. "Within emptiness are stored myriad beings; within quiet there exists a heaven and earth." If people can reach the point where not a single thought is born and not a single thing affects them, then the original positivity spontaneously grows, the original energy spontaneously arises, and endless transformations, endless states, are also freely accessible therein.

When the Green City school transmits the path of the higher vehicle, what they give is just nothingness. And in the end, even the nothingness is not there. Everything is put down: there is no sky and no earth, no others and no self, no beings and no things, nothing established and nothing destroyed, nothing gained and nothing lost, no imagination and no thought, no mind and no ideas, no method and no path. This is uniting with the universe as eternally indestructible space.

The Master of Green City said, "The method of culling supplements does not refer to the practice of sexual yoga whereby feminine energy is culled to supplement the masculine. It has to do with culling the energy of heaven and earth to supplement one's own energy, culling the vitality of heaven and earth to supplement one's own vitality, and culling the spirit of heaven and earth to supplement one's own spirit. Based on the evolution of heaven and earth, one makes one's own evolution; based on the life of heaven and earth, one extends one's own life.

"Since the energy of heaven and earth does not cease, therefore one's own energy also does not cease. Since the evolution of heaven and earth do not stop, therefore one's own evolution also does not stop. Since the life of heaven and earth does not decay, therefore one's own life also does not decay. Based on the endless creativity of heaven and earth, one develops one's own endless creativity; therefore as the life of heaven is always new, so also is one's own life always new."

FOCUS ON OPENINGS

Among Taoist meditations, there are those that involve focusing on openings, and there are those that do not focus on openings. There are those who do not focus on openings but do focus on emptiness, and there are those who do not focus either on openings or on

278

emptiness. Focusing on openings is easy to get into, but final realization is hard. Not focusing on openings is hard to get into but final realization is easy. It is easy to give instructions for focusing on openings, hard to give instructions not focusing on openings.

Fu Hua-i

THREE SELVES

The purpose of Taoist practice is to cultivate three selves.

The first self is the physical body. Although the first self is temporary and unreal, attainment of the Way depends on it. Therefore when inactive it is best to be calm and light, and for action it is best to be cultivated through exercise. Breathing exercises, energy induction exercises (*yin-tao/yindao*), the "course in transformation of the musculature" (*i-chin-ching/yijinjing*) and "absolute boxing" (*t'ai-chi ch'üan*) will all do.

The second self is the vital spirit. This means using the methods of quiet sitting to refine this substance, in which dark and light are mixed, into a pure serene body of balance and harmony. Singleminded concentration on the infinite whatever one may be doing is what is called "the supreme state in which even nothingness does not exist."

The third self is the fundamental essence. It neither increases nor decreases, is neither defiled nor pure: it is the true emptiness that is not empty. When you understand mind and see its essence, only then can you know its original state and be the primordial true master.

All beings have the same source; to look back for the fundamental essence is something that both Buddhist and Taoist classics discuss.

SHAMBHALA CLASSICS

Appreciate Your Life: The Essence of Zen Practice, by Taizan Maezumi Roshi.

The Art of Peace, by Morihei Ueshiba. Edited by John Stevens.

The Art of War, by Sun Tzu. Translated by the Denma Translation Group.

The Art of Worldly Wisdom, by Baltasar Gracián. Translated by Joseph Jacobs.

Awakening to the Tao, by Liu I-ming. Translated by Thomas Cleary.

The Book of Five Rings, by Miyamoto Musashi. Translated by Thomas Cleary.

The Book of Tea, by Kakuzo Okakura.

Breath by Breath: The Liberating Practice of Insight Meditation, by Larry Rosenberg.

Cutting Through Spiritual Materialism, by Chögyam Trungpa.

The Diamond Sutra and the Sutra of Hui-neng. Translated by Wong Mou-lam and A. F. Price.

The Great Path of Awakening, by Jamgön Kongtrül. Translated by Ken McLeod.

Insight Meditation: A Psychology of Freedom, by Joseph Goldstein.

The Japanese Art of War: Understanding the Culture of Strategy, by Thomas Cleary.

Kabbalah: The Way of the Jewish Mystic, by Perle Epstein.

Lovingkindness: The Revolutionary Art of Happiness, by Sharon Salzberg.

Meditations, by J. Krishnamurti.

Monkey: A Journey to the West, by David Kherdian.

(Continued on next page)

The Myth of Freedom and the Way of Meditation, by Chögyam Trungpa.

Narrow Road to the Interior and Other Writings, by Matsuo Bashō. Translated by Sam Hamill.

The Places That Scare You: A Guide to Fearlessness in Difficult Times, by Pema Chödrön.

The Rumi Collection: An Anthology of Translations of Mevlâna Jalâluddin Rumi. Edited by Kabir Helminski.

Seeking the Heart of Wisdom: The Path of Insight Meditation, by Joseph Goldstein and Jack Kornfield.

Seven Taoist Masters: A Folk Novel of China. Translated by Eva Wong.

Siddhartha, by Hermann Hesse. Translated by Sherab Chödzin Kohn.

Spiritual Teaching of Ramana Maharshi, by Ramana Maharshi.

Start Where You Are: A Guide to Compassionate Living, by Pema Chödrön.

T'ai Chi Classics. Translated with commentary by Waysun Liao.

Tao Teh Ching, by Lao Tzu. Translated by John C. H. Wu.

The Taoist I Ching, by Liu I-ming. Translated by Thomas Cleary.

The Tibetan Book of the Dead: The Great Liberation through Hearing in the Bardo. Translated with commentary by Francesca Fremantle and Chögyam Trungpa.

Training the Mind and Cultivating Loving-Kindness, by Chögyam Trungpa.

The Tree of Yoga, by B. K. S. Iyengar.

The Way of the Bodhisattva, by Shantideva. Translated by the Padmakara Translation Group.

The Way of a Pilgrim and The Pilgrim Continues His Way. Translated by Olga Savin.

When Things Fall Apart: Heart Advice for Difficult Times, by Pema Chödrön.

The Wisdom of No Escape and the Path of Loving-Kindness, by Pema Chödrön.

The Wisdom of the Prophet: Sayings of Muhammad. Translated by Thomas Cleary.

The Yoga-Sūtra of Patañjali: A New Translation with Commentary.
  Translated by Chip Hartranft.

Zen Lessons: The Art of Leadership. Translated by Thomas Cleary.

Zen Training: Methods and Philosophy, by Katsuki Sekida.